LONG
TIME
COMING

LONG TIME COMING

A Black Athlete's Coming-of-Age in America

BY CHET WALKER
with Chris Messenger

GROVE PRESS
New York

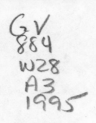

Copyright © 1995 by Chet Walker and Chris Messenger

Published simultaneously in Canada
Printed in the United States of America

FIRST EDITION

Library of Congress Cataloging-in-Publication Data

Walker, Chet.
   Long time coming: a black athlete's coming-of-age in America / by
Chet Walker with Chris Messenger.—1st ed.
   ISBN 0-8021-1504-7
   1. Walker, Chet.   2. Basketball players—United States—Biography.
3. Afro-American athletes—United States—Biography.   I. Messenger,
Christian K., 1943–   II. Title.
GV884.W28A3   1995   796.323'092—dc20   94-42161

Grove Press
841 Broadway
New York, NY 10003

10 9 8 7 6 5 4 3 2 1

For Regenia Walker

Acknowledgments

I never thought my life would be interesting enough for someone else to want to read about it, but I've discovered there *is*
something of lasting value in all of our lives if we simply look for
it, recognize it, acknowledge it, and then have the courage to
share what we've found with others.

When I tried to come to terms with my life, it occurred to me
that I never really understood the complexity of my experience.
As a sports figure, my self-image had always been defined for
me by others. Sportswriters, coaches, and the public in general
persisted in telling me who I was and what I was supposed to
become. Even though I rarely agreed with those views, eventually I was persuaded to accept them and allow those expectations to define my public persona. It is my purpose in writing
this book to finally define who I am for myself.

It is not easy to bare one's soul in a public forum, but I feel
that African-American men need to take the initiative and make
full use of every opportunity to define who we *really* are, to define ourselves. This is not only a story about Chet Walker. It is
my life history, but this is a story that reflects the conditions and
situations many African-American men face throughout their
lives, whether they are in or out of the limelight. I hope after

reading *Long Time Coming* you will have a better understanding of who I am, but I also hope you will have a better understanding of what it's like growing up in a society where black men are associated with certain stereotypes. Like all groups of people, we are a diverse body of individuals. Yet there are common threads that bind all black men together. Ironically, sadly, it is precisely these threads that we too often find we must compromise in order to succeed. Still, I find a positive message in my story, and I hope it will serve as an inspiration to young black males for their future.

As I progressed through different "self-revelations," there have been many people who have helped me come to a broader sense of how "self" can be defined. I am not able to mention them all, but I would like to thank some of them for the positive influence they have had in my life.

I can never appreciate my family enough. The strength, courage, and spiritual guidance I received from them is what gave me the motivation to succeed. The incredible support I received from my many friends provided an inspiring source of encouragement, too.

I would like to thank my teammates from my high school days, my teammates from my college years, and the wonderful men I had the privilege of playing with during my professional career. We shared many thrilling moments of success, and together we were able to survive those moments of failure. These relationships will always be a part of my life.

I would also like to thank a few of the many college classmates I had: Roger, Skip, "Roach," Havard, Bobby Joe, Chuck, Ray, Al, and Mack. We shared a great deal together in a place where we depended upon one another to survive. My cowriter, Chris Messenger, brought invaluable professional skill to this project. His assistance and support provided cohesion and structure, and I thank him and his wife, Janet, for putting up with my late-night telephone calls to discuss ideas the moment they popped into my head, ideas that just couldn't wait until the next day. Thanks, too, to our editor, Jim Moser, whose patience and wisdom guided us both.

Lastly, I would like to thank my dear friend Luretta McCray, who gave me both initial encouragement and the motivation to bring this project to fruition.

Chet Walker
December 1994

Contents

Prologue

"**B**oy, you'd better learn to stay in your place!"
Over and over I heard these words and every possible variation whenever I'd get into mischief or question something or behave too boldly or just do the things a little kid does. It was the Deep South, the 1940s.

I was just a child, and I couldn't understand why the folks were telling me, "Stay in your place." Maybe they were playing a game with me. That could be it. Perhaps my father and mother and older sisters and brothers knew about a secret place that was mine alone, and it was my job to find it. What kid couldn't warm to that task?

I wandered around our farm in the Mississippi hill country, searching for that place. First I'd look for somewhere I'd be safe, safe from people calling me for chores, from grown-ups arguing, from sisters teasing. Other times I thought maybe I'd find a place for adventure. I'd picture gold in some rickety treasure box. I'd crawl under the bed to search there. Or I'd look in the closets behind all the stiff, adult-smelling garments. In my most serious excursions to find that place, I'd take our old hound dog into the rich brown-red earth under our house. We would hide there for hours while *I* pretended to dig and hunt.

I never did find that magical place although I looked for it for a long time. Gradually I realized what everyone had meant about "my place." I discovered that "place" had many meanings and locations. For the older men and women in my family, it meant knowing the places of black and white people and where the lines had to be drawn, which spaces were ours and which were *not*. Knowing there was nothing you could do but keep a wary eye out for boundaries that would suddenly loom.

This growing awareness of "my place," of these outside limitations and constraints upon freedom of movement, came over me gradually, sadly, inevitably, as it would for most black children. In time, I became shrouded in it, paralyzed within place. But that young seeker was and is still me. Searching, hiding, looking for "my place."

It's always been hard for me to open up. Even when I competed in basketball, the most public of sports, I held my cards close to my vest, kept my own counsel. By nature and nurture I'm private about most things. So it's been hard to write this book, to take you to some of the "places" I've visited. Mine is a story about the coming of age of a black athlete in America during the 1950s and 1960s, how I worked to find that place within myself, and how I learned about other places and people as well. It was the most telling period of my life, when I came the furthest and learned the most about myself and my country.

Twenty years ago I was an All-Star in the National Basketball Association (NBA) and the offensive leader of the Chicago Bulls. But in the NBA time is telescoped, and twenty years is an eternity. That's why it's always important to see beyond the forty-eight-minute game, beyond the long seasons, beyond making a career out of playing a game.

The unreal world of sports beckons seductively to residents of that other unreality, the isolated ghetto. Many of today's black athletes have lost the ability to see their lives in any frame larger than the court. Young players today seem to move in an endless present of replays without memories. They are often unaware of the struggles of my generation or of those who went before us. The black sociologist Harry Edwards points out that younger black athletes don't understand how to meet the challenge of being a black person in society. They think sports is a way of avoiding it. They rarely hear stories of earlier generations of successful men and women who used sport as a vehicle for larger successes. As Edwards says, "They can't put their hands on it, can't feel it."

Then as now, just like many young players, I saw basketball as my chance. In that tough time, poised between a segregated past and an uncertain future, I had to find myself. There was no place mapped for a black athlete during the Civil Rights era.

When I see today's NBA player looking out of a television screen and urging kids to stay in school, I worry that all kids see is a hero who probably dropped out of college for the money the pros offered. What these young people *need* to see is how he got there. And I'm not talking about the car. The kids need to know how he got from grade school in a black community to the suburban fortress he most likely lives in today. I want to tell how I made my way from a Mississippi farm and a Michigan housing project to the NBA before most of today's stars were born.

There's no question that a black athlete endures racial injustices, but it's hard to complain or talk about them when he's making so much money, for a few years more money than almost anyone in the country, certainly many lifetimes of money for any working man in his family's past. He's an athletic hero in America, which society feels is a very privileged role.

So he convinces himself he's overreacting to slights and prejudice, that he's too touchy. The only thing he can feel good about is the money he makes, but that comes with its own guilt, akin to that of survivors of some tragedy: What do my people think of me? Why am I *here* and what must I make of my life?

Seeing people's lives in terms of stories is my business, has been for the almost twenty years I've been a movie producer. I always thought that one day the story I would love to tell is my own.

In 1988, I'd just won an Emmy for producing *A Mother's*

Courage: The Mary Thomas Story. This story of NBA star Isiah Thomas's mother, a good mother and a powerful black woman raising her children against all odds on the tough west side of Chicago, touched me because it was so like my own family life with an indomitable mother helping her children become strong men and women. I had brought Mary Thomas's story to the screen, putting together a story treatment, negotiating the film rights. Emmy in hand, I let the loud applause carry me back to my seat in the packed auditorium. As the applause faded away, it was my own mother's name ringing in my ears. How proud Regenia Walker would have been for me at that moment. To win such an award, and to win it for telling the story of a family. It was the night of the Emmys that I had the first intimation that I would write this book about myself and my own family.

To the worlds of basketball and Hollywood, I'm Chet Walker. To my mother and the rest of my family, I was always just Chester. This story is written by both of them. I've had my moments in the spotlight of big-time sports—an NBA title, selection as an All-Star, clamorous fans, big money. I've also felt very lonely in that crowded arena, exploited, running on empty. But always I kept alive the faith that had been taught to a little boy named Chester. I had my chances to discover my place and came through, and my hope and survival is what the journey in this book is about. It's been a long time coming.

1.
Bethlehem, Mississippi: A Death in the Family

One of my earliest memories is of myself at age seven, a little boy lying on the back of a wagon loaded with cotton, watching a plane flying overhead, wondering where it was going. I thought airplanes only went to New York City because I knew that's where boxers fought in Madison Square Garden. At the same time, flocks of geese would lazily cross the shadow of those airplanes as the birds flew south escaping the northern winter. They would often swoop down to get food, and we'd hunt them with shotguns. Their decision to stop was final! North and South. Back and forth. Flight from one place to another.

They say your personality and your consciousness are indelibly stamped in the first five or six years of life, and my first ten years were spent in the rural South.

I was the youngest of ten children born to Regenia and John Walker, and I spent my early years on our farm helping to plant and pick cotton. In 1950, in Bethlehem, Mississippi, schools for black children were open for only five months of the year and then were closed so that children could help with the spring crops. Education was not a priority for children in cotton country.

Our one-room school went through the eighth grade. With

my brothers and sisters, I walked the two and a half miles there. I loved that long walk through the piney woods. Back and forth, every day, I ran with the squirrels and rabbits and put them in my games.

On Friday nights the family gathered around the radio, our one luxury, listening to boxing matches. We eagerly followed the fights of the great black heavyweights such as Joe Walcott, Ezzard Charles, and Joe Louis. Even as a very young boy, I knew they were champions and somehow I identified with them.

In tiny Bethlehem, we could pretend we were in Madison Square Garden. On Saturday afternoons after the Friday night fights, my friend Henry and I would go to town and sit in front of the country store. Some of the white men there would pay us to box each other. Henry was always Joe Louis, and I was Jersey Joe Walcott. We would cuff each other for five or ten minutes. The winner would get a quarter, the loser a dime. But it didn't matter who won or lost, because we would decide ahead of time to alternate winning and losing. When the "fight" was over, Henry and I would split the thirty-five cents, and off we'd go to buy two Royal Crown Colas and a bag of peanuts. We poured the peanuts into the sodas and sat down to enjoy our Saturday treat. We were boxing heroes. We had put on a show.

Bethlehem, and the area for miles around it, was in the middle of the Holly Springs National Forest in north central Mississippi, about forty miles south of Memphis. It was no more than a crossroads with a country store and a church. Naturally, I didn't know it at the time, but I was born right in the middle of William Faulkner country, the area that he made part of his fictional Yoknapatawpha County. The Tallahatchie River flowed south of town, and we often went there for catfish. We were just off the eastern edge of the rich Mississippi Delta land that runs from Memphis down to Vicksburg.

Our house was simple, three or four large rooms, including a kitchen and two bedrooms where we all slept, the boys several to a bed. As the youngest son, I wore well-patched hand-me-down overalls and regular farm shoes, which were rough and heavy, with high tops. The house sat on top of beams, which were tall enough for me to walk under. I loved to make up games that I'd play with our dogs under the house, which could become any magic place I imagined it to be. We had well or stream water to drink, and we boys took turns hauling it in. Since we had no electricity, our radio ran on batteries, and we used kerosene lanterns. My mother always cooked on a wood-burning stove, and one of my chores was to chop wood and tote it in for her.

The one fireplace was in the room where my parents and sisters slept. On cold December or January mornings, we'd all crowd in there, carrying our blankets and turning our bodies toward the warmth as though we were on a barbecue spit. The roof leaked, and when it rained, we'd catch the water in pails. Some of the holes in the roof were so big that I could look out at night and see the stars. My family's life in Mississippi in the late 1940s had few modern conveniences. All the farming was done by mule- and horse-drawn plows. We had a truck for a while or we'd ride with a neighbor to Holly Springs, about twenty-five miles to the north on the road to Memphis. Everything in Holly Springs was marked WHITE or COLORED.

I had no one to measure myself against except my brothers and father. Then, too, I had nothing to measure the outside world by, no television, no newspapers, no magazines, no other places. Only the radio. Besides the Friday night fights, I remember the family listening regularly to the *Amos 'n' Andy* show. It was amazing, a show about black people who lived in fabled New York. We had no idea that Freeman Gosden and Charles Correll, the creators and voices of the black characters, were white. I don't think we would have cared that much if we'd known. They made us laugh till we cried.

I was the baby in the family, but on a poor farm that didn't accord me any privileges. By the time I was seven, I was cutting wood, picking cotton, and working behind the plow. I also helped my mother in the kitchen. I used to watch in awe as she'd snap a chicken's head off with just one twist. The headless bird would hop around to the noise of our astonished squeals, and my mother would dunk the chicken in boiling water to loosen its feathers. We would all help in the plucking.

When a farmer in Bethlehem had a good crop, all of his profit went back into farm equipment. When he had a bad crop, he had to borrow money to tide himself over until the next season. The bank would hold his farm for collateral. If his situation got worse, the bank could slap a lien on the property, take it over, and then lease it back to the farmer so that he could sharecrop his own land. It was a harsh life and seemingly the only one we could look forward to. Jim Crow was telling us to go north in many ways.

My father always owed money but never lost the farm even though we were dirt poor. This land was a parcel from the original forty acres and a mule given to his father, Pegues "Rice" Walker. My grandfather gave the land to my father as a wedding gift. Like his father before him, my father planned to give his sons land to work and to feed a family. We sold corn and potatoes from the farm and took the cotton to gin although the crop was often destroyed by pests or rain or drought.

October was a special time in Bethlehem when the last of the cotton crops were harvested. Picking cotton was cramped and uncomfortable work. You had to work in a crouch or on your knees since the cotton bolls were attached to the plant at waist height. The cotton bolls had thorns on their stalks that cut up your hands. You'd shove picked cotton into a long canvas sack that trailed off your shoulder as you worked your way down the endless rows. "Sacks of woe" was what the black fieldhands called them. With just a few hours' pickings, these sacks dragged heavily behind us. Once a week we'd load them onto the wagon and take them to gin at Bethlehem, where the bolls would be separated from seeds and weighed. The cotton was put into bales, and my father would get paid on the spot.

Although my father and grandfather had always rallied after bad years, often there was little difference between the financial situation of a tenant farmer and that of an owner like my father. Both were at the mercy of the weather and the banks and the setting of cotton prices. Both simply tried to break even year after year. A working farm under these conditions was often a place of great frustration and few rewards. It was some of the hardest work imaginable, with almost no way to get ahead.

I remember my grandfather as a kind and gentle man. He was also very tall, about six feet four inches, which is probably where I get my height. My father was about five feet eleven inches, wiry, with a thin, pointed face and high Indian cheek-bones. He was a hardworking man, determined to make that farm pay out for all of us. His brothers had all gone north, some of them to Michigan.

My father was poor and controlled by forces outside himself. He took out his anger, powerlessness, and frustration on his own family, the only people he could control. Bethlehem was about 50 percent black and 50 percent white, but there was absolutely no social contact between the races. My father couldn't look at a white woman without risking physical attack. Every white man he met was "Mister" or "Boss." Even old black men had to call little white boys "sir."

So my father took out his anger on us, those he was supposed to protect and love. I tried to understand what made him so mad all the time. He whipped all of his children for the usual misbehavior. Yet it was my mother who bore the brunt of his verbal and physical abuse—when he was at home, that is. But often he wasn't there because John Walker was a roamer and a womanizer. He had dalliances with many women in the county, and everyone knew about it. He was a country Baptist preacher, but even the solace of religion seemed to fail him. He knew he was enslaved to that farm six days a week, and the Sabbath couldn't make up for that.

I grew up hearing stories of black men being lynched for even looking at a white woman. At the same time, the reality of my daily life on the farm was to watch my mother being abused by my father. Lynching was a nightmare in the realm of possibility, but John Walker's anger toward us was real and present. All I knew for sure was that my father was a hard, hard man.

My mother, Regenia Walker, was a tall, stout woman, about

five feet nine inches and big boned. She had a warm, lovely smile and a calm voice. I never saw her in a hurry. A Baptist in the South, she was searching for truth, both in this world and in the next. She'd had about as much education as a black girl in Mississippi could get at the time, going through the tenth grade. That made her eligible for a state teaching certificate. And that's how she came to Bethlehem in the first place—as the schoolmistress of the one-room schoolhouse. After she married my father and the children started to come, she stopped teaching at the school but never at home. She also passed on her curiosity and love of learning to her children, especially to my sister Alter and me. She'd say, "No matter what, you can always better yourself. Take advantage of your opportunities."

She was always sewing patches, either on our clothes or into quilts. We'd take baths on Saturday night in preparation for Sunday school and church the next day where the preaching and singing could raise the rafters through most of a hot Mississippi day.

By 1950, most of my older brothers and sisters had already headed north. My father was becoming apprehensive over who would be left to help him run the farm. My oldest brother, Emmett, had run away in 1941 when he was fourteen years old. He lived in Missouri, Chicago, and Indiana before settling in Benton Harbor, Michigan. My second oldest brother, John Henry, was the first Walker son to be married and out of the house. He lived down the road. My brother James, a World War II army veteran, headed for Benton Harbor when he couldn't readjust to Jim Crow in Mississippi. My brothers Moses and Fred and my sister Lydia followed James to Michigan, where the brothers found work in the Benton Harbor Whirlpool plant, part of the growing factory economy after the war. Still at home were Robert, called "Duke" (thirteen years old); Alter (fifteen); and me (ten). Our sister Anna Laura boarded at a black high school in Holly Springs.

Anna Laura was a lovely girl named for both of our grandmothers. She was a year younger than Alter. Tall and spirited, she even stood up to our father. My sister Alter remembers a time when our father had stayed away in Memphis for a while with some woman. While he was gone, our mother became desperate for food money. So she took sacks full of cotton seed to gin and kept us fed with the $10 that she was paid. But John Walker wasn't having any of it when he returned home and she told him about the sale. He began to beat her unmercifully until Anna stepped between them and took his blows on her own back. She went to her grave with those three long, deep scars.

Anna Laura came home from school when she contracted tuberculosis and was confined to total bed rest. In 1948, hospitals in Mississippi were not integrated. Only a limited number of beds were alotted to black patients; and their names were put on a waiting list. Meanwhile, a person either got better or died. Anna Laura Walker was on a hospital waiting list with more than two hundred names. While waiting for Anna Laura to be admitted to a Mississippi hospital, my mother tried desperately to get her into a sanitarium south of Memphis, but she failed to meet a state residency requirement.

I'd never seen my mother so helpless as when she nursed my sister. I watched a beautiful girl turn into sixty-five pounds of skin and bones. Many times I stood at the end of Anna's bed and saw my mother rub her chest with cod-liver oil while she faithfully appealed to God with prayers and songs. Amidst the awful smell of the mucous Anna spit up, I wondered why my sister was allowed to lie in bed and waste away while no one did anything to save her.

Every night when I came back from the fields, I went in and watched Anna Laura. As the disease progressed, she spoke less and less, every word an effort. One Sunday night I walked into her room to find my mother applying the cod-liver oil and yelling at Robert in an anguished cry, "Go down to Grandpa Rice's house and fetch him right away." Then in a softer voice, as if whispering to herself, she admitted, "I think we're going to lose her." I saw the tears of love and frustration well up in my mother's eyes. I didn't want to understand the urgency all around me, but Anna Laura was dying and my mother knew it.

My mother began to pray. She asked the Lord if He saw fit to give us just one miracle. If He didn't, she would understand. I remember seeing Anna's eyes roll up in her head, only the whites showing. I watched the motions of my mother's hands as she closed Anna's eyelids and placed a quarter over each eye. This was her way of surrendering a dead person to God. All of a sudden the room turned bitter cold. I ran into the kitchen and stood in front of our stove, shaking as if someone had completely covered my body with ice.

The Walker family gathered for Anna Laura's funeral. My brother James reluctantly came back to Mississippi. He had served for two years in the South Pacific and was wounded in Guam, where his leg was shattered in three or four places and he had become addicted to the morphine prescribed for the pain. James came to the funeral in Bethlehem by bus from Memphis and had to ride in the back, in full uniform, with his medals showing. That was too much for him. After the funeral, he left the South immediately.

After Anna Laura's death in November 1950, my mother was determined that no other child of hers would be lost to Mississippi. At Anna's funeral, as we all turned away from the grave site, my mother said softly that she thought she would go to Michigan for a while with the younger kids. My father angrily replied, "Well, if you do, don't come back!" She backed down a little and said, "Well, I'll be back." My sister Alter remembers praying under her breath, "Please don't change your mind, Mama."

My father could see the writing on the wall and was afraid of losing the rest of his family. Nevertheless, on the night after the funeral my mother calmly and determinedly got all our things together. We helped her pack our belongings in cardboard boxes and wedged them into my brother Fred's Ford, which he'd driven down from Michigan.

My mother and father began arguing all over again. She proclaimed that she would not allow her children to stay in Mississippi and be tormented and killed. "They're my children, too!" he shouted. The next morning Robert, Alter, and I were assembled in the front room and asked one by one whether we wanted to stay on the farm in Mississippi or go north to Benton Harbor for good. We all chose to go. I was only ten and terribly frightened as I looked at tight, angry faces and tearful eyes all around me. What was going to happen to us?

My father was desperate about the loss of the family he'd abused and particularly about the loss of his youngest sons, whom he had counted on to work the land with him as we grew older. He made one last plea to my mother to stay. She refused, and before she knew what was happening, my father hit her so hard he knocked her onto the hood of the Ford. The side of her face instantly swelled up, and her leg was badly bruised against the fender. As she got back on her feet, my father moved toward her again. This time my brother Fred pulled my father's arm back—it was a tense moment. Whole worlds were coming apart for all of us. My father still had a vision of our family on that farm, but that vision was an illusion to my mother. She'd taken enough from him. Without a word, she steadied herself, slowly opened the car door, and said, "Come on, y'all, let's go."

Before my frightened eyes, my mother seemed to expand, to grow taller, to become big enough to oppose my father. My mother showed great courage that day, and she did it for her children. She wanted us to be in a position to have a better life. As the car rattled away from the farm and Mississippi, from the backseat I turned to see my father and the dogs standing there in the middle of that dusty, old road. He was so angry. I wondered what would happen to him now and to us.

2.
Living the Great Migration

I guess the Walker family looked like something out of *The Grapes of Wrath* with boxes tied on top of the car and onto the fenders. We'd become part of the Great Migration. Between 1940 and 1970, five million American blacks moved from cotton country in the Deep South to large northern and western cities such as New York, Detroit, Chicago, and Los Angeles, and to smaller cities such as Benton Harbor. The lure was the factories offering real jobs at real wages. Even rural Mississippi was on the pipeline to Memphis, where the great railroad networks stretched north in a grid to Chicago, Cleveland, and Detroit. The greatest promise of all for southern blacks was to move out of deeply entrenched segregation and into a new freedom of opportunity.

On our trip north, we were jammed into that Ford so tightly we couldn't have been pried out with a crowbar. But I felt secure, surrounded by the warmth of my sisters and brothers and comforted by my mother, who silently kept her eyes on the road. In Indiana, we drove into the middle of a huge snowstorm. I'd never seen snow before, and it seemed white as cotton, piling up fast. People's cars were stuck in ditches where they'd skidded off the roads. Farmers came out in their tractors to help pull the cars back onto the pavement. Later that day when we stopped for gas, my mother bawled me out for not using the station's bathroom. I hadn't because I couldn't find the bathroom door for us, the one with the COLORED sign on it. I'd assumed that the woods were my fate and had tinted the white snow.

It was mid-November when we rolled into Benton Harbor. The town sparkled with Christmas lights that were reflected by the snow. How beautiful it was! I thought Benton Harbor was fairyland.

The Walker children already in Michigan had rented a large house owned by a Chicago woman, so we moved in with them. Our new home! It was so wonderful and strange. I'd never seen anything like it. I was a ten-year-old rural southern kid, and it was the first time I'd used a bathroom inside a house. The first time I used a telephone. I switched the electric lights on and off until my mother told me it was driving her crazy.

Our next-door neighbors were a German family who spoke English with heavy accents and might have recently emigrated themselves. I wanted to play with their son, Eddie, but my shyness held me back. We had one hell of a time communicating because he didn't really speak English and I quickly found out that I didn't speak English either, certainly not in the way it was inflected and spoken in the North. With Eddie, I first discovered that, in my new world, the way I spoke and the words I used put me at a disadvantage in school and social situations. Words and phrases that were second nature to me made me an outsider here.

Eddie and I played together a lot for several weeks until one day when we were out back, his father called him into the house. Their conversation was in German, but I knew what was being said—or thought I did. Sure enough, from that day on, Eddie wasn't so eager to play with me. I believe his father got the message from someone that black kids didn't play with white kids in this country. Here he was, a refugee, but this man already seemed to know where he stood in relation to me and my family.

Eventually our landlady came from Chicago to Benton Harbor to check on her properties. Upset at finding so many children living in her house, she demanded that we leave. In the next six months we moved a lot because nobody wanted to rent to a family with so many children. We had to split up because it was too difficult to find a place for all of us. My older siblings lived all over town while my mother and I lived in the back room of a house belonging to a lady my mother met at the Seventh-Day Adventist church. My mother was hurt and frustrated. Having made the decision to leave the farm in Mississippi, she never intended to scatter her family. She still tried to cook for everyone and to bring the family together at mealtimes.

Because we had arrived in Benton Harbor so close to the holidays, I was kept out of school until the second semester, which started in late January. With little to do in a fascinating new place, I went exploring. The winter weather nipped through my thin clothes, but I kept on the go and spent a lot of time downtown. I listened to people talk in the streets and looked in store windows. I wondered at all the lights and new cars in town. All the hustle and bustle. People moved so much faster in the North, darting here and there.

I made the fortunate discovery that I could sell milk bottles and get two or three cents apiece for them. I roamed the back alleys looking in trash cans and collecting bottles to make some money to help buy food. Only occasionally was there enough left over for me to buy a treat like a candy bar; but sometimes I went into the biggest drugstore in town just to watch, because I couldn't get over the fact that blacks could sit down at a lunch counter next to whites.

I had gone to the movies once in Mississippi, but blacks had to sit upstairs in the balcony while the whites sat downstairs. One day in Benton Harbor, I was determined to go to the theater downtown and satisfy my curiosity about the movies there. I collected enough milk bottles to pay the admission price, and I hesitantly approached the theater with my ten pennies in hand. Inside the huge, dark building, I looked for the balcony but discovered there was none. Everyone, blacks and whites, sat together!

I became fascinated with Westerns. I'd go as often as possible and many afternoons found myself the only person in the theater. My favorite heroes were Gene Autry, Roy Rogers, and Randolph Scott. I rooted hard for them, never thinking I might have something in common with the Indians. I didn't see any black cowboys on the screen, and it never occurred to me there might be some. I was so curious about the source of the images that one day I got up enough courage to sneak behind the screen to see for myself if all those horses and cowboys were back there acting up a storm in clouds of dust and sagebrush. That was when this country boy learned there must be some other way that all these images came alive.

Everything in my life in the strange, cold North was an adventure. I was on a free pass until school started. In February 1951, I enrolled in the fifth grade in the predominantly white Jefferson Elementary School. I was frightened to be sitting in the same classroom with white children. In fact, the ingrained prohibitions against racial mixing were deeper than anyone in the North could possibly imagine. In Mississippi, I sometimes walked down a road past a white farmer's house where a little girl named Marie always played in the yard. Since I had heard stories at home that a black man could be lynched if he were caught even looking or staring at a white woman, I would walk past Marie's house, not daring to turn until I was well past her gate. Then I would get behind a big tree and peek back at her. I was afraid she'd catch me looking or, worse, that someone else would.

That first day at Jefferson school in Benton Harbor, I found myself sitting across from a little white girl. I was stunned and very insecure and couldn't speak to her or anyone else. I already knew that my English wasn't correct and that the other kids had trouble understanding me even when I could get the words out. I did poorly in class because I was afraid to speak and thus had trouble showing I could learn anything. It was a real downward spiral. Many times I knew the answer to questions, but I was afraid to raise my hand. On top of all the instinctive and learned fears, I was a stutterer. I felt inferior and completely out of place.

Back at Jefferson school, I always hung back during recess, never thinking I would be chosen to play in the other children's games. I was too shy to walk up to a group of white kids and become part of it. But one day in the schoolyard when no one was around, I picked up this big round ball you were supposed to shoot through a hoop. I did it; then I did it again. This was great—a game I could play by myself! All that was required was me, the ball, and the hoop. From the time I discovered basketball, I felt more comfortable. Since I now had a skill, I knew I could play with the kids now if I chose to, if they asked me. I developed a real fondness for the game. It was something I could control. I could play by myself and not look like an outsider. Sometimes I could almost become hypnotized by shooting for that perfect circle.

I loved the grain of the leather basketball and the grooves in the material. I could pick it up and balance it on different parts of my hand, feeling it on the heel of my palm, on my fingertips. The extension of my arms, the arch of my wrist, the clean feel of its release. I don't think there's another competitive team sport that can give you such deep satisfaction as when you dribble and shoot, just practicing by yourself. I knew very early in my love affair with basketball that this solitary play satisfied a deep part of my nature. You can become hypnotized by making ten, fifteen shots in a row. No one else needs to be there. Then again, you can pretend you are both teams and play a game by yourself, taking all the shots, inside and outside, as well as providing your own running commentary. No team sport transfers to solitary play as well as basketball. In football, you're always looking for some-one else to hit. In baseball, if you hit the ball, you must retrieve it. Basketball can be a very private game and still be a delight.

Then again, I longed for acceptance by others. Sure enough, about a week after I started shooting the basketball, I was asked by a kid if I wanted to be on the baseball team. I quickly said yes.

Michigan in spring is a blooming feast, so unlike the red clay of Mississippi. Someone gave me an old bicycle, and I rode around admiring the blossoms and thrilled at the color and beauty of the northern spring. That summer we moved into an apartment in the "projects." That's what everyone called the housing developments in the black, east side of Benton Harbor. To me, the projects were heaven. The apartment was big enough for all the younger children in the Walker family to live together. Plus, it had a bathroom, and I had my own room.

The projects were barrackslike housing of a kind built in a hurry all over the United States after World War II. They were often called veterans housing and sprang up in city parks, in vacant lots, in unincorporated areas to accommodate the hundreds of thousands of veterans who came home to settle down and begin families. Benton Harbor even had white projects on the west side of town to complement the black developments on the east side. The projects were single buildings of attached row houses, and each building had four units. We had an end unit, which was the most desirable because it had three bedrooms.

It's hard to believe by today's standards, but in those days coming from a single-parent home in the projects made me an exception. I was always looking for a father figure, either inside or outside of the house. This was unconscious on my part, but I know now that I always craved and needed that kind of support in my life. I was able to draw a lot from my older brothers Emmett, Fred, and Moses, but they were grown men, already holding down jobs and looking to start their own families. None of the men in the Walker family could concentrate on me alone.

Everyone who was working in our family contributed to the rent and food. My brothers could barely read and write then because of the poor schooling they'd had in Mississippi. But they made decent wages in the Whirlpool plant although no black could be promoted to foreman at that time. My sister Alter was in high school, and Robert was in the eighth grade. Later Alter joined my sister Lydia who had found work as a nurse's aide in an integrated hospital. They helped my mother raise me and became strong, independent women themselves. Fred was in and out of the place, working as a barber on weekends to help out with my mother's rent. During the next decade my brothers and sisters married southerners who'd migrated to the Benton Harbor area just as we had.

Sometimes, if a boy is lucky, in the closeness of a place like the projects, he finds that male figure in someone else's family who spreads his wings a little wider to shelter the child. I found that man in Mr. Mosby Yarbrough. I was fortunate to have his son Mickey as one of my best friends throughout my school years. He was one of the few guys who came over from our church-league basketball team to be a starter alongside me on the high school team. Another son, Arby, was a good friend, too. Where you would find one of us, you would usually find the other two.

Mickey and Arby lived with their family in the unit next to ours in the projects. Their father, Mosby, was the epitome of the strong black man who cares deeply for his wife and family, a large one, like ours, with eight or nine kids.

The Yarbroughs had migrated from the Deep South like most families in the projects. Mosby was the only guy in the projects with his own truck, a battered old affair with slatted sides, which growled its way through town. He did everything he could think of to make money with that truck. He hauled garbage and scrap metal all day long and would do any number of odd jobs. He seemed tireless, and his presence, huge.

One source of supplementary income for many families in the projects reminded me of farm life in the South. Fruit orchards abounded in the counties south and east of Benton Harbor, providing seasonal work picking fruit—everything from strawberries to peaches to cherries to blueberries. I started working in the fields during my first summer in Michigan. Summer mornings, the men would head off to the factories, and the women and children would go to the fields.

Every morning in the summer Mr. Yarbrough's old flatbed truck would cough itself awake at the projects around 5 A.M. My mother and I would be outside along with many other people, and we'd climb aboard for the ride to the fields. Some boys would hang on the frame or the running boards while our mothers and sisters warned us to be careful. The farmers treated us pretty well, giving us water and food breaks in the blistering heat. Each of us made up to ten dollars a day. I worked alongside my mother in the fields until I got summer jobs in high school. Such work was familiar but a far cry from southern sharecropping. We were working toward a better life for ourselves.

Mr. Yarbrough would pick us up at the orchards late in a long day. When we'd stagger off the truck at night, almost bent in two by our day of picking, the Yarbrough house always had great smells coming from it, and we'd head there for chow. Mickey's mother was a great cook and as dedicated to her family as her husband.

Mosby Yarbrough was the most powerful black man I knew in Benton Harbor, a big bear with an outgoing personality. When we messed up in any way or got into any trouble, he never hesitated to discipline me along with his own boys. Yet he would do it firmly without making me feel he was bossing me. He would also call my mother to tell her exactly what I'd done and what he'd said and done about it. In that way he kept her respect and mine. He wasn't overstepping any bounds. I actually craved his care and concern.

He was also a deeply Christian man, who passed that on to his family. No matter how tired we were on Sunday morning, he would roust us to go to church with him. Most of the Yarbrough kids went off to college and got good jobs. Mr. Yarbrough knew how to make ends meet and was the most successful man in the projects because he was his own employer. Since he didn't bring a lot of anger home from the assembly line or from having taken guff from his foreman, there was little resentment to take out on his family.

The Yarbroughs added to my sense of stability in the projects and were our role models. Such experiences helped me survive after Benton Harbor. I could always summon up home, if only in my mind. Such calm and structure remain part of the life of your spirit into adulthood, if you're fortunate enough to experience them.

We were still very poor by northern standards, but to us life had taken a sharp turn for the better. We didn't even think about cars or new clothes. We didn't think we were poor. Poor to us in Mississippi was having no food to eat, no clothes to wear, the bank throwing you off your land.

The projects themselves, although isolated racially and ethnically in all the ways that are known to be detrimental, were *stable*. I think that the southerners who came to a town such as Benton Harbor re-created a sort of village atmosphere, like a small hamlet or southern crossroads community. The projects were all one-story buildings, so no one was stacked on top of anyone else. At the most, three or four hundred people lived there at any time. We were homogeneous racially, in our roots, in our religion, and in our dreams. Yes, we were segregated and knew it, but we had a lot going for us in the 1950s.

I know total integration is part of the American dream and the law, but often it can cause black people to lose much of their identity. When a person is forced into someone else's environment, there's rarely any true comfort or peace. To be at home, in our own place, with love and concern flowing around us, that was the beauty of the projects in the 1950s.

I started the sixth grade in the fall of 1951 at an all-black school near the projects. My mother was worried that I would get an inferior education there, but, among my peers and with the encouragement of the teachers (all of whom were white), I did much better than in the few mute, frightened months I'd spent at Jefferson school on the west side. I was beginning to learn how I fit in a northern world of black people, and I was more at ease. In a lot of ways, I was poised to be the most "Northern" member of the Walker family since much of my schooling and most of my coming-of-age would be in the North.

When I was about thirteen, I started getting into bad arguments with Percy, the local bully. Percy was a year older than I, and he enjoyed showing how he could boss me around although I was already the tallest kid in the neighborhood for my age. He had a passel of sisters, who were tall, skinny, and even meaner than he was.

The key to his success in fights was that he always got in the first punch—always. You'd be standing there with him, just woofing, when all of a sudden, on an offbeat, with no warning, he'd sucker punch you in the eye or nose and stun you for a minute or two. Worse than that was the humiliation of all the guys and his stringy sisters razzing you afterwards.

One day Percy beat me up pretty badly. I had a swollen eye and blood streaming from my nose. After the commotion died down, furious and hurt I stumbled back to our house. No one was home but as I walked around stopping the blood with toilet paper and peering at my bad eye with the good one, something took hold of me. I went to the closet where I knew my brother Fred kept a shotgun, a single-action, double-gauge gun that I had fired on occasion when I'd gone out with Fred into the woods. Holding it down behind my leg, I walked back outside. I was thinking, Something is going to happen right now.

I was floating in my anger. At first it seemed that I could touch it; then it was inside me, then outside, as though it were happening to someone else. I walked halfway back across a yard toward the group of kids among whom Percy was still holding court. I stood behind a thick telephone pole and slowly drew the gun up into firing position. I pointed the barrel right at him and squinted as best I could with my swollen eye. He was in my sights. No one was looking in my direction.

I don't know how long I stood like that, for thirty seconds maybe. I don't know how close I came to pulling the trigger. It felt like both the easiest thing in the world and the hardest. My trembling stopped, then almost began again because I was frightened of where I was pointing the gun. I walked back home and quickly put the shotgun back in the closet and out of sight.

I began studying Percy as I would a basketball problem, how to take proper advantage of an opponent's weaknesses, something in which I later took great pride on the court. If he always attacked before the other guy was ready, I would have to just wade in earlier. A few weeks later I saw the opportunity I craved. I approached him so quickly, started jawing with him so fast, that it caught him off guard because everyone thought of me as a tall sphinx of a kid. But this time I began by socking him in the eye, then just kicked the crap out of him until he was almost unconscious. I went overboard that day to cast out my own fear of that shotgun and my anger about what I had almost done to myself as well as to another person.

After that experience, I became a very good observer of other people's behavior. I'm a watcher and waiter. I hang back. It's my nature. On the court over the years I could pick up the slightest deviation or eccentricity in other players' games. Little cues when they would drive, shoot, go left or right, where they were vulnerable. For example, when it came time for his team to set up a play to allow Jerry Lucas to shoot, he'd always unconsciously lick his fingers; then I'd get up real tight on him and fight extra hard through screens to stay with him, for I knew that although he had unlimited range, he couldn't go around me. Rick Barry would always begin to fiddle with his wristband. Then I'd prepare for him to fake a jumper and try to blow by me. I memorized a mental card file of the ticks and quirks of my opponents. But it all began when I stanched my anger and renounced that shotgun.

I used my head and prospered, at least most of the time. I wore out the hoop tacked on a backboard by the manager's office at the projects. Then from seventh to ninth grade we had a club called the Panthers. I suppose it was really a gang, but this was before gangs were synonymous with weapons and drugs. Most of the Panthers' activities revolved around sports, and in the spring we had a softball team. We were the best in Benton Harbor, an all-black team playing guys from throughout the area. But our equipment was so shabby that we were ashamed. Not one of us had a new glove or a decent bat.

A team from St. Joseph, the all-white town directly across the St. Joseph River from Benton Harbor, was our opponent in a Saturday championship game. Late on Friday afternoon the Panthers went shopping downtown at a sporting goods store, where we proceeded to steal all the equipment we needed to play the next day—gloves, bats, and balls. We wrapped up our heist before closing time at 6 P.M. The next day we took the field eager to play with our new supplies, but the game was interrupted in the fifth inning when the police showed up and confiscated all our paraphernalia. The store clerks must have figured out we had something to do with the missing merchandise. The police took our names and said we would all be contacted Monday morning. We finished up the game with St. Joseph anyway. Some of us had to play bare-handed, but we still won. The Panther victory was soured by the fact that we'd been thieves and that our folks had to pay for what we had stolen, because the store would not take back used equipment.

My mother was really angry with me, and I had to work extra hours in the orchards to pay back the ten dollars she paid to the store. Her anger made me hang my head. But when you're poor, it's tempting to take what you want because people with so much are all around you. You just yearn for something new and good to make you feel important, feel right.

Life for the Walkers in Benton Harbor wasn't easy. However, we stuck together, and each of us looked to the fulfillment of a promise that he or she hadn't known before. I found a game to call my own. In Adventism, my mother found a religion that gave her a deeper peace than any she had known before. My brothers and sisters established themselves in the post–World War II economy. We all had chances but not equal rights, and we were thankful for these opportunities. They were a start. The absolute prohibitions of Mississippi faded somewhat from my memory. The North was so exciting, so new, that I often overlooked the signs of still-prevalent racism. As a young boy, I could not tell that my life was different only in degree. I accepted that it was different in kind as well. As the baby brother and youngest son, I walked in an innocence more complete than any I would encounter later. I had been delivered out of bondage in the South. But this deliverance was partial, and my education was just beginning.

3.
An American Schoolboy and Neighborhood Hero

I grew up, lived, worked, and played in the 1950s in a different era from today. Opportunities were both better and worse for black kids coming of age. In the 1950s, there was a more widespread segregation that erected firm barriers at certain stages. We didn't have vast horizons. Factory jobs seemed amazing enough.

Fathers headed most families in the projects. A black workingman could feed his family with a factory or railroad job. Everything revolved around the economic success of plants like the Whirlpool factory, which prospered to the extent that it ran three full shifts per day. For most workers in Benton Harbor, these were the best jobs of their lives. Of course, nobody owned his own home. It was unthinkable that a black could get a loan to buy a house in Benton Harbor, though he or she could get a loan to buy a car.

You could make a living by the sweat of your brow, with your own two hands, work that you, your family, and society at large respected. There was no rising black middle class that I knew about as a kid. Then again, I didn't feel I was a member of an underclass or that I'd been left behind. I didn't know any well-off black people. Black criminals in Benton Harbor weren't drug lords or pimps. They were the local gamblers and numbers runners who constituted an underground economy and had families like everyone else.

The men in the projects were the working poor that today's American conservatives like to remember so fondly. We all felt that times were getting better for us. We had shoes, a roof over our heads, electricity, food. The folks there were religious, hard-working, and thankful for the step up from the abject nature of the southern sharecropping life. Besides, Benton Harbor was just a larger town; it was no Chicago or Detroit.

My friends and I loved to poke around for treasures in the trash of the town's wealthier white residents. We also walked through the alleys so that we wouldn't be harassed on the streets by the police. I knew from a young age that police could and would stop black kids for no other reason than their being black. It didn't matter what you did or didn't do. Just *being* black was suspicious.

In the autumn before my sophomore year in high school, we were coming back from the YMCA one late afternoon after playing ball. We came upon an open meat truck parked in back of a grocery store. We couldn't see anyone around, so we stuffed our gym bags with hot dogs and sausages and took off. By the time we got to a park with our booty, we wondered what to do with it all. One of the guys said he wanted to take his share of the haul home because his family never had any meat in the refriger-ator. I knew my mother would kill me if I brought home stolen food. We decided to have a barbecue in the park. After eating our fill, we began to pelt each other with the rest of the sausages in an outdoor food fight.

Toward eight o'clock, out of the dark came the strangest sight any of us had ever seen—an attractive white woman in a full-length fur coat walking slowly through the park. She had us transfixed. About ten yards from us she stopped and opened her coat: she was stark naked. My friend Mickey hollered, "Setup, Setup!" We fled that park faster than if she'd been the police. This was too bizarre to imagine! We thought we were losing our minds. Who was this white woman? What was she doing there?

When I got home sweating and shaking, my mother had a

late dinner waiting for me. When I told her I wasn't hungry, she was immediately suspicious, because usually I shoveled it in. So I told her I had eaten some sweet rolls on the way home. My conscience was tugging hard. If she'd known about the meat truck "job," I'd have received the whipping of my life.

But the meat truck didn't stay on my mind after being mesmerized by the white woman in the park. Emmett Till replaced the figure that had floated through the dark. If you were a black teenager in the Midwest in the fall of 1955, Emmett Till haunted your dreams, no matter how you pushed thoughts of him from your mind.

On August 28, 1955, Emmett Louis Till, a fourteen-year-old black kid from Chicago, was shot to death and mutilated beyond recognition while visiting relatives in Money, Mississippi. Supposedly, Till made a remark to a white woman, according to her, "How about a date, baby?" or maybe he just whistled. In any event, her husband and his half-brother were tried for Till's murder. Later that fall, an all-white jury took one hour to find them innocent. A month after the trial, in an interview published in *Look* magazine the men admitted they *had* killed the young man.

"Lynching" remains one of the most powerful words to black men since it reminds them of their inability to control or stem the power of the white man when he turns his full gaze on them. My mother followed the Till case closely. She constantly reminded me and my brothers that it could have been us with our skulls bashed in if we had stayed in Mississippi. She wept at the newspaper photos of Till's grieving mother, who fell to pieces at his funeral in Chicago and draped herself over his coffin.

The fate of Emmett Till was the darkest of my imaginings as a teenager. Most of my days were spent becoming a basketball player and becoming somebody. The two seemed interchangeable for a long time.

At Bard Junior High in 1955, I was six feet tall in the eighth grade and a fairly good player. The next summer I grew another four inches. I'll never forget the look of amazement on my mother's face when she got out my one good suit a week or two before school started. She thought she was just going to let the cuffs down on the sleeves and pants legs as she usually did and that everything would fit again. My arms and legs dangled from that old suit like stalks. She just couldn't believe how I'd sprouted, and neither could I.

We didn't have any extra money to buy me a good basketball, so each evening I borrowed one from the junior high when the gym was closed. Sometimes I would dribble the ball all the way from home across the river to St. Joseph, where I would practice and play at the St. Joseph Catholic High School gym on Tuesday and Friday nights. The trip was about three miles each way. I had no bus fare, but I had my borrowed ball, so I would just start dribbling home. I wanted to play every chance I got. I even remember making the trip with snow up to my knees. Basketball never seemed like work because I loved and became obsessed with it. The town of St. Joseph had a youth program, and I could get in a lot of time against older players. When you're junior high school age, your body is so restless and goes through so many changes. I could have just played all day and all night.

I didn't care about football or baseball as much as basketball, because those sports couldn't be controlled by one player. You had to rely too much on other people, and that always tensed me up. I liked basketball best when I could move on my own.

I was always hanging back as a player until I could figure out my angle of attack in a given game. I never wanted to take the reins of my team at any level—high school, college, or pro. I was a solitary kid who tried to understand an opponent as a puzzle to be solved.

But my solitary status was about to change. Ordinarily, a high school sophomore does not get to start on the varsity basketball team, but Coach Don Farnum made me a starter. He was also my biology teacher, and the first white man with whom I really developed a personal relationship.

As I was about to begin my high school basketball career

and a long life in the public eye, no one really knew how good I was going to be, including me. I knew in practice before my sophomore season that I was holding my own against the seniors. This was significant because the year before, Benton Harbor had gone to the state finals. Also, I had played with the older guys for several years in the playgrounds and during summers, so I knew I was growing into my height, that my skills were there.

At that time the Benton Harbor Tigers still played their home games in an old navy armory in town. Our high school gym was tiny, but the armory could hold about 2,500 people. At the start of each game, we had what today would be a real low-tech opening ceremony, but it was very special in 1955. At the end opposite our bench, there was a large hoop on the floor, and stretched tightly across it was a snarling papier-mâché tiger. The first Benton Harbor player to come out on the court would burst through the paper tiger dribbling a ball and go down to the other end and lay the ball in. The rest of the team would follow, hopping through the tiger hoop, and we would start our pregame warm-ups.

Coach Farnum came up to me right before we went out and told me to lead the way through the tiger. That was an honor I hadn't thought would be mine. Jim "Jelly Bean" Reynolds, our senior center and an All-State candidate, got uptight about it but not seriously.

I didn't have time to really think about what I would do before we filed out. A ball was shoved in my hands, and suddenly there I was, busting through the hoop and going full tilt toward the other basket. Most of the fans probably didn't even know who this tall, skinny kid was. They were used to the heroes from last season's team.

Then I finished off my dribble with a move that surprised myself as much as anyone else. I just went up as high as I could and dunked the ball, and the place changed from a low hush to absolute bedlam. The fans went bananas, cheering and stomping their feet. As a very shy kid, I didn't know whether to hide,

smile, or raise my fist. I had just done what came naturally. Remember this was a very low-key time in organized basketball
with everything under a coach's tight control. Nobody on a Benton Harbor team had ever dunked the ball in a game or in warm-
ups. We would fool around with dunks a lot on the playground
and in the projects, but it was still a mutation in the game.

Seven-foot players would "stuff" (as it was then called)
every now and then if left alone under the basket. But no one
thought of the shot as an offensive weapon, and no one could
have foreseen how the mythology of the dunk shot would totally
transform the aura of the game by its power and balletlike
beauty. Wilt Chamberlain in a few years would dunk so often
(the "Dipper Dunk") that the shot became commonplace. The
National Collegiate Athletic Association (NCAA) became so apprehensive of the power and authority of the dunk shot that it
was actually banned while Lew Alcindor (later Kareem Abdul-
Jabbar) and Bill Walton were at UCLA, but this was absurd.

The next step in the shot's evolution was the constant and
more artistic dunking of midsize players of great leaping ability
such as Julius Erving and David Thompson. The American Basketball Association (ABA) in the early 1970s featured a more
wide-open game where even average players such as Darnell
Hillman of the Indiana Pacers would receive the nickname of
"Doctor Dunk." Finally, in the late 1970s, Darryl Dawkins of the
76ers proved a poet by giving fanciful names to his arsenal of
dunks. At all levels of the game, the players have never looked
back.

I got to start at forward in my first varsity game, which was
very close. Before the game, I'd been real scared. I'd seen few
familiar faces in the largely white crowd. My brothers and sisters
didn't care about sports, so I was pretty much on my own. I was
and always would be "Chester" at home. Since my mother had
become a Seventh-Day Adventist, she could never watch me
play basketball. The Adventists prohibit any recreational activity
from sundown Friday to sundown Saturday, even cooking, and
most of my games were on Friday nights. Besides, she had very

high blood pressure, and I didn't know if she could survive one of our close games.

I scored twenty points, and we pulled it out in the last few seconds. After the game, I was swarmed by my buddies from the projects, who saw me as the new neighborhood hero. We all piled into a car and went to the Roxy Drive-In in town. We ordered a slew of burgers, Cokes, and fries, and one guy said he would pay for it all and came up with a fistful of bills and change. I wondered where he'd gotten all that money since most of us were always scrounging a couple of bucks from each other.

The next morning I was anonymous in town no longer. My name was on the front page of the Benton Harbor paper, and my picture was inside. It was my first good review. That morning I went down to the corner store to get something for my mother. I'd been in there dozens of times, but the owner of the store hadn't known me from Adam. On this day, I strolled in to hear him say, "Oh, you're Chester Walker. Well, I'll be." He came over and pumped my hand. Scoring points and winning games would prove to be a partial cure for invisibility.

I learned later that day that the guys had lifted the cigar box of money from the concession stand during the excitement of the last few seconds of the Friday night game when all the action was at the other end of the court. Then they'd eased out the side door before the game was officially over. So that's where our burger feast had come from! What was I to do? I know had this public role, but I also had my friends. Would I have to choose my friends according to some new criteria or standard? These were the guys I'd been with all my years in Benton Harbor, with whom I felt safe and accepted. When I began to limit our contacts, not consciously as a result of this incident but inevitably because of my celebrity and time constraints, they accused me of acting like a star, being distant. One of the hardest things about success on the larger American stage is you end up leaving people behind. And with so few black people achieving success, other black Americans are always left behind.

My dunk shot and the cash box. These are the two elements

that stay with me from my first night before a paying audience. The gulf between the great athletic move and the "heist," the worlds that would bind and separate them. When you move to another level in sports, the pressures build. After you're a hero, people ask you for money, rather than taking cash for hamburgers to celebrate with you. So if you're naturally wary and private and shy as I was, you withdraw even more.

The economics of my success and the team's drawing power enabled Benton Harbor to convince the taxpayers to build a brand-new high school gym, and we moved into the facility in my junior year. The place seated five to six thousand people. The freshness and wonder and small scale of that first night and first dunk were lost. I now dunked regularly in warm-ups and games and would continue to do so before my knees started giving out in college. Benton Harbor received more notice. The gate receipts and gym gave the school more clout. I had begun to bring in the cash before I had made any of my own.

As I grew into my basketball skill, I found people, both black and white, were relating differently to me. I went from a person who actually had no public identity at school to someone everyone recognized in a particular way. A lot of the better-off white kids at the high school were curious about our bringing something *different* to the school environment from the other side of town—our clothes, our language, our music.

As for me, despite my local celebrity, my interaction with the white kids was still very limited. I only really knew the guys on the team. We had little social contact. Occasionally, someone would offer to buy me lunch, but it was all based on my athletic status. There was little that was truly personal about it. I was never asked any questions about my family and life, or where I'd come from. For my part, I just assumed that all white kids were well off and wouldn't be interested in my roots. As for my black friends, we would kid about my putting on airs, but these were my friends whom I'd played with every day since I was ten years old. I was no mystery to them just because I'd become a star athlete.

I sensed I could get away with a lot because of my athletic status. One day, for no particular reason, I cut to the front of the lunch line in the high school cafeteria. No one said a word. The next day, I bopped in and sauntered to the front again. No response. I was taking what seemed to be mine. Nothing else ever made me feel so powerful and immune as this early recognition for my basketball skills. This was a heady experience for a kid. The project kids didn't care about my celebrity. If I'd tried to cut in front of the black girls, they would have slapped me silly. I couldn't put on airs with them because we all went home to the same place on the east side of town.

Teachers cut me a break if I hadn't done the work, because they admired the jocks in the school, or perhaps they assumed I couldn't do it because I was an athlete and black. The double force of the identity of "black athlete" meant that I could get by with less effort in class, and I took advantage of that, too. I flunked algebra twice, but I managed to accumulate enough credits to apply for college. In 1958, I became the first child in the Walker family to graduate from high school, which made my mother very proud. I learned the same doggedness in the classroom that I'd developed on the court, but I learned the hard way.

As a teenager I had this ingrained belief that black people weren't supposed to be intelligent. I remember my first and only session with a high school guidance counselor when I was a sophomore. She told me to "try" and finish high school: then the best I should hope for would be to enlist in the army. Since she was an authority figure, I felt she wouldn't have any reason not to tell me the truth and that she had my best interests at heart. I didn't have any college-boy role models in my family. Instead, my brother James had been wounded in World War II, and my brother Fred had served in Korea. When you figure out at a young age that sports can get you a passing grade, that all your coaches and teachers are interested in is your athletic performance, you go right along. When you're young, you believe what people tell you. When my high school guidance counselor told me in tenth grade that the army was what I should shoot for, that the military was my upper limit in life, I believed her.

I had one English teacher in high school who encouraged me to do more than just get by. A German-American lady, Mrs. Breidenbach was a stern disciplinarian. She would keep me out of basketball practice until I'd completed my assignments. She would say, "Chet, I know you can do this work. Don't tell me you can't." The important thing was that she allowed me to make mistakes without making me feel less of a person. Many teachers have no idea how fragile their students are and how enormously grateful these young people would be to receive equal treatment, to have the chance to prove themselves, as long as they're not labeled hopeless from day one.

I had other unofficial teachers. Wyatt was an old black man who sat in the door of the local poolroom in Benton Harbor. Wyatt was the look-out. The look-out has been an unofficial job category that you won't find in employment notices or the want-ads. I don't even know if "Wyatt" was his first or last name. I suppose he knew my name, but he used to call me "Long, Tall Drink a' Water" because I was one skinny, tall kid. While people were shooting pool in the front room, Wyatt's job was to watch for the police, who might come by and raid or harass the guys gambling in the back room. When Wyatt gave his loudest and shrillest whistle, the guys inside closed up shop for a while. He gave me a great piece of advice: "If you listen, you can hear everything."

One afternoon Wyatt called out to me, "Come here, you long, tall drink a' water, let me tell you something. You know, you could go someplace in life. You could make something of yourself. But there are two things you have to do. First, keep your ass out of this poolroom. Second, whatever you do, NEVER TRUST THE WHITE MAN . . . NEVER."

When I was playing high school basketball, Wyatt warned

me, "Long, tall drink a' water, don't you turn into a thug on me
now." He then spit a straight-as-a-string line of tobacco juice out
of his mouth. I couldn't figure out what he meant. I thought it
had something to do with being a clean player. Wyatt explained
that Joe Louis had become a thug ruled by people who just
wanted him to be a killer, that Louis had lost his humanity.
Wyatt was telling me to remain a human being. True enough, the
further you go in big-time sports, the more coaches tell you to
knock someone's head off. It starts as a figure of speech for aggressive play. Then sometimes it becomes second nature, and
you forget how to play with respect for your opponent. In the
end, you end up with less respect for yourself.

Black coaches, white coaches, the message is the same. You
have to learn how to play with the coach's command for aggres-
sion ringing in your ears and to decide what sort of player you
want to be.

I never could play that way. I never wanted to check my
humanity in the dressing room. I was always fascinated by the
finely tuned mechanics of the game. How to execute an offense.
How to work fakes on an individual opponent. I played the necessary contact game but was blessed with enough skills that I
didn't have to resort to much in the way of thuggery. I hope
Wyatt was proud.

When I got to high school, Coach Farnum put me at forward, my natural position, because our senior captain, Jim Reynolds, was a fine center. This was actually a blessing. Many
times, the kid who stands six feet six inches ends up at center
because he's the tallest player on his high school team. But that
does him no favors, because in college he'll generally be down-
sized one position. This transition is sometimes impossible if a
player hasn't developed a versatile game. I learned how to play
the corner spot from the beginning. I didn't have three inferior
players collapsing all over me in the middle as many outstanding young post players do. I always knew how to play facing the
basket and knew how to create my action on the baseline and
cutting through the lanes. I had my coordination from the begin-

ning, and ball handling was no problem. I liked faking opponents into the air and watching them stumble as I moved past
them. I looked like a lazy player at times because I would approach offense so methodically. I wanted to get the job done. The
easiest way for me to score was the least flashy. Two points is
two points. Farnum wasn't a great basketball coach, but I thank
him for making me a forward.

What sorts of "life" knowledge do high school coaches im-
part to kids? Farnum was obsessed with the fact that players
should never have sex before a game, and I believed him absolutely. Not until I got to the pros with the 76ers did I ever break
this prohibition, and, even then, I waited for some absolute judgment by the god of basketball! I didn't have a real schoolboy romance when I was in Benton Harbor. Just several exploratory
one-night stands in the back of a borrowed car. Sports took up
too much of my time. Besides I had no money at all, and I had
nothing to impress a girl with beyond my status as a basketball
star. I think that in the 1950s, girls didn't run after athletes as
much as they did the guys who had lots of time and money to
spend with them, the guys with flashy cars. Besides, girls really
went after guys who were smooth dancers and loved music.
Dancing was never my thing, and I was too shy to get out there
very often.

The white girls *were* more interested in the athletes, or so
Coach Farnum thought. He feared that the black players would
have sex with the white girls who hung around the gym, his
worst-case scenario. But sports is a macho world. Basketball is an
intimate game with players running around half-naked, glisten-
ing with sweat, muscles rippling. Players are taught from day
one to mistrust women. They are told how destructive women
can be to them. Athletes have great physical success on the court
so they believe they can have physical success with anyone off
the court, too. Winning becomes an object; athletes look at
women as objects to be won. And the women looked right back,
even in the 1950s.

Amid the beginning of all this athletic immortality came

other reminders of how fragile my life was. One highlight of my weekends was our regular Saturday morning touch-football game with all the guys from the projects. The wraps were off then; no coaches telling us what to do, no white folks in the stands. We played in rain, in snow, in every kind of weather. In fact, we had some classic games in the snow. One of my best friends was Richard Davis, who lived just across the alley from us. He was the star of our games, no matter what sport we played. He was the only boy in a family of five so he got everything he wanted from an indulgent father.

During one Saturday game, Richard just collapsed. No one was even near him; it was eerie. He got up by himself and went home. We didn't see him for two or three weeks, but word got around that Richard had multiple sclerosis. He went to a sanitarium for a stay, and when he came home, he could barely walk. He just got weaker and weaker until he died. Richard was a high school sophomore, like me. He was my friend and could have been my teammate, perhaps reaching greater heights than I did. Sports was not strong enough to save him.

Those pickup games at the projects evoke happy memories. In fact, some of my favorite times in basketball have been away from school or professional competition. The most fun I had in basketball as a kid was playing for a church team in the summers. We were sponsored by the African Methodist Episcopal Baptist Church. We were an all-black team coached by a black guy, Charles Gray, who was a social worker at the local YMCA. He let us play the way we loved, the way we played in the schoolyard and at the projects. We played other all-black teams in an informal league all over Michigan. We would play against teams from Grand Rapids, Detroit, Lansing, and Battle Creek. We would play our hearts out, then join the fans and families of the players to dance, eat, and socialize at the church.

We would do all sorts of fancy stuff like behind-the-back dribbling that no school coach would allow. The whole network of teams and fans took place outside the structure of organized ball. We played in tiny church gyms packed with local people. I never had so much fun. We were free to strut, which was called "globetrotting" in the 1950s after the style of America's master basketball showmen, the Harlem Globetrotters. We were both proud of the Globies and wary of their reputation as black clowns. No black high school player aiming to make it to a college program wanted to be labeled a "Trotter." Unless you were Bob Cousy, and white America thought you were a wizard, or you were another colorful white player like Hot Rod Hundley, if you dribbled through your legs in high school or college in the 1950s, you stood the risk of being benched or cut. The best basketball is actually a mixture of elements: small, subtle moves; a team working together as one person, then a sudden, wonderful individual feat.

In the 1950s, there was one game for the white coaches and another for the playgrounds. Our game belonged to us and had varying degrees of difficulty, like a diving or skating exhibition. You tried the most wonderful stuff you could think of to score on your friends and make them remember it. It was art, it was survival of the fittest, it was theater.

We were a diverse bunch. Only a ninth grader, I was the kid of the team, but I had proved myself in order to play. As such, I was protected by some of the older guys, both on and off the home court, especially Carl Brown, our local enforcer in the projects. Carl was a few years older than I and the toughest, meanest friend I ever had. He would have been a fine high school player at six feet four inches, but his attitude was wrong as far as coaches were concerned. He was as much a mentor as a protector. He realized my potential as a player and wasn't going to let anyone rough me up.

One of our guards was John L.—that's all we ever knew of his name. He was about seventeen and supposedly a fugitive from justice in Chicago. He lived in Benton Harbor with his aunt. We accepted him as long as he could play, and he accepted us as long as we didn't ask many questions. Charles Gray led us all with calm and equanimity, and we respected him.

At one tournament in Kalamazoo, we made it to the cham-

pionship game against a team from Grand Rapids. We faced
their amazing star player, a kid who had only one arm. His left
arm had been amputated at the elbow. But the crowd loved what
he could do with that right arm. He would dribble wondrously,
then somehow get shooting room where he would put the ball
on the stump of that left arm and sling it off with his right arm
just when you wouldn't expect it. He was a deadly shooter with
such a strange, unpredictable rhythm that no one knew when he
was going to put the ball up. So Coach Gray assigned J.T., our
toughest defensive player, to guard him. J.T. was a very muscu-
lar kid who played high school football. All J.T. had to do was sit
on the kid's left arm to knock that carefully calibrated shot away.
But in the first half, the one-armed kid just killed us with long
shots. He looked unstoppable at halftime as we trooped into the
church basement, our makeshift locker room. We couldn't believe we were six or seven points behind at the break.

Coach Gray couldn't believe it either. He paced in front of
us. We knew Coach Gray as a mild mannered, very religious
man whose whole life was dedicated to ministering to young
people. But there was something forceful about him as he
walked back and forth, and we couldn't take our eyes off him—
all of us except J.T., who glued his eyes to the floor. Charles said
softly, "J.T., I don't understand. I know you're a better defensive
player than you showed. What's the problem?" His head still
down, J.T. answered, "Coach, I feel sorry for the guy. I can't
bring myself to be more physical against him." Charles gently
put his hand under J.T.'s chin and drew his face up. He said,
"Look at me, son. I want you to know one thing. If you don't go
up there in the second half and put the clamps on that guy, I'll
personally take you out in the parking lot and beat the shit out of
you."

We were all amazed, the burly J.T. most of all. Charles had
never cursed or raised his voice to us before. After that halftime
shock, the game was already effectively over. J.T. totally destroyed that poor, gallant boy in the second half and never let
him get off a shot. Suddenly, Christian charity coexisted in my

I came in and went straight to the kitchen. My mother fried up something that looked like a hamburger and placed it between two end pieces of bread on a plate she set in front of me. She was very quiet, as if she wanted to apologize for not having more food in the house. She just stood there avoiding my eyes as I avoided hers, not wanting to make her feel any worse. Finally, she just softly put her hand on my shoulder and left the kitchen. She knew that I knew that she knew how poor we were and how sorry she was.

From my gym bag, I pulled a bottle of orange juice that I'd lifted from the school cafeteria at lunchtime and ate the burger in silence. If you wonder why players on signing their first big contracts so often mention buying houses for their mothers, you can multiply scenes like the one in the Walker kitchen many times over. Such moments are prime motivating forces that sustain the family and keep it together through lean times.

We were talked down to by our teachers and harassed by the police; we had no decent clothes and no spending money. So we would find ways to act out. When we played towns like Grand Haven and Holland, all-white teams of Dutch kids, we just wanted to crush them.

What people don't often realize is that organized sports can be a vicarious way for black men to get even with white guys. Sure, it's all symbolic but so are most public activities. Night after night, black manhood is legally on display in a physical sense in only one arena of American life: organized sports. That transaction is culturally approved and experienced. But every young black kid on any team, on any court, always carries more than his own burden. He's bearing a legacy that stretches long before his time and that underlies every move he makes.

There is an area in which black men are considered not only equal but dominant: speed and jumping ability in American sports. I've been living the myth of the "natural" superiority of black athletes and hearing about it ever since I was a kid.

Black kids are runners. They spend much of their lives running to something or away from somebody. As a boy, when your mother calls you to dinner, you rush along, afraid if you're late, there'll be nothing left to eat. If you're in a fight, chances are you're chasing a kid or being chased by him. When we were young in the projects, "chasing girls" meant just that, and they were usually faster than we were! Later in life, you might be running from a rival gang or from the police. In any case, life in the ghetto is always run, run, run, most often to take evasive action.

Just drive through a large housing complex and watch kids at play. Take that energy and refine it, and you have entertainment. Am I talking about natural rhythm? Not really. It's not that simple. Black people do have a fundamental rhythm, and it's to a drumbeat. All sorts of half-beat and offbeat syncopations. I'm convinced that it goes all the way back to African musicians and the hip, arm, and leg movement in tribal dancing.

Black American music comes from a drum rhythm. A spectator can see such a rhythm manifested in a sport like basketball when he or she watches a black guard take the ball up the court. Chances are the guard is throwing fakes even when no one is in the way. All the movements veer left and right, hesitating and putting on a burst of speed. Black style in basketball is not some inborn rhythm. It's part of our cultural background (the drums) and historical circumstance (slavery, slipping the yoke, running from the man).

Why can't white men jump? It's not so much that they can't run or jump but that they seem to perform at a different rhythm. Not a defective rhythm or without rhythm but another one. I think of orchestral music that goes back centuries, music with strings and long, flowing lines. White people listen for the melody, not the beat. Watch white players bring the ball up court. They move in straight lines, always in control. There's no body movement, no feints, no head and arm fakes. No body part is *loose*. Nothing moves to a drumbeat or an improvisational rhythm.

It's the difference between NBA greats Jerry West and Earl

Monroe. West had a giant first step that could free him to his right for a jump shot that was deadly accurate. His game was all sharp, blunt angles, as ruler edged as his face. But the Pearl couldn't keep his body from twitching when he got the ball down low. Every part of his torso would make a different move. Then he'd spin and be free. Evasive action. Both players were enormously effective but moving to different music.

I can't give the medical explanations for why some people can jump and others can't. But I do know that, as a rule, most black players have really slim legs, long ankle bones, and stringy muscles. These muscles contract the achilles tendon to produce the explosive jump. Most white guys I've played with had much heavier legs and thicker ankles. They couldn't get up as high or go up again as quickly after coming down. Is this nature or nurture? Have black people been outrunning their enemies for too long? I think of all the great jumping animals in the kingdom— kangaroos, gazelles, leopards. Their legs are long, stringy, and powerful.

I like to think that running and jumping have a lot to do with the way black people approach life. Somebody in some way is always demanding either "Bring this in a hurry" or "You'd better get out of here fast." I guess I'll leave it at that. What is a stereotype anyway but a mixture of nature and culture?

I do get angry when black basketball style is attributed to nothing but "natural ability" whereas white players are generally "tireless workers" or "always thinking on the court." I had my share of natural gifts, but I guarantee you that I worked as hard as any player and out-thought most on the court. Any outstanding athlete at a high level of performance is always a mixture of talent, hard work, and intelligence. It's foolish to think otherwise.

I always used my intelligence to enhance my game. I hated to lose so much that I wouldn't play until I'd figured out a way to beat my opponent. In my early teens, I was always playing ball with older kids around the projects. If they beat my team, I'd have a number of defensive reactions. I would go off and cry where they couldn't see me. Or I would make an excuse to go home. Or I would sit out and quietly figure out a strategy to win when we had the next game on the court.

When you play on a playground, you always wage a series of individual battles against your opponent. You don't think of the team as much as in organized sport with its different work ethic and cooperation. When did black players ever have the luxury of giving up the ball? Instead, we watch our opponent's moves for the slightest hint of a weakness in his game.

If you're a black kid, it's not good enough to shoot from outside. You like to break people down by taking it to the hole. Such moves come from anger and frustration, from competing and trying to be on top, from struggling all your life. Only people who have something can afford to be unselfish, unless you're a saint. In the ghetto, you often must take what you can before someone takes it away. Moving the ball around so that someone else can take a better shot often appears to be a virtue from another world. Soaring over an opponent, driving in at him, then *looking* at him to say "I crushed you"—that's control. Perhaps the only place a young black player can feel it.

Another more practical reason that playground players want to go to the basket has to do with playing outside on bad surfaces in wind or cold or with bad lighting, bent rims, and dead backboards. Graceful jump shots aren't much good in a war zone if they clang off the rim—long, short, left, right. So you start by trying to take the drive away from your opponent. As a kid, I was almost always taller than anyone else, so I should have been able to block a lot of shots, but it was very hard to block shots on the playground because the other guy would always call "Foul!" Then arguments would start, and fights would break out. So you try to use the *threat* of blocking the shot to make the guy do something else he doesn't want to do. You sort of steer your opponent toward his weaknesses without letting him realize that it actually *is* a weakness: make a guy go left when he wants to go right; make him put it on the floor when he doesn't want to dribble; back off the weak jump shooters; know their routine entry passes or passing lanes; cut off his receipt of the ball if a guy doesn't move well without it; know whether he wants his shot or looks to someone else all the time.

A person's basketball game is a blueprint of his personality and a clue to his character. That's what makes competition in sports so interesting. That's why any sport, even the dazzlingly quick game of basketball, is a thinking man's game at its best.

In some ways, black kids in Benton Harbor did things that just provoked the cops to come after us. But at the same time the cops let us know they would go out of their way to harass us. So we had a real give-and-take. It wasn't enough to stop us downtown or on our way home from school in groups. They had to let us know where we stood. If we were caught snatching fruit from a stand or trying to sneak into the movie theater, it was never a stern lecture or just a firm hand or a warning. It was "Get your black ass out of there, you little black son of a bitch." The cops' responses were always humiliating.

One lazy summer Saturday afternoon before my junior year in high school, a group of guys had just finished working up a sweat on the basketball court and sat down in the park to play blackjack at a penny a hand. We liked to cap our sports day with this high-rolling activity. But this day would be real different. Before we knew what was happening, two cops pulled up in a squad car and arrested us all for gambling.

We were always very careful not to cross any of the real or imagined boundaries that existed in town. I don't remember ever hearing about any blacks voting in Benton Harbor or talking about elections. There were no black politicians or city officials. There was one black cop, and he was the guy who booked us for "gambling in the park." When I told him we were only playing for pennies, he cut me short with a bark and a shove, Saying, "You're lyin', boy. You were gamblin'." He wanted to prove to us and his police pals that he could be as tough on black kids as any white cop. This cop was a real hard-ass. It's my opinion that many blacks put in positions of authority by whites have to exaggerate their toughness. It's part of a colonial mentality: identify with your oppressors, put on a uniform, and no one can get at you anymore.

So there we were, in jail and as incommunicado as if we lived under some third-world dictatorship. The court system was closed for the weekend, so we couldn't be arraigned. The jail didn't allow visits on weekends, and we couldn't make phone calls. The authorities finally let one kid call out, so all our families would know where we were.

We were thrown in a cell on Saturday afternoon with the drunks and the thieves, and we stayed there until Monday morning. We sat on a concrete floor because there were no bunks, no benches. Some of the drunks were pissing and puking onto the floor. The place stank and was stifling. One guy crawled over to me on Saturday night and insisted that I move, that I was crowding him. When I wouldn't, he spat on me. I stood up and kicked him in the face as hard as I could. He just groaned and fell over. I was afraid I'd killed him, but he was so drunk he had just passed out. On Monday morning we were all arraigned before a judge, fined eight dollars apiece for gambling, and warned not to do it again.

My mother understood why I'd been arrested but not the gambling itself. If you were a black kid in the ghetto, you almost automatically had a police record while still in your teens. But my mother, who understood the clashes between black men and police very well, was angry with me for going against what she considered a religious teaching. That took precedence for her. Even if I was gambling for a penny, she thought I was abusing the Lord. The Benton Harbor police and courts didn't matter as much to me as did her opinion of me.

In Monday's Benton Harbor newspaper after our weekend in jail, only my name earned a mention in the story headlined "Benton Harbor Basketball Player Chet Walker Jailed for Gambling." Such was my introduction to yet another downside of celebrity. From that moment on, I realized I would be held to a different standard. I also knew deep down that I had been arrested and held only because I was black. It was the black *athlete* who made the newspaper, but it was the *black* athlete who'd been arrested with his friends.

One of the results of my arrest that fall was a downward spiral into real self-hatred. I don't think I ever felt so ashamed of who I was or of just being black in a white society. I kept fantasizing about being someone else.

I'd gone to see *Rebel without a Cause.* I identified completely with the James Dean character. He seemed so cool and free of all hypocrisy and status games, a strong, gentle kid who stood up for his friends. In the film he wore a lightweight red jacket with the collar turned up. Wanting to be James Dean, I saw that same jacket in a downtown store and worked weeks to save enough money to buy it.

Just like the Dean character, I wore it constantly but never told any of my friends or my mother how strongly I felt about this white movie star. I was extremely upset when he died in a car crash when he was only twenty-four. But even that death—mysterious, sudden, violent—was somehow cool, a "movie death," and part of his mystique.

Not until later that basketball season, after I'd become established as a team leader and emerging star, did I begin to feel like myself again. I grew more comfortable in my role and started to forget about that weekend in jail and about James Dean. The red jacket was left hanging in the closet.

At the beginning of my senior year I started receiving letters from colleges and universities throughout the country. That was when I began to believe I had options. No one had prepared me for all this attention, not my coach and certainly not my family. The whole experience was overwhelming. In the summer after my junior year, cars began mysteriously showing up at the projects with white coaches wanting to establish contact with me and my family. Recruiting wasn't as invasive or sophisticated as today. My mother didn't have to endure slick-talking assistant coaches at her kitchen table. She wouldn't have known what to make of these aliens though I'm sure she would have been gracious and offered them something to eat.

It's not surprising that no one else in my family had the time or the opportunity to become involved in sports. Since my brothers had come to the North as men looking for work, and they didn't play school sports, I didn't have shoes to fill on the court.

Most of the visiting coaches made assumptions about what I could and couldn't do just as the high school counselors and teachers had. They figured they would have trouble with my intelligence and motivation levels. As a senior in high school in 1958, I wasn't cynical, and I wasn't suspicious of other people's motives. I had been vaulted into prominence in a small arena and was feeling pretty good about myself. I didn't know what an agent was; there weren't any. There were no shoe contracts, no television exposure in high school. I had no idea that I would have a shot at professional basketball. My life as a sports hero did not seem predetermined to me.

Today, player prospects are identified in junior high schools and become subjects of recruiting wars by competing high school coaches. In the 1950s, young black players were painting themselves on a virtually empty canvas. I experienced the rewards and dangers firsthand without the advantage, or disadvantage, of foreknowledge. My athletic career developed just as sports grew to great prominence in American society because of television and the expansion of college basketball. The sport I began to play at Benton Harbor High School in 1955 had only a passing relation to the game I had played with delight as a kid to please myself and to combat loneliness and isolation.

When scouts came around to look at me in high school, I felt as if I were a young racehorse. These guys sit in small groups at games or stand around in the projects. Everyone knows who they are. They are easy to spot: they have clipboards, note pads, are always doodling and writing. They're making notes on your body fat, skin tone, flexibility, jumping ability. They're checking the size of your hands and feet. They would like to find some prototype of the perfect animal. We should be glad they don't ask to see our teeth; maybe we could whinny for them. This process calls to mind one of the racial nightmares of black people: the slave auction, where bodies and health were everything.

To be judged solely on your physical attributes is unsettling for anyone, man or woman, black or white. Surely white players feel much the same uneasiness about ownership of their bodies. But the history of black people in this country is based on our physical survival. The uncomfortable truth is that we were bred for physical strength by forces outside our control. It may be true that a grim eugenic selection lies at the heart of black physical dominance in sport. Furthermore, not many of us could have made it through to the present if past generations hadn't had the physical heartiness, not to mention courage and endurance, to survive.

I was an all-conference tight end in football during my junior and senior years in high school and received a few offers of football scholarships, but football wasn't really my game, not like basketball. In my junior year, we made it to the state semifinals in basketball, where we were beaten by Muskegon Heights. When I was a senior, Benton Harbor advanced to the Class A finals in the Michigan state tournament. At the time, Michigan's high school tournaments weren't as well publicized as those in Indiana, the hot-bed of high school basketball. In this championship game we played in Lansing against Austin High, an all-white Catholic school from Detroit led by Dave DeBusschere. Dave and I were to battle each other for the next two decades in college and the NBA.

Nothing is as exciting in an athlete's life as a high school championship game. You're playing before people you've known for most of your life. In college, it's a four-year crowd, and in the pros, you don't know who you're playing for. But in high school, your friends and family appear in great numbers.

Many black people drove to Lansing from the projects for this game. They would cash their paychecks or use the money made working in the orchards to charter buses in order to watch us. At that time high school sports triggered a lot of community excitement because they weren't competing with a full slate of televised college games or other sports entertainment. The team and the game belonged to the whole town.

We lost the game 71–68. I managed to foul out DeBusschere and score twenty-five points; but I was so keyed up that I must have missed ten foul shots, and I couldn't help feeling I cost us the championship. I cried after that game, just sobbed, because the game had drawn everyone who was woven in the fabric of my life except for my mother. It was personal and local. We wanted that game for our team, our town, ourselves, and our friends and families. Such a moment happens very seldom in sports.

High school sports unite individuals from the disparate groups who live together in a small town. For example, a great friend of mine in Benton Harbor was Sheldon Radom, a white man who owned a farm-supply store. Shel was a walking encyclopedia of Benton Harbor High School basketball, who had seen all the games for twenty-five years, including mine. I called him about a summer job when I was in high school, and he found me work in a canning factory. Later, he wrote me regularly when I was homesick at Bradley and gave me a summer job driving his truck to deliver chemical supplies to farmers in the area. I'm not sure how our paths might have crossed without sports.

My mother got to share in one of my athletic triumphs only once. In 1960, when I was first named an All-American at Bradley, the Benton Harbor downtown merchants sponsored a Chet Walker Night at the all-white Elks Lodge. It was a banquet I'll never forget. My mother had never made a public statement in her life, but she came through with flying colors. When she told them I was a good boy, I cried right there. My mother wanted her children to grow up to be good citizens and good people. To that end, my mother had worked and, most important, had prayed for all of her children. Her religion defined her life and therefore shaped mine to a great extent.

I have not been a churchgoer as an adult but consider myself a religious person. Deep spirituality existed in my home as a child. For black people, religion has always been a vehicle to maintain our sanity. Having said that, I also believe religion has persuaded blacks to be passive in the fight for freedom. Since the beginning of slavery in what is now the United States, frontal attacks on racism have caused death to blacks. Christianity has been called a slave religion. But what else did slaves have? What chains ever bound the philosophers who talk about free will? Freedom in the hereafter is a comfort when you're getting your skull bashed in the here and now. But I never entirely trusted organized religion. It transformed too much anger and hatred into resignation. My soul told me to fight, but my common sense told me it was of little use.

It's like Malcolm X said of Dr. King: he had great respect for a man who would tie his own hands and walk out into a violent and dangerous world without the ability to fight back. Malcolm said he respected the view all the more because he didn't understand it.

4.
A Basketball Abduction

In Michigan, I began to see that I could use basketball to go a long way from home. Would it change who I was? I didn't know. I thought that was still in my hands alone. My brothers couldn't help me decide where to go to college. What did any of them know about college recruiting? My mother was suspicious of any white man who came to her door.

So I was on my own dealing with these college basketball coaches. They talked basketball nonstop, how I would start for their team right away as a sophomore, how I would become a famous player. They said nothing about my education or my development as a person. I took campus visits to Bradley, Michigan, Michigan State, Western Michigan, Navy, and Nebraska. These trips suggested the new life opening to me because the only traveling I'd done before was in Michigan in groups with the AME church team and later with the high school team.

The University of Michigan intimidated me with its size. The campus was huge, winding through and around the town of Ann Arbor. I might have gone there, but in the end they pursued other high school seniors. The idea of going to the Naval Academy intrigued me for I'd read about sea captains and naval battles and imagined becoming a military hero. I went to Annapolis and was amazed at the sight of those famous battleships and cruisers. I was a little over the limit of six feet six inches, but they would have waived the regulation for me if I'd played ball. Who knows? I might have been the first David Robinson. But Annapolis scared me off, too. There were no girls anywhere in sight, the discipline looked really strict, and I was afraid that academically I would have washed out.

On the other campus trips I would usually be shown around by the black players—if there were any—or at least by athletes. Our conversations always revolved around playing, the social life on campus, the prestige of a college degree. Everyone was very polite. I never brought up any questions about race, about where I could get a haircut or soul food or find a black community or someone who might advise me. Race might have been fundamental, but back in the 1950s, it simply wasn't something you could talk about to someone you just met. I knew I was expected to be deferential and grateful for everything and just keep my mouth shut.

My campus trips were not the hard-sell, totally scripted scenarios that universities put on for today's talented high school seniors. I was not offered under-the-table deals or indirect payments. Each time I went to a campus I returned a little more bewildered from all the attention, but I didn't have the knowledge or the confidence to take control of the process.

I drove down to Bradley in Peoria, Illinois, in the summer and was shown around campus by their black senior center, Joe Billy McDade. It was a pleasant little campus but made no deep impression on me. I did like the fact that Bradley had been a national basketball power and had several black players from the Chicago area.

McDade didn't try to sell me too much on Bradley's basketball success. He talked instead of academics, of what they had meant to him as a person. That impressed me more than any recruiting talk. I knew I'd just done what was necessary to get by in school in Benton Harbor. But here was a guy only a few years older than I was who had a whole future opening up to him beyond basketball, beyond Bradley. He was an outstanding student and later became a prominent lawyer and judge in Peoria.

As time wore on, Nebraska really put the move on me. Nebraska's athletic director, Bill Orwig, was a former Benton Harbor High coach and a college friend of Benton Harbor's mayor. Joe Carver, a wealthy auto dealer in town and Orwig's friend, gave my brother Robert a job. The summer after my senior year, Orwig arranged a job for me at a cold-storage locker. It was owned by a religious cult in Benton Harbor called the "House of David," famous for fielding a barnstorming baseball team whose players never shaved their chins or cut their hair or ate meat.

Two weeks after I graduated from high school, I began the job with the House of David cold-storage plant. This was the first real job I had other than working in the fruit orchards. I worked the night shift, 3–11 P.M., and I had to miss a lot of social activities in the evenings.

Because of my "clout" as a basketball star, I never had to go into the storage lockers to store fruit like the other employees. My job pretty much consisted of playing checkers with Tom, the owner, who reminded me of Bluto from the Popeye comics. I spent the summer trying to beat him, but I never did. For playing checkers, I earned eighty-five to ninety dollars a week, quite a lot of money for a summer job in 1957. By helping me get that job, Orwig almost earned himself a Nebraska recruit. A summer job may not sound like the strongest reason to choose a college, but since I hadn't even imagined a college career until very late in high school, I just wandered into the decision. I had no strong allegiance to any team and no great academic ambitions. No national magazines or newspaper reporters were hanging on my decision.

My mother had little to contribute to my choice but a lot of reminders. Through the years of my young life her message sounded in my head: don't get in trouble, behave yourself, be a moral person.

***

I was growing out of Benton Harbor now, thinking about the larger world. My thoughts strayed toward romance though I knew it wasn't the time; but it was summer, and the sap was rising. Against my better judgment I fell for a girl named Shirley, a tall, beautiful "stallion girl" as we called a girl like that back then. I was reluctant to admit to myself how much I was thinking about her. I'd spent four years fighting off girls, pleading I didn't have time or money. And now with the prospects of a four-year college scholarship as an All-State high school star, I saw myself as someone who could call his shots.

But I couldn't shake my dreams about Shirley, a high school junior, so we tentatively began to go together. At the time, a big deal in the 1950s was to take late-night hayrides to the dunes at the beaches on Lake Michigan. There were all sorts of unplanned and amorous adventures in those dunes in the summers.

I got up one Friday morning and called Shirley, who told me about a hayride that night. She wanted me to take her. I said I couldn't get off work until 11 P.M., and she then insisted I take the night off. She asked what was more important, her or the job. I asked why she couldn't wait until eleven and then we would drive out to join everybody. She said she couldn't wait, and I agreed to meet her at the dunes.

I felt sort of manipulated by Shirley. We'd come close to sex several times when I'd made moves on her, but then she would back off insisting she was a virgin, that she was waiting for marriage. She made me respect her, and though I was frustrated, I liked her that much more. The romantic in me considered her all the more special.

I drove out to the beach late that night in the cooling breeze coming from Lake Michigan. I parked and walked up the trails through trees to the high, bulky dunes from which I could see small bonfires and hear laughter. I greeted some friends but couldn't see Shirley anywhere and asked where she was. Everyone got real quiet before one guy said in a low voice, "I think she's across the road down behind that big dune." Excited, I ran up the immensely shadowed dune, feeling the burn in my legs as they dug into the coarse sand. I scrambled to the top, the stars blazing over my head, only to look down to the beach, where two people were entwined in a blanket. It was Shirley and Harold, a kid I didn't like because he had the nicest car and was the best dancer in our crowd.

I felt a terrific pounding in my heart, the combination of my run up the dunes, my hurt, and my anger. I could have charged down that dune like someone from the Light Brigade and taken Harold out, then dealt with Shirley. But I didn't, and they didn't see me, busy as they were under that blanket. Instead, I took my shock and ran down my side of the dune to a waiting group of curious friends. I put on a really brave front, didn't lose my cool, brazened it out about how little she meant to me, called her a few choice names. Then I got out of there as fast as I could before Harold and Shirley could return up the dune.

I was Mr. Everything in Benton Harbor, and I was damned if I would let anyone see that a girl could affect me so much. I was the man, the star. After I drove my brother's car home to the projects, I found myself almost hyperventilating for the first time in my life. I lay down in my room with all my clothes on, unable to sleep. I couldn't understand how this could happen to me. Not in my wildest dreams did I believe a girl could make me feel this way.

On Saturday morning I dragged myself to breakfast but wasn't able to eat under my mother's sharp gaze. She looked at me and said, "Boy, what's wrong with you? Are you sick, got a cold?" "No, just not hungry," I whispered. She put her hand on my forehead to see if I had a fever, then slowly took her hand away and sat in her chair, looking at me.

"I know what's wrong with you, you're in love, aren't you?" she said.

"No," I lied. "No, Mama."

"I said I *know* what's wrong with you, Chester. I know what you're going through. It's a wound. But it will heal."

I knew I was reacting with a mentality that is common for young males. That no woman could ever really touch me, that I had to be cool and in control. As athletes with so many females throwing themselves at us, we refuse to believe that our hearts can be captured. I had just learned otherwise, and it hurt so bad. But my pride took over. I was too big to let this happen to me.

This incident at the end of high school had a profound influence on my relationships with women for a long, long time. Later, if I found myself with strong feelings for someone, I would always break off the relationship, not because I was a compulsive rover but because I was sure I would be hurt in the end. And my pride as a star simply couldn't take that. Everything I did socially was in a fishbowl. What if somebody *found out* I'd been dumped? I couldn't be vulnerable. Vulnerable meant leaving myself open to loss. What if emotional defeats carried over to the basketball court? What if I got soft? Would my game be taken away from me? Then where would I be?

I talked to Shirley a few days later. I knew she'd found out I'd seen her with Harold. Tentatively, she came around to that night, but pretty soon she was ragging me: she had been hurt and disappointed that I wouldn't go with her earlier that evening; nothing had happened under that blanket with Harold on the beach; please, couldn't we just pick up again as if it hadn't happened. I looked deep into her eyes and saw what she saw. Her ticket out of Benton Harbor—a would-be college man and basketball star. She wasn't really looking at me. Now I'm not so sure. I know my *pride* refused to believe her. That was enough when I was eighteen. I dropped her cold and did not see her again.

This would not be the last time in my life that I ended a relationship because of my conflicts and roles. I never had any idea, as long as I was playing basketball, who I was for other people and whom they were looking at when they saw me. In the summer before my college life began, my wariness kept me more alone than I could have imagined.

***

In early September 1958, my mother sent my trunk ahead to the University of Nebraska at Lincoln, and soon I was all set to leave myself. My brother Fred was going to drive me to Midway Airport in Chicago on a Sunday, where I would catch a plane for Lincoln. As if summoned from a dream, Joe Stowell, an assistant coach from Bradley, pulled up in front of our house at 6 A.M. that Sunday morning. Now, Stowell was the kind of guy who could recruit a dead man! He said he was on his way to Chicago too and volunteered to drop me off at Midway. I knew something was up and almost shivered as I gave my mother a good-bye hug.

As we drove toward Chicago, Stowell worked hard to change my mind and get me to consider switching to Bradley. He knew how to lay it on. I got even more attention when we stopped for breakfast in Three Oaks, Michigan, at Al Benson's cottage near Lake Michigan. Benson was a disc jockey and evangelist from Chicago and a great persuader. He had already tried to get my mother to let me choose a college—Bradley—on religious grounds! Together, Stowell and Benson had a mean one-two punch.

I was getting scared and apprehensive at Benson's and asked to call my mother. Benson's wife said the phone wasn't working. After breakfast at Benson's house, the cast of characters in my little drama grew. Jim Brown, a legendary black Chicago basketball coach at DuSable High School, "happened" to drop by. He had almost won the 1954 Illinois State High School Championship with an all-black starting five. I knew he had sent his players such as Shellie McMillon and Curley Johnson to Bradley and that they had both earned their degrees. Everyone was pushing *Bradley, Bradley.*

Stowell and Brown dropped out of the picture at this point, probably to keep their noses clean if they were ever held to account. Al Benson then took over as my next handler, driving me the rest of the way to Chicago. Somewhere along the way he gave me some money, three or four hundred dollars. I didn't even want to look as if I was counting it. I was afraid that if I didn't take it, he might drop me right there on the road. I don't remember even telling him I'd decided to go to Bradley. Perhaps it was assumed. Perhaps I was just hoping it was true. An eighteen-year-old kid was about to, hoping to, go where he had wanted to in the first place. I admit I didn't think of the morality of the move or the people who would be angry or let down by this change in destinations. I let it happen. Once again I was going along with other people's plans, only this time these plans agreed with my own.

In Chicago, we didn't drive to Midway Airport but to Meigs Field, a small landing strip next to Lake Michigan, near downtown. There, to my surprise, were the Bradley athletic director, Dutch Meinert, and the Bradley head coach, Chuck Orsborn, standing next to a propeller-driven plane. It's hard to imagine now how easily I was passed along, but the next thing I remember I was on that little plane taking off, then rolling and rattling down into Peoria about forty-five minutes later. I looked out the window and saw a huge, flashing red sign: JOHNNIE WALKER RED, Peoria's most famous distillery. In my nausea, I imagined my father, John Walker, glaring at me with a big, red eye, disapproving of the mess I was in. It was an almost biblical message. Dizzy and sick to my stomach, I arrived in Peoria, Illinois. I was a college man.

Too chagrined to call and tell my mother I was at Bradley, I laid low for a couple of days. My mother received a terrible shock when the Nebraska coach called her to ask where I was. Naturally, her first thought was that my plane had crashed and I was dead. She was totally surprised and disappointed to find out that I was at Bradley. Feeling that they'd stolen her baby boy, she was angry at Bradley. She felt I was obligated to Nebraska since its athletic director had secured jobs for Robert and me. She felt that by my agreeing to go to Nebraska, she'd given her word and that it had been broken by Bradley and me. To Regenia Walker, her word was her bond. I convinced her that at Bradley I was closer to home and that I would work hard to make her proud. Since the whole recruiting process had been a mystery to her from the start, she finally accepted my fate.

Meanwhile, I was getting pretty rank with only one change

of clothes and one pair of shoes because my trunk was still at Nebraska. When I called there to have it returned, the university refused. We finally got the Peoria chief of police to call the Lincoln chief of police to handle the matter, and after a week or so I had more than one change of clothes and one pair of shoes.

I can see now that I let the whole affair happen because I wanted it to. It was a heady feeling for a young man to be the center of attention. So much action taken by adults I respected or wanted to please flattered me.

I know it all sounds tame compared to recent horror stories about recruiting. My abduction didn't involve sex or drugs or huge sums of money; yet it's not such a far cry from what happens today. Colleges then, as now, intruded on the lives of vulnerable young men whose great skill suddenly turned the spotlight on them. A spotlight that can be turned away or off just as fast if the coaches and schools are ready to discard their eager recruits when they're not tough enough or good enough or disciplined enough to survive in a very strange new world. I was lucky. I worked very hard at Bradley and earned a national reputation and an education. In the end, it was all up to me.

A black athlete does not see sports as "a way out of the ghetto." This sort of comment is insulting to the player as well as to the so-called ghetto. What is a player to do? He can't bring everyone "out" with him. Why should he forget his family and friends, the very culture that has raised and nurtured him? Does the "way out" mean he must leave everyone and everything behind to crumble and die? Does he go to a world where everything is foreign to him and then deny his past?

Today there's no place for a young athlete to be a kid anymore. If he lives and plays in the ghetto, chances are he's seen it all by age fifteen and is a very old teenager whose goal has always been to survive and stay away from gangs and drugs. Everything moves so much faster now, the pace of basketball as well as the recruiting and media games, not to mention the pace of the degeneration of a young life. There's no time to learn what a player needs to know. No one to tell him to slow down.

I never did find out how much money Al Benson got for handling me. The whole "kidnapping" was strange from the start, and I should have smelled a rat. Here's how the pieces fell into place for me. Al Benson had been seen in Benton Harbor buying a round of drinks at a bar a few weeks before. Orsborn's recruiter-assistant coach Joe Stowell might have called Jim Brown at DuSable to help him get me to Bradley, but Brown would have insisted that if he helped, Bradley had to take his star player, guard Poochie Moore, who stayed at Bradley for one year. Stowell probably agreed to the deal, and I guess Brown called in Benson to help him snare me. They had a relay system set up to get me to Chicago. When Joe Stowell appeared by magic at my door at 6 A.M. on a Sunday morning, in a Bradley station wagon, I wonder where he spent the night? Parked down the street in the projects? Not very likely! Joe Stowell was a good but fast-talking guy. When I was inducted into the Bradley Hall of Fame in 1976, he didn't come to the ceremony though he was head coach by then. I think he suspected I was going to reminisce in public and spill the beans.

Orsborn's name was never mentioned by anyone that day, not even up to the moment I got onto the plane and saw him and Dutch Meinert, the athletic director. I guess today the whole caper looks amateurish in light of what goes on in recruiting, and, of course, the NCAA would be all over a sports program that used such tactics.

In my four years at Bradley, I don't remember that Orsborn ever asked me about my mother, my family, my hopes, my fears. Of course, it was a two-way street. I never expected he would want to know anything about me. So I did what I usually did: stayed in my proud shell. His indifferent attitude was the same as the rest of the athletic staff: we black players should be thankful that we were allowed to be on campus. Their only fear was that we were going to make some girl pregnant and get the coaches in trouble.

Years later, after I was traded to the Bulls, I saw Al Benson outside Chicago Stadium after a game. The night was freezing, and the stadium parking lot was almost empty. Benson suffered from diabetes and had had both legs amputated. Confined to a wheelchair, he was a shell of his old, obnoxious self. I couldn't believe my eyes. Benson said, "I remember you when you didn't have decent shoes on your feet or clothes on your back. I need some money." I went to my car and wrote a check for three hundred dollars. Benson had his pride and was still reminding me of my beginnings at Bradley as I wrote the check, eyes down, avoiding his. He took the check and wheeled himself into the darkness.

Bradley was no household name in Michigan though I knew of its basketball prominence. In Peoria, I found myself at a campus in a town about which I knew very little. When I arrived in the fall of 1958, Bradley had about three thousand students, more than 85 percent of them from Illinois and 30 percent of them commuters. There were only about sixty male and five female black students on campus, two of whom were Jehovah's Witnesses, so case closed there! Most of the young men were basketball, football, baseball, and track athletes. When I was a freshman, Bradley had no black organizations, no black fraternities or sororities.

All the black athletes on campus lived in one dormitory, Harper Hall. My first roommate was Al Saunders, a big-city kid from Chicago, who was a sophomore. I thought he was real slick. The first time I walked into our room, he reached into a bag and pulled out a pint of cognac. I had never seen an athlete drink before. Not only did Al drink but he also smoked! He took me up to Chicago and introduced me to the jazz and blues there, and we became strong friends.

Freshman year I spent trying to survive academically. The classes were painfully difficult for me. I was frightened all the time but worked hard on my writing with some tutorial help. I was still handicapped after all those years by my southern dialect. Freshman English proved especially difficult, and I worried about flunking out but pulled through with a C minus. Again, I felt as out of place in class as I had at Jefferson school in the fifth grade in Benton Harbor. I felt that if I opened my mouth in a college classroom, the topic of conversation in the fraternity and sorority houses that night would be, "God, that Chet Walker is so stupid. You should have heard him in class today." My shyness paralyzed me. I was scared of being called on even when I knew an answer.

I was shy, but I was just too big to hide. I was so visible at six feet seven inches and black. I was embarrassed by my clothes, my beard, my mustache. I thought everyone on a small campus knew what I didn't know. I know I could have worked harder. However, countering this inferiority complex was the conviction that I was pretty important to this school. I was going to be the next Bradley basketball meal ticket. Just wait until I stepped out on that court. The truth was that all the signals were mixed. The Bradley campus was the first environment I'd lived in that was mostly white except for those few months in the west side of Benton Harbor when I'd attended Jefferson school. The cord to home was cut: after all, what could my mother or my brothers tell me about college? I was years behind other Bradley students I met in terms of knowledge about the larger American culture. They could negotiate situations I couldn't even guess at.

I experienced the sensation of being noticed *and* ignored, but finally rejected, in a nice, middle-class way. Nothing is worse than rejection on the grounds of race because there is nothing you can do about it. If you're a bad person, you can try to change. If you need education, you can study and learn. If you're sick, you can obtain medical attention. But if God created you black, you can't change that. You can only appeal to the humanity of other people. If they won't recognize you as a person, you begin to build a wall around yourself so the hurt doesn't get in as often. It looks like hostility to the outside world. But to the black person, it's essential self-defense, a necessity for survival.

On occasion, you can trick yourself into believing you've beaten the rap, especially when you're an All-American something-or-other or when you sign a large contract. So racism takes a backseat in your life until the next slight, the next inhumanity. Maybe it's that look of fear or suspicion when you enter a store or walk down the street. Or the frustration when basketball is all anyone wants to talk about with you. It is so easy to rationalize and label everything that happens to you as discrimination. Against our wills, an enormous amount of energy is taken up in just being black. You cycle through your rage and come back to fight again, always hoping that fairness and opportunity will someday be truly realized.

Bradley was an island of pleasant white people who didn't connect with me very well. Since I was so shy and had no small talk, I couldn't begin to change that. I know people either thought I was too proud or just plain dumb. Language, clothes, background, culture—all functioned to isolate me. I didn't know how to make college live up to the promises whose fulfillment I had so hoped for: that I would be accepted as an equal in that environment. Remember, I'm speaking of 1958, an almost prehistoric period in race relations, given the speed with which various eras and social climates have evolved since then. Blacks and whites lived with an attitude of incuriosity about each other. Blacks didn't feel they could demand anything. Whites hardly saw the need to grant anything. Everywhere were unwritten rules, places a black person didn't go, things he or she didn't do. Socially, there was almost no interaction between the races at Bradley.

Peoria was a river town that had conflicting views about slavery. Peoria was a key stop for escaping slaves on the Underground Railroad, but many times abolitionist rallies in the 1850s were met with armed resistance. On October 16, 1854, on the steps of the Peoria courthouse, Abraham Lincoln and Stephen A. Douglas had the first of their impassioned and historic debates about slavery. Five years later, when the great black orator and abolitionist Frederick Douglass gave a speech about his life as a slave and his heroic escape, no hotel in Peoria would give him lodging. Douglass walked the streets all night to keep from freezing.

In the 1940s, blacks were still denied rooms in Peoria hotels and could not attend most theaters and restaurants in the central city. They were limited to one day per week in the municipal swimming pools. There was the usual quota of complaints about police injustice and poor treatment from government agencies. All this was changing slowly by the time I arrived on campus. We quickly learned the places that would and would not serve us. The local chapter of the NAACP was very active when I was on campus, bringing suits to end housing discrimination and working to enlarge job opportunities. Playing basketball was the only way I could attend Bradley. There was no college outreach to minority students in 1958, no affirmative action programs. No offices of minority affairs or black studies programs. I was curious about college, knowing nothing of what to expect there. Most of the white students from totally segregated backgrounds were as indifferent to me as if I had been invisible. I was truly on my own.

It was basketball that put Bradley on the map after World War II. Even though the college basketball scandals of 1950–51 deeply tarnished the university's image, it was still felt that basketball could remain a significant feature of Bradley's development as long as the university could monitor the program and the players could keep their noses clean. Athletes were steered into the easy courses, such as physical education classes. Coaches also guided us in certain directions to certain teachers who would cut us a break. If we were pulling below a C in a course, we were assigned tutors, seniors hired by the Athletic Department, and we would be expected to go to study table with them. This concern about our grades was not about our academic or intellectual development but about our basketball eligibility. College coaches generally treat their athletes as fellow employees of a lower rank. They play good cop-bad cop with your life to make sure you conform to what the team is supposed to accomplish for the university. Coaches care about an athlete only as a part of a team that wins games.

That's why it was so important for me to find Professor Romeo B. Garrett, the first black professor at Bradley when he was named to the faculty in 1947 and the first black teacher I had in the North. A sociologist, he made me believe not only that I had academic potential but also that black people belonged in the university setting. Since he was born in Natchez, Mississippi, where his grandparents had been slaves, I felt we'd made the same passage to the North. He'd been a Jackie Robinson of sorts on the Bradley campus.

Professor Garrett brought liberal ideas to a very conservative faculty. He was the most learned black man I had ever met. To me he was majesty itself as we sat and talked in his booklined office or as I listened to him lecture. He always implored me not to put my future in the hands of athletic departments and sports. He pointedly challenged me to have the character and discipline to improve my studies and to get a real education. The words meant a lot to me coming from someone who knew exactly what it took. Dr. Garrett was also pastor to the Zion Baptist Church in Peoria. By 1977, seventeen scholarships for minority students at Bradley were endowed in his name. There's now a Garrett Black Cultural Center on campus as well as black Greek letter societies and a famed gospel choir.

The black population of Peoria doubled and redoubled between 1940 and 1960 to about 10 percent, following the pattern of so many small northern cities like my own Benton Harbor. Rural people from the South came to Peoria hoping for manufacturing jobs in the large Caterpillar tractor plant or in related industries. Peoria was the world capital of earth-moving machine production.

Most of Peoria's ten thousand blacks were crammed into an area on the near south side, living in conditions not of their own choosing. Only about forty black students graduated from Peoria high schools each year. Peoria looked like Benton Harbor all over again. Peoria was surrounded by all-white towns, including

Pekin, the home of the former Illinois senator Everett Dirksen. Pekin, with a population of thirty thousand, actually boasted that it didn't have a single black citizen. In 1935, there'd been one black guy in Pekin, and when he was jailed on a larceny charge, the *Peoria Journal Star* headline observed, "Entire Negro Population of Pekin in Peoria Jail." That passed for humor in Peoria.

One of my first thoughts on arriving at Bradley was to get to the gym and try out my game against these fabled college stars. I both looked forward to this new level of competition and felt apprehensive about it. For the first week or so, I spent lots of time in the gym checking out the other players' games as they did mine. But the player I really wanted to see and go up against was Bobby Joe Mason, Bradley's senior guard and leader.

Bobby Joe was the Bradley player I knew the most about in Benton Harbor. But, as far as I could see, he never came on campus. I later learned that he lived down the hill with the Peoria native Richard Pryor, who was an opening comedy act in local clubs. Bobby Joe would come to campus on the first and fifteenth of every month to pick up his meal and expense money, and that was it.

When he did arrive at the gym one day, everybody began buzzing. I looked around and saw a thin guy, all of six feet two inches, with hair slicked back like Cab Calloway. He proceeded to turn us all inside out on the court and left us with our mouths open. Then he left, just like that, and we didn't see him again for two weeks. Bobby Joe was a smooth mystery to us.

Bobby Joe was somewhat of a street guy back then, not into illegal stuff, but he liked the nightlife in Peoria. He was the first successful black man I'd known who played the white system like a tune. I realized he was able to function best in the system after he'd totally given up on it having anything to do with him. He just didn't care if he succeeded in the white world or not. Bobby Joe capped off a brilliant career at Bradley by being drafted by the Los Angeles Lakers, but he considered pro basketball too demanding and regimented. He couldn't play in a coach's straitjacket.

Bobby Joe was looking for a life he could define that placed less responsibility on a player to win and lose basketball games. He was a true showman and signed with the Globetrotters in 1960. He played with them for sixteen years, traveling the world several times over. I never saw him upset by anything that happened on or off the court. The coaches couldn't reach him and neither could his opponents.

The Globetrotters were still a real option for black players in the late 1950s. Wilt Chamberlain left Kansas after his junior year to play with the Trotters in 1958–59 for about as much money as he made a year later with the Philadelphia Warriors. They paid as well as the NBA and were even more established. In fact, from 1939 to 1948, the Globetrotters played every year in the World Professional Basketball Tournament held in Chicago Stadium. Professional players acknowledged the winner of the tourney as World Champion, even after 1946 when the NBA (which began as the Basketball Association of America [BAA]) began play. The Trotters annually played a few exhibition games against the new NBA, tended to business, and held their own. As the NBA tried to put its own barnstorming past to rest and to include a few black players on its rosters, it put some distance between the league and the Trotters. In effect, the integration of the NBA marginalized the Trotters though they remain a worldwide attraction.

In essence, the game the Trotters played—tremendous athleticism punctuated with showmanship—became the game the NBA finally sold to the American public in the 1980s, minus the overt clowning and combined with muscle and fierce competitiveness. Bobby Joe would have been an NBA All-Star in this sort of game.

Bobby Joe had the cool to play the various styles of basketball like a veteran jazzman. He could improvise from a variety of basic moves. I wish I'd been able to adopt an on-court mentality like his. Basketball is, at bottom, a game of spontaneity. A team's success depends on how players react to unforeseen situations on the court. Coaches who overcoach and restrict the instinctive reactions of their players very seldom win championships.

The most important part of any game is the last three minutes. All great teams must have one or two players who can control the game at this time. These are the players who will attack defenses and not freeze up. This is what I brought to the Bulls in 1969, and it is a characteristic I first noticed in Bobby Joe Mason. Every team needs a finisher, such as a Bird or Magic or, in my era, a Walt Frazier and Earl Monroe.

Players drop off at all levels of basketball, making for a smaller and smaller top of the pyramid. Few can withstand the various pressures. As the game gets bigger, more is on the line, and more is demanded of you. In college, you could be injured, get in wrong with your coach, not like your school, have trouble with academics, miss your family, become emotionally involved. All along, the bottom line is that you are expected to come and perform at your highest level every night. The pitfalls were there in the 1950s as well and are probably normal for a college kid who participates in organized sports. Today there are bigger traps waiting for young kids who don't even have the family support and basic literacy that I brought with me to Bradley.

The mellow Bobby Joe always knew how to beat all that. He was a fine player, as good a guard as I ever played with anywhere. He wanted to steer his own course and be in control. For Bobby Joe, that meant seeking a world where his game could be totally within the confines of black basketball.

Social life on the Bradley campus centered on the fraternities and sororities, which in turn followed the football and basketball seasons to schedule their dances, big weekends, student productions, campus beauty contests, and the like. My years at college (1958–62) were the lull before the storm, the last supposedly innocent time of college life before Vietnam, drugs, and campus protests. I was excluded from this life, but nobody knew

or cared about that but me. In 1960, a campus discrimination report came out identifying the fifteen Bradley fraternities that
didn't accept black students. The fact was not one black student
who participated in fraternity rush at Bradley had ever been accepted as a member. The fraternities' feeble defense was that
many of their charters expressly forbade black members. The fraternities always argued that we didn't want to join and very few
blacks even went through the rush system. Our answer was
"Why put yourself in for humiliation?"

In four years at Bradley, I was never asked to a fraternity for
dinner or as a guest at a fraternity party, not even when I was
first team All-American. Once I went with a couple of the black
players to a non-fraternity party where there was a lot of illegal
drinking going on. I heard one white kid reassure another, "It's
okay, they won't kick us out, because they'd have to kick out
Chet Walker." I left quickly after that.

However, late in my freshman year I received an invitation
from a fraternity to come to breakfast. I was amazed. I told my
friends, "Hey, this is some kind of breakthrough here." We were
never invited to anything by anybody. Here I was actually being
noticed as an athlete who might be a person too.

When I went to breakfast, I expected a large order of ham
and eggs, something to stick to your ribs. Instead, I was initiated
into the mysteries of lox and gefilte fish. To me, they tasted
awful. I lamely tried to joke: "What is this stuff?" They said it
was "Jewish soul food." I was stunned. I didn't even know this
was a Jewish fraternity. I felt like the dumbest person in the
world. But at least we all could laugh, and that broke the ice. The
incident brought me to a renewed awareness of just how naive I
was about the world I inhabited. Before college, I had not known
any Jewish people. For the longest time I thought that all Jewish
people lived in Israel, that they didn't live anywhere else. My
mother had studied the Bible and had told me all about David,
Moses, Jesus. I figured I knew where they were from!

It turned out the fraternity had a program to invite a minority student to breakfast once a month. That was a true sign of

liberal good intentions in the 1950s. Actually, I made a terrific friend, Rick Golding, from that fraternity, with whom I am in touch to this day. In getting to know him, I realized there were other minority groups on the Bradley campus. We shared some problems of discrimination; but we could not share others.

After I became a star, I was invited to the homes of Bradley boosters, primarily because I was a hero to their kids and Dad could look pretty tall if he brought me home. Every time I got free eats, I would load up on the extras and take them back to Harper Hall to distribute later. I was experiencing culture shock so fast I couldn't tabulate the results. I was entering the celebrity phase of my life without ever having any stable middle ground between anonymity and fame. I had no idea who or where I was.

People wanted to be seen with me in certain places, in controlled situations. Now that I was becoming somebody, I felt awkward all the time and out of place. I had no idea of a black middle class; I never had met anybody who lived there.

From the start, my world at Bradley was off campus in Peoria itself. I had to find the black community and become part of it. To get a haircut. To eat food I could taste. I hung out a lot at Big John's Barbecue Pit "down the hill." Down the hill was a black community of single-family homes, a nice working-class neighborhood on the near south side of the city below the Bradley campus.

The fact that we weren't able to participate in the social life of the Bradley fraternities turned out to have an upside. I had a classmate at Bradley named Adrian Hinton, one of the few blacks from Peoria on campus. Most black college hopefuls from Peoria couldn't afford Bradley and went to Illinois State or Southern Illinois. But Adrian lived at home with a large family that included six brothers and sisters.

On many weekends, the black students on campus would trek down the hill to the Hinton house, where we would party in the basement while Adrian's mom kept us in food and drinks. She was sensitive to our situation on campus and knew what we were facing away from home and our own mothers. She opened her home and her heart to us. As far as I was concerned, it didn't hurt that Adrian's sisters were really fine-looking girls. In fact, I chased one of them for three years at Bradley but never caught her.

We would dance to all the Motown tunes of the early 1960s and work out dancing the Stroll and the Mashed Potato. I know we had more fun than we would have had at a fraternity gathering. A couple of white Bradley students who loved to dance always hung with us at the Hinton house. We never felt awkward about including them.

Every young man or woman deserves a college experience that is a time to stretch—to learn about new things, meet new people, explore new places, hear new music, and examine how all these new things can fit with the old self. Certainly, athletes on college campuses should be able to socialize more with the larger student population. But athletic departments want to keep their athletes segregated from the larger college population. In general, they're afraid athletes might begin to think for themselves too much or be exposed to so many ideas or opportunities that their fixation on sports will dwindle. Athletic directors and coaches want players to keep at their business.

For this reason black athletes end up doubly segregated, by both a housing and an academic situation, which reinforces their feeling of immunity from college work. First, they feel alienated and fearful about the white majority at their schools. Then, the athletic departments sequester them, in many ways denying them the larger curriculum and life of the university. The fame they achieve in games gives them a false sense of power and freedom that disguises the truth: that black athletes are still coming in the backdoor to universities, forced to work like field hands and denied the full benefits of college society.

In the 1950s at Bradley, we felt that *not studying* was getting away with a lot. We could not imagine what else we might get away with. One example shows this clearly. Bradley players had to wear matching blue blazers on the road. I thought we looked like choirboys and got pretty sick of that uniform. So in my junior year in 1961, I wore a suit on our first road trip. I thought this was a rebellious action. I was actually scared of the consequences. Wouldn't you know, no coaches even noticed? In the mid-1960s, coaches and athletic directors freaked out (to use the language of the day) when athletes began cultivating beards, growing Afros, and speaking out about social issues. This was the period of real terror for the power structure in sports. An athlete with a cause beyond winning itself is a dangerous athlete for he can't be controlled so easily. In many respects, I feel that athletes today are even more conservative than those who played in the 1950s. We were the silent pioneers. Then came the activists.

Now the only word that seems to matter is *money*. Huge amounts of it, more money for one year in the NBA than many of us, even star players, could have imagined making in an entire career. Any time that millions of dollars become the focal point, you have the makings of a conservative. Even a brilliantly talented ghetto kid knows he has to keep his mouth shut about his treatment if he wants to get the money. You don't have to look much further to see why black athletes aren't way out ahead on civil rights. They might lose their one chance in life to radically improve their situation and that of their families.

In 1958–59, freshmen didn't play on varsity teams, and the freshman teams played a limited schedule of games, freeing them from the big-time pressure of today with major travel schedules, holiday tournaments, and television games. Our freshman team went 15–0. I led the team in scoring in every game and averaged 23 points and 16 rebounds. We didn't travel a great deal but easily defeated teams all over Illinois. We played against other freshman teams as well as against junior colleges and teams from army bases. I was able to get my feet on the ground at Bradley before I had to major in basketball. I had a lot to learn off the court, including survival in the classroom and adjustment to my new environment. I believe that college players should not play varsity ball as freshmen so that they have the opportunity to adapt to their new situation.

The Bradley varsity team had another fine year but lost an

overtime thriller to St. John's in the National Invitation Tournament (NIT). Since it was a sophomore-junior squad, almost everyone would be back for 1959–60. Therefore, hopes were high with the addition of our undefeated freshman squad to a strong nucleus of veteran players. After my college debut on December 3, 1959, I could not be labeled just another promising player. At home in our season opener against Abilene Christian, not exactly a big-time foe, I picked up where I had left off in Benton Harbor. I found the zone and left the court with 44 points in only twenty-five minutes in my first varsity game. I broke the school scoring record held by Curley Johnson. I followed up this performance with 33 and 34 points in my next two games, so that three games into my varsity career I was actually leading the country in scoring. The Peoria sportswriters nicknamed me "Walk the Stalk," a terrible derivation of "Wilt the Stilt" Chamberlain and one that quickly died as I got older and gained some weight, which didn't leave me exactly stalklike. I had arrived although my scoring now settled in the low and middle twenties as coaches began to set their defenses to stop me and I was forced to pass out of double-teams.

Now that I was playing for the varsity, my future looked limitless. I had convinced myself that I could be an outstanding player at this level. I had veteran teammates who knew how to win. I had a national stage on which to perform. The abduction was complete, and I was a willing hostage. I was ready to play ball.

5.
On the Road
in the South: 1960

In my sophomore year (1959–60) at Bradley, I scored 111 points in my first three games. I was elevated from being a former high school basketball hero in Benton Harbor to a campus hero at Bradley, and the national press began to spread the news. We were ranked fourth in the nation behind the University of California, Cincinnati with Oscar Robertson, and West Virginia with Jerry West. I felt that I was about to join the basketball elite. Such was the high point of my optimism about equality through sports.

With all this attention, I began to feel pretty good about myself. Maybe my celebrity meant I no longer had to feel inferior. Maybe we *were* all equal. Basketball really could take me a long way in American society. But I lost that notion on my first road trip in the Deep South, where I had been born.

As we prepared to take our first extended trip of the season to St. Louis, Houston, and Denton, Texas, Coach Chuck Orsborn called in the black players on the team—Al Saunders, Bobby Joe Mason, Mack Herndon, and me—to remind us that we had to expect racism and offensive treatment, that it was just the way things were and there was nothing he or we could do about it. Implicit was the idea that we better not cause any incident that would reflect badly on the team or on Bradley. The message was that the South was going to be different because we were different: this is your lot, accept it, don't make waves if you want to play.

Orsborn was in fact warning us about what was to come. I heard him but didn't really believe it. The warnings sort of went in one ear and out the other. I thought I was on my way to being an All-American. I was bigger than all this race business. Orsborn had been through this sort of discrimination against some of his black players in previous years. But this was a kind of *black*mail I didn't yet understand. Our white teammates gave us little sympathy; if they gave it a thought, they seemed just to accept Orsborn's views because they never said anything about it.

Bradley's first road trip in 1960 began in St. Louis. Before the game that night, the St. Louis University band marched out playing "Dixie," and we came out on the court surrounded by a sea of waving Confederate flags, which almost made me sick to my stomach; to me, going onto that court was like running head-long into a military rally. But we had a great strategy to counter the fans' attention to the band. We would commence to dunk everything in sight during lay-up drills. We would throw stuff down off spins and swoops, and jam balls up to our elbows. That would make the people stop listening to and wailing "Dixie." They would start oohing and aahing at our moves. When we'd totally distracted the Confederate singalong, we would stop just like that and make sedate little lay-ups, and everyone would say, "Awwhh . . ." Once the game began, however, it was business as usual. With racial taunts and slurs stinging our ears, our 81–71 victory was doubly sweet.

After the game, Al, Bobby Joe, and I went for dinner at a Chinese restaurant near the hotel. We went in and sat down, amidst all the lanterns and little miniature pagodas. I felt like a real man of the world. The smells coming from the kitchen were delicious. Through the swinging doors to the kitchen we could see the skinned ducks hanging feet first just ready for the pot. But I became aware that other customers were giving us strange looks. Before we could warm the seats of the booth, the cook, who I assumed was the owner, came out of the kitchen screaming and yelling. He didn't speak English very well, but we all understood what he was saying: "No serve color, no serve colored." Some white customers seemed to take great delight in seeing this tiny Chinese man run big colored boys out the door. To them it was entertainment.

Bobby Joe Mason and and Al Saunders didn't have the same intense reaction to the Deep South that I did. Bobby Joe was from Centralia, a town in southern Illinois, and Al was from Chicago. They certainly knew racism. But for me, going back to the South was a nightmare. Everything from my early years in Mississippi came back as if I'd been returned to jail. What was another slight for them was deeply painful to me. I was naive to think I'd left it all behind.

The three of us went back to the hotel and stayed hungry because there was nowhere we could eat. We were not allowed in the hotel restaurant, and it was too late for room service. I tossed and turned with my stomach growling. It didn't help to know that our white teammates probably had a good meal and a good night while we were hungry and depressed. Yet we were supposed to carry on as if nothing had happened and, not incidentally, carry the team. Why didn't we protest? We knew if we did that Bradley University might accuse us of being troublemakers. We would get the blame. We felt our only choice was to let the incident pass and wait for breakfast.

The road trip moved on to Houston, Texas, where the team was refused hotel accommodations because of our black players. So we were all moved to the student dormitories at the University of Houston. The only reason the black players got to stay with the white players was that because it was Christmas vacation time at the university, the administrators made an exception for us "under the circumstances." So we stayed in the girls dorm at Houston, but we still had to get our meals across town at Texas Southern University, a black school.

Such endless maneuvering just to eat and sleep *somewhere* took its toll on us. During warm-ups for the Houston game, fans threw lit cigarette butts on the floor at us and screamed, "Nigger!" I was in a state of great confusion and frustration, and scored only one point in the first half, wondering why I was subjecting myself to such abuse. At halftime, Coach Orsborn had a different take on my game. He was all over me in the dressing room. He berated me, yelling "Don't quit on me, Chet. Just don't quit on me!" With a final sneer he concluded more softly, "All-American, my ass!"

Well, there it was, the accusation that I didn't have what it took when the going got rough. He didn't care about the trauma of this trip to a nineteen-year-old kid. He just wanted to win, and I was supposed to help him. To Orsborn, I could see I was basically a black kid who played basketball well. I wanted to put all the blame on him, but I knew it was my shock at my new life coming apart. My fleeting sense of equality was gone. Heaven help me if I permanently lost the ability to play basketball. I came out and scored more than 20 points in the second half, but we lost a close game.

Our last stop on the trip was North Texas State in Denton, Texas, a real pit. By that time our anger had reached the boiling point. The night before the game, Al, Bobby Joe, and I left the hotel (where, of course, we couldn't eat) to get some burgers at the White Castle down the street. As we walked back and stood on the corner waiting for the light to change, a car full of white guys slowed to a crawl, and a low voice growled out the car window, "Nigger, I don't want to catch you on the street after dark."

Without saying anything, we all knew now that someone would have to pay for this whole road trip, but we also knew we could exact this punishment only on the court. At the arena in Denton, we faced the usual screaming, hostile crowd. The Missouri Valley Conference crowds were almost always all-white, but in Denton, we could see a few black fans huddled in a high corner. A black player notices things like that when he's on the road.

Two minutes into the game, a big redneck on the North Texas State team jammed Saunders in the throat with an elbow. It was just the incident to set things off. Al threw one of the prettiest right hands I've ever seen in my life and laid him out. A free-for-all began, and both benches emptied. Police came on court to break it up, and our team was escorted back to the locker room. After a fifteen-minute delay, the game continued with police holding hands and ringing the court. Stowell and Orsborn were scared to go back out on the court, but I never felt so good in my life. All the tension from St. Louis and Houston was let out. It was a small vindication. We went back out and played a great game, and I scored 40 points. We always had a mission to get after teams in these racist strongholds on the road.

I vividly remember my white teammate Ed Wodka, a great big Polish guy from Fenger High School in Chicago, fighting beside us in the Denton melee as if he felt our pain. He fought for us, and with us, as if it were the last moment of his life. Somehow he was with us. We never talked about that moment. Al, Bobby Joe, and I never discussed race with our white teammates. We didn't know if they wanted to talk about it, and we all would have been uncomfortable if they had.

I will never forget those games, those fans, those towns, and the way I felt. After we returned to school, I called my mother and told her I wasn't sure that I could keep going. Everything had turned so ugly. I said I couldn't stay at Bradley.

When she was able to get a word in, she said, "Let me ask you a question. If you leave school, is that gonna change racism? If you leave school, is that gonna change the coach's opinion?" I said, "Nope." "So why are you going to leave?" she asked. "Chester, it's not a perfect world. You have to find the good and enjoy it, make the most of it. Chester, we survived living in Mississippi. We survived living in the projects. Chester, you mean to tell me that you can't survive three years in Peoria?"

Despite my mother's attempt to brace me, I was so upset that my mind raced through various scenarios—all of which revolved around my getting away from Bradley, from Peoria, and from the specter of more southern trips. I thought of transferring, especially to Michigan State, which would have put me closer to home in Benton Harbor. One day, Orsborn called me into his office and told me Fordy Anderson, the Michigan State coach, was on the line. Anderson said it would be in my best interest to stay at Bradley and that he wouldn't accept me as a transfer student. The two coaches had rigged the deal, and I could see that Orsborn was not about to lose me to some other team.

I became desperate enough to consider flunking out. If I couldn't play for another school, I would just fail and go home. Of course, my lack of self-confidence had taken over. Like countless black kids before and after me, I'd been placed in a white society that seemed unnavigable. I had no support systems. I was lonely. My options were zero. I remember taking a music appreciation course that spring. For the final exam we listened to recorded selections and then identified the composer, such as Mozart or Bach. I scrawled across the top of my exam, "The only music I can appreciate is the Blues," and left the rest of the paper blank. The professor gave me a C and wrote on the exam that I showed "great vision." So I was caught. Bradley would never let me flunk out! It sounds ridiculous today, but that's how I felt. Bradley had me as its employee; they had me as a commodity for as long as I was of use. If I publicly expressed my anger or desire to leave, they would destroy me.

Of course, once I found the resolve to stay and get everything I could from the experience, I was glad in a strange sort of way that I was so important. I was valuable as a sports hero. But not as a young black man. Not as a man. I knew that.

My time in the public eye lasted for roughly two decades, from the mid-1950s to the mid-1970s. During that time I experienced a constant ebb and flow of confidence and fear of failure, of shyness and suspicion coupled with a need to be liked and to trust people. One minute I was an All-American basketball player as full of myself as a powerful young man could be. But the next minute, I was reduced to the nigger in the doorway. No amount of sports heroism in America could change that. Early on I understood this doubleness and that it would never truly change for me.

On that rainy night in Houston, back at the girls dorm where we finally stayed without incident, old Wyatt's words came back to me from the poolroom in Benton Harbor with such clarity: "Never trust the white man." But it wasn't that simple. In my frustration I was furious at the fans, at my coach, at myself for letting all the incidents bring me down. This would not be the last time that I would dredge up Wyatt's advice. Sometimes it helped me. Other times it only contributed to my self-defeat. Like any strategy, it couldn't be applied to all the games I played. Wyatt's words were a hollow and bitter consolation. Late at night in that dorm, in tears, I wondered if my dream had already come to a dead-end.

All I could think about was getting back home to my family where I belonged, where I could be safe with whatever knowledge of the larger world I possessed. But that impulse might lead me straight back to Wyatt's first piece of advice. Would I become just another guy hanging out in the poolroom, making excuses as to why society had beaten me?

In St. Louis, after we were chased out of the Chinese restaurant, I thought of Jackie Robinson and his legacy to black men and black athletes. He was a hard man to follow for all of us. Jackie had to hold all his pain and anger inside himself for so long. People praise Branch Rickey for combing the minor leagues to find just the right combination of brains, heart, talent, and character. He then told Jackie that he wanted a fighter but one "who had enough guts not to fight," who would turn the other cheek at all times when events and hatred become unbearable. Jackie was college-educated and militant enough to have been court-martialed for leading a bus boycott in the army. But Rickey knew Jackie was well spoken and mentally tough.

Sometimes I feel Rickey should have given Jackie permission to punch somebody's lights out. The incident might have resulted in a race riot, the end of the "great experiment." But suppose not? Suppose that Robinson's courage had validated an outward expression of just anger? Suppose it was acknowledged that Jackie had a right to express that anger instead of being lionized for withholding it? Because Jackie had the great strength to endure, he set a precedent. All black athletes since have had to live up to his powerful dignity and forbearance. But my soul died a little each time a nightmare like that southern trip had to be lived through.

6.
Juiced at the NIT

My mother persuaded me to stay at Bradley after our southern trip, and I went on to lead the Braves to a 24–2 regular season, which resulted in a bid to the NIT at Madison Square Garden in New York. This tournament ended with the most famous and bizarre incident of my basketball career, one that would leave me with a lot of questions and lifelong physical problems.

My sophomore season at Bradley remains the most vivid of my three varsity campaigns not only because of the trauma of our southern road trip but also because of some thrilling games. We were down 19 points at Wichita State and rallied to win. We beat St. Louis 81–71 at Kiel Auditorium, breaking an eight-year winless streak there. We destroyed Notre Dame 86–65 in Chicago Stadium.

I finally got to play against people who were legends to me. The game that made me feel I belonged at the top of the college basketball world was when the senior Oscar Robertson led the Cincinnati Bearcats into Peoria to play us in midseason at the old Robinson Fieldhouse, our barn of a home court. Cincinnati was 79–9 in Oscar's three years, and he was on his way to averaging 33.7 points per game for the season. Cincinnati came in unbeaten and ranked second in the nation whereas we were ranked fourth.

That night, the whole American sportsworld focused on Peoria. At first I was just glad to be on the same court with him. At six feet five inches, he was athletically perfect with a body that moved like some efficient basketball machine. I had to resist the impulse to just watch him. Oscar could always get whatever shot he wanted. If he was fifteen feet out, he would bang, back in, and put up the short, sweet turnaround jump shot. If he was eight feet out, he would go in and get fouled. He was always taking the ball forward and was both regal and economical in his moves. A large, fluid, rhythmic cat.

The game itself was a classic. Cincinnati led by 10 points late in the first half, and only Al Saunders's fine shooting kept us in the game. We fought back in the second half, and the score began to inch closer. The Bearcats were bigger than we were with hulks like Paul Hogue at center and Bob Weisenhahn at forward. But we were quicker. With 2:35 minutes left, I drove around Hogue for a lay-up, and we were down 82–81. But since I had 4 fouls, I couldn't play Hogue tight on the defensive end and had to let him go for an easy lay-up. Then Mike Owens hit what must have been a 25-foot shot to put us down 84–83. The Bearcat forward Larry Willey drove hard for a lay-up, but I switched on him, blocked the ball in midair and grabbed it. We pushed the ball hard, and Al threaded a bullet pass to me between Oscar and Hogue for a lay-up. We finally were ahead in the game 85–84. I was jockeying for rebound position under the basket when Oscar dropped in a jump shot from the corner to make it 86–85 Cincinnati. The shot was like a missile that floated toward me and just exploded through the net with a loud pop. Bobby Joe raced down and made a turnaround 15 footer, then Oscar drove the length of the court for a lay-up. Cincinnati led 88–87 with forty seconds to go.

The crowd that night had been amazing. Every time we scored, they rose to their feet as one. Then when Oscar retaliated, he would sit them down. They were up again screaming when Bradley countered with yet another hoop. With the ball in my hands and eight thousand people on their feet, tearing the roof off with their noise, I faced down Oscar at the head of the key. I faked and drove around him. As Hogue loomed, I evaded his block and backhanded the ball in for a lay-up to put us ahead 89–88. Now it was Oscar's turn. Coach Orsborn was on his feet, the veins popping in his neck as he yelled at Al Saunders to force Oscar into the middle, but none of us could hear the bench instructions over the crowd's roar. We were playing on instinct. Oscar eluded Al and wheeled in on the baseline, seemingly putting the Bearcats ahead. But Jim Enright, the lead official who was also a sportswriter in Chicago, was right there looking at Oscar's feet. Enright weighed about three hundred pounds, and there he was, down on one knee, dramatically pointing to the spot where Oscar had stepped out of bounds. Enright waved the basket off.

Mason and Owens then put on a dribbling exhibition until Mike was fouled and hit two shots. Oscar's last-second basket didn't matter. We won 91–90 in the most exciting college game I ever played. I'd walked with a god and found out we at least belonged on the same court. We gave Cincinnati all they could handle while I was at Bradley. The next two seasons they won the NCAA tournament and lost a total of five games. We won two of those games and lost 73–72 on their court when I was a junior.

At the end of my sophomore season, Bradley went back to the NIT in New York City, its familiar March stomping grounds. Until the late 1960s, the NIT tourney was on a par with the national NCAA tourney in prestige and caliber of teams. Five of the top ten teams in the nation vied with Bradley in the 1960 NIT field. I was thrilled to be in New York City for the first time, to be in Madison Square Garden where Wolcott and Louis had fought as my family and I listened on our radio in Mississippi.

After we arrived in New York, I threw my bags in our room and went into the streets of the fabled city. I knew I just had to go to Madison Square Garden to see the place and pay homage before we went there for practice and games. I used my player's pass to get in. The empty building was like a majestic tomb with only the noises of custodians and cleaners disturbing the quiet. I found a seat high up in the lower stands and mused about what a journey it had been to get to this palace of my dreams. It's funny how when you think about a place, you believe you'll never get there. When you're finally there, all you can remember is the dreaming. For me, Benton Harbor had been my first great journey. Now I was struggling to make it in Peoria. But once I made it to the Garden, I didn't need the Arabian Nights. I was living it.

There I was, sitting in the stands of the empty mecca of the sports world. For most Americans in the 1950s, the old Madison Square Garden was *the* arena where the big games, the big fights, the memorable championships were to be won. The Garden had its own personality; it wasn't one of these faceless, tacky new arenas of today. I sat there in a Garden that smelled of beer and decades of cigarette and cigar smoke, and closed my eyes to dream of Joe Louis, the ultimate warrior who had owned this city during the 1940s.

I wanted to tell everyone back home in Benton Harbor and Bethlehem, Mississippi, about this experience. I knew that I too had joined a small privileged class of sports heroes and had been carried far away from my family, even as my family had been carried away from Mississippi. Some kid back home would watch me play on television and dream about the Garden as I had. The journey had been long and hard, and the price was high. A sister dying. My mother crying. My father's anger. And an old Ford that huffed and puffed its way through the snow moving north to the Promised Land.

I wished for some way that my family could share this moment with me, even as we had shared those Friday night fights on the radio when we were still a farm family in Mississippi, eating the peanuts we'd grown and pulling sweet potatoes out of the hot ashes. When this memory washed over me in that cavernous building, I felt more alone than ever, and I was scared. I wanted to go back to where I had been safe. Or second best, I wanted to get out on the court where I was always at home. I couldn't wait for the tournament to begin and allow me to get out some of my feelings and shake my nerves.

In our first NIT contest, we came back after a rocky start to put Dayton away 78–64. I scored 22 points and got rid of pretournament jitters. Earlier that day, eleven thousand people had been in the Garden in the afternoon to watch the New York City high school legends Connie Hawkins and Roger Brown square off in a city championship semifinal game. Neither player would ever play a minute of college basketball after being banned for not reporting bribe offers.

Before our semifinal game with St. Bonaventure, Al Saunders and I spent the afternoon relaxing in our hotel room. Around five o'clock a bellhop brought two glasses of orange juice, compliments of Coach Orsborn. I downed about half of mine, but Al held his glass and remarked it was awfully strange because Coach Orsborn had never sent us any before. We quickly put down our glasses and called the coach; he knew nothing about any bellhop with juice. We panicked when I began to feel really ill, going to the bathroom constantly with severe diarrhea. Al called Orsborn, and he and Dutch Meinert, the athletic director, rushed to our room after calling the police. In short order, our hotel room was filled with coaches, the hotel detective, and four of New York's finest. They were all ready to label the affair a prank.

They ran a preliminary test on the leftover juice and found no narcotics, common sedatives, or toxic substances. Of course, that didn't rule out hard-to-trace poisons and other stuff. Police were supposed to run more sophisticated tests on the juice with the results available in a few weeks. I never heard the results of any such tests.

Orsborn and Stowell took me down into some sort of Madison Square Garden medical office where the house doctor examined me. He said he could find no signs of abnormal blood pressure, fatigue, or loss of reflexes. The doctor and coaches practiced a kind of deft cruelty on me. They just wouldn't do the humane thing and tell me not to play, that risking my health wasn't worth it. The coaches wouldn't speak up but just stood there. They knew how much I wanted to play. I just had a tube poked down my throat in the Garden's medical facilities, but they knew I would never beg off from playing, even though I had cramps and nausea, and no one knew what was the matter with me.

I now think that they were afraid to go into the big game without their key player. But my worries were of a different weight. *I* felt I might be dying. If a horse had been in my condition, I bet his trainer would have taken him out of the Kentucky Derby. Yet when Ozzie—Coach Orsborn—asked me how I felt, I told him, "Okay, I guess." I was lying. To me, the game and the NIT gave me the ultimate opportunity to be a hero.

Meanwhile, the game was set for that night at 7:30 P.M. Would I be able to play? I was so weak. I girded myself up by telling myself I would be playing in the house where Joe Louis had fought, playing in a televised game in which people in Mississippi and Michigan could see me. I couldn't miss this opportunity. Even if it threatened my life, this game meant more to me than my life. This is how you think when you're twenty years old.

On my way to the Garden that night in pain, I saw the front page of the *New York Post* already blaring: "Bradley University Star Poisoned." Bradley had been favored to win by seven points but that headline caused the point spread to drop like a stone in a two-hour period. Some people lost a lot of money on that game. Because they didn't expect me to play, they probably bet Bradley would lose. They underestimated my desire and determination. At the same time, my coaches undervalued my health and convinced me to do the same.

Ozzie reminded me, "This is our most important game ever." And I thought, The game, THE GAME. It's always about the game. The game always takes precedence over the player's well-being, mental or physical. This game was the semifinal. We lose and we're out. We win, and we have a chance to be champions. If Bradley made it to the NIT finals, the university would make more money, the coaches would get a raise, the recruiting climate would improve. Bradley would receive national exposure, which could lead to an increased enrollment.

Then Ozzie said, "If you can't play, don't go out there." I could tell he didn't mean it. He wouldn't even look me in the eye when he said it. I remembered during the halftime at the Houston road game when he had questioned my courage. He had the same look on his face now. It was a look that said, "Don't quit on us."

I know it looked absurd that night to see me running off the court every few minutes heading for the locker room. All through the game, Coach Orsborn kept a player at the scorer's table ready to go in for me. Despite my urgent departures from the game, I managed to score 27 points in twenty-three minutes, and Bradley beat St. Bonaventure 82–71. I was in a cold sweat all the time on the court. The lights and the smoky haze over the court made me dizzy. The fans seemed to tilt in and out of focus as I performed almost on body memory alone. After the game, I was totally spent and could barely make it back to the hotel on my own. No one seemed to take my situation seriously. For a day or two, people were interested in the orange juice story but called it a "prank" or suggested I was simply scared before the big game. I was scared all right—scared of dying.

I don't remember much about the game against St. Bonaventure itself except for the stabbing pains. I do know I felt awful and so weak that I probably shouldn't have played in the finals two days later. When a player gets warmed up, he always thinks he's in better shape than he is; the adrenaline takes over, and his emotion and concentration mask the pain and stress. Only after he cools down can he tabulate what he has done to himself.

There I was, twenty years old, in my dream arena. This was the NIT and the Garden. The show had to go on. In the NIT final, we made a great comeback against Providence led by Lenny Wilkens. Owens and Herndon were terrific. We won 88–72, but I had no energy and scored only 9 points. This game was of great importance to Bradley's image because it was nationally televised on a Saturday afternoon. I could have become an innocent victim of the fixers and gamblers or been implicated with them. It wasn't easy at that time to keep from being sacrificed to the greed and crime surrounding the college game.

Even thirty years later the whole story of that day in the hotel and at Madison Square Garden looks more and more like a cover-up to me. Orsborn was quoted as saying I always had a nervous stomach before games. That just isn't true. Lots of guys threw up from nervousness before games, but I didn't. My "nervous stomach" became the official explanation and was even picked up by *Sports Illustrated* in their line summary of the game, ignoring the possibility of gamblers and fixers having drugged me.

The NIT was protecting the reputation of the tournament. They were afraid of the public reaction if what happened to me became an official police matter. So many gamblers swarmed around Madison Square Garden that they practically owned the telephones inside the lobby.

We were naive back then about personal encounters. It would have been ridiculously easy for a gambler to gain access to a player. People were always asking for autographs or to have pictures taken. Next thing a guy knows, that photograph is part of someone's evidentiary file with a caption "Photographed with prominent bookmaker Joey Bananas" or something like that. If a regular fan asks if he can have a photograph taken with a player and the athlete refuses, the guy may get angry and call him stuck-up or worse. We were warned to "stay away from shady characters" and "keep your nose clean." But in real life, shady characters don't lurk in the shade or wear signs announcing who they are. We were all ripe for the picking.

I'm convinced our "bellhop" with the orange juice was no ordinary fan. Sure, he asked for an autograph, which was no big deal, and he wore a bellhop's uniform, or what looked like one with a red jacket and black pants. Al thought it was suspicious that he hung around waiting for us to finish the drink. He also asked us a lot of questions, such as how I was feeling, how much the room cost. Now why should a bellhop make that his business? And why would he want to watch what happened to a guy he had just brought an order to?

Other odd occurrences surrounded that game. In the early afternoon, the papers had us as 1½ point favorites to beat St.

Bonaventure, but there was very heavy betting all that afternoon so that by game time, the Bonnies were installed as 1½ point favorites to beat us. That's an incredible shift in betting action in one afternoon, considering I didn't drink the juice until 5:00 P.M., or two hours before game time. What did the gamblers know or think they knew? What information about me hit the street before the attempt to drug me had even gone down?

Supporting my belief that this orange juice incident was anything but a prank is the information that came out the following year in the betting scandals. It turned out that some of the heaviest wagers on college basketball games were placed by the very New York City detectives who were investigating alleged fixers like Jack Molinas and Aaron Wagman. The detectives had so many wiretaps on the fixers' phones that they accidentally got their own money down too early in one-sided action. So Molinas in his death-wish fashion actually had to double-cross some of the investigators to protect his own operations, infuriating them further. With well-placed erroneous overheard instructions to his confederates, Molinas made sure that New York's finest took a bath on some of the college games in 1960–62. No wonder no one wanted to do any serious follow-up to my being drugged. It's possible the orange juice caper was a small-time and heavy-handed attempt to muscle in on some of the action. We'll never know. But why anyone would take on faith any college basketball game played in Madison Square Garden during this period is beyond me.

My great night at the Garden left me with health problems that continue to this day. I damaged the blood vessels in my left kidney by playing in a severely dehydrated state. For years after that and periodically throughout my career, I would have similar problems and finally be hospitalized during my last year with the Bulls. Even today I must be careful to drink a great deal of water to keep my system flushed or I feel sluggish.

I shouldn't have played that night, but how could I have made that decision for myself and for my team? I was a kid on the biggest night of my life. I was in pain and frightened and had to put myself in other people's hands. We're talking about 1960 here. I had no agent, no lawyer, no leverage. A kid from the projects, I was still constantly trying to prove myself worthy of all this attention and opportunity.

One year to the day of my being juiced on March 17, 1960, the Manhattan district attorney Frank Hogan disclosed a new college basketball scandal and said that when revealed, it would spread from coast to coast and dwarf its 1951 predecessor. In that earlier sordid mess, college basketball almost went under. It was proved that from 1947 to 1950, 86 games had been fixed at Madison Square Garden and in 22 other cities in 17 states. Gamblers had given bribes to thirty-two players from seven different schools. Thirteen convicted fixers went to prison, and five players received jail terms. Programs were wrecked at City College of New York and Long Island University while Kentucky and Bradley were sent reeling.

The college basketball scandals of 1951 had been bad enough. They had engulfed eastern powerhouses such as LIU and CCNY, and taken down the stars from Adolph Rupp's dominant Kentucky teams, Alex Groza and Ralph Beard. The scandal had even reached as far as Bradley. Three players, including the star guard Gene Melchiorre, had been recruited to shave points in selected games, beginning in the 1949 NIT Tournament in Madison Square Garden and continuing through the 1951 season. Bradley was actually ranked number one in the nation at the end of the 1950 season. The disgrace of its nationally visible basketball program had left a deep scar on this small private university on the make. Peoria and Bradley had been very wary about again building the reputation of the university on the strength of its basketball program.

In the 1961 scandal the first known players implicated were Art Hicks and Hank Gunter of Seton Hall. St. Joseph's of Philadelphia, coached by Jack Ramsay, had to return its third-place NCAA trophy when its star players Jack Egan, Vince Kempton, and Frank Majewski were implicated and expelled from school. The team captain Egan had been drafted by the Warriors and

Kempton by the Knicks. Their college degrees and professional careers were swept away.

Their crime was shaving points so that if their team was favored, it would either lose or win by a lesser margin than anticipated. In some cases, bribe offers were rejected by players because the athletes were facing traditional rivals or their teams were playing in sectional tournaments. In other cases, players did their "dishonest best" to please the gamblers but failed to meet the requirements and had to return the bribes. All players eventually received immunity from prosecution from the grand jury and were named as witnesses for the state. Their penalties came not from jail sentences but from being exiled to live with themselves outside the sports world they had betrayed.

In the investigation I, too, was called to New York City. After the end of my junior year in the 1960–61 season, I was placed in Hogan's hot seat. Bradley had been ranked second in the regular season to the Jerry Lucas powerhouse Ohio State team. Then we failed to win the Missouri Valley Conference tournament and were knocked out of the NCAA tournament, which at the time had a very small field of only sixteen teams. We naturally turned our eyes to the NIT, where we were the defending champions, but, inexplicably, Bradley turned down its invitation. It's probable the school didn't want to risk another New York trip after my drugging incident and the fact that talk of scandal was everywhere. Could that stop any team from playing today with millions of dollars at stake? Hardly, but today the team is separate from the school.

After the end of our disappointing season, Orsborn called Al Saunders and me into his office and questioned us about our possible association with gamblers. Not one white player was called in. Of course, no white players could have significantly influenced a game's outcome after Mike Owens and Dan Smith graduated along with Bobby Joe Mason. So the finger was pointed at us. We were suspect because we were vulnerable and poor and, it was surmised, perhaps immoral to boot.

I sat across from Orsborn, who gave me no sign of sympathy or understanding my fear or position. All he said was "Chet, if you're involved in this, it would totally disappoint me." I don't recall that he said anything about the school being on my side, about being innocent until proven guilty, about any trust he might have in me after three years of my giving everything for his team. This from a man who, if I had told my recruiting story, could have been in trouble with the NCAA. A man for whom I had played at the NIT in great pain. As usual, the coach seemed to hold all the cards. He couldn't extend the simplest humanity to me. All he could do was make me afraid.

When Hogan flew Al Saunders and me into Manhattan, we were put up in the same hotel where I had been drugged the year before! When we arrived at the district attorney's offices, his hallway was filled with very scared and nervous college players from all over the country. I knew and had played against most of these guys, but no one was talking. No one wanted to look at each other or crack jokes or fraternize with the guys in that hallway. We could have easily fielded a couple of All-Star teams with this group. Guys from the Atlantic Coast Conference, (ACC), the Big Ten, the east coast, the west coast. Even squeaky-clean Player of the Year Jerry Lucas was there to show that Hogan was leaving no stone unturned. I sat on a chair in the hectic hallway. No one had an adviser or counsel or anyone looking out for them. The schools had thrown us to the wolves while we held our breath.

Finally, my name was called. I entered a room with only one chair in the middle of the floor. Circling the chair were two New York detectives with their jackets off and their guns bulging from shoulder holsters. I felt as if I were in a Humphrey Bogart movie as they played the classic good cop–bad cop routine with me.

The good cop began by saying he saw Bradley win the NIT the preceding year and congratulated me on playing such a great semifinal game despite the circumstances. I was too frightened to do anything but nod my head. He went on, "You're not being accused of anything, you know. The reason you're here is to see if you have any information that might shed light on this situation."

My eyes stayed riveted on a spot on the floor.

"Do you know a fellow by the name of Jack Molinas?" he suddenly asked. Molinas would turn out to be the master fixer of 1960–62, a former NBA Rookie of the Year for the Pistons. He would later serve time, become a west coast gang guy, and be killed in Los Angeles in 1975. But at the time his name meant nothing to me, and I said so.

"Do you know Art Hicks?"

I said I'd never met him but that I knew he played for Seton Hall.

"Do you know Hank Gunter?"

I gave the same answer. No.

"Did your roommate, Saunders, ever talk about Hicks and Gunter?"

I said I knew Al had known Hicks when they played high school ball in Chicago.

"Did you wonder why Saunders didn't drink his orange juice last year when you got sick?"

I didn't want to overreact and get Al in any difficulty. But I thought to myself, So that juice *must* have been connected to fixing games if this guy is still pushing about it. I said no, that I didn't wonder about Al.

Finally, he came to his last question: "During the NIT last year, did anyone bring women to your room?" Evidently call girls had been supplied by some of the gamblers. Again I said no.

Then the bad cop took over, immediately changing the tone. "Chet, we know that as a teenager you were arrested in Benton Harbor for gambling and spent two nights in jail."

I could feel my heart jumping out of my chest. They'd run a background check on me in Benton Harbor and had come up with the two nights I'd spent in jail for the penny-ante game in the park. I couldn't believe that this incident would come back to haunt me. I figured these big-city cops knew the circumstances, knew I'd been fined all of eight dollars for my sins. But what they implied was I'd been found guilty of gambling!

Now these cops had me scared. They began to ask about specific games in my junior year, about the Minnesota game in which we'd been favored to win by ten and had won by only four. They followed with a series of questions about other games in which we'd been heavily favored but had just snuck through. These guys were searching and trying to break me down.

After starting out with high expectations, our 1960–61 season had been very shaky. But it wasn't due to gamblers or shaved points. We had lost two very mature leaders on offense in guards Mason and Owens, and we didn't have replacements for them. Al was now playing guard but was really a forward. Mack Herndon and Tim Robinson were both talented forwards but undisciplined on the court. We just didn't have the poise it took. But the detectives wanted another explanation, one I couldn't give them. They finally let me go and even said, "Thank you for coming. You've been a lot of help." I could breathe again.

Al Saunders admitted being contacted by a gambler over the summer before his senior year. That was all. He never took any money or tried to influence anyone to shave points. He had never told me about it, as much to protect me as himself. But Bradley suspended him from school only weeks before his graduation. The next year, he returned to Bradley at his own expense and lived with me off campus while he finished his degree.

College players were totally at the mercy of the colleges and the NCAA. We had no lawyers, no agents, no well-placed friends in the university or the legal system. Ours was a lonely and fearful heroism at all times. The NIT games and the investigation only reinforced my belief that what I had could be snatched away with one wrong move or an accusation.

When I returned to Peoria, Coach Orsborn called me in and told me I had been cleared of any wrongdoing and that I had nothing to worry about. He said, "It turned out the way I thought it would." That's not what I remember him saying before I left for New York.

7.
College Fever

In March 1960, I came back to campus as the heroic center of a championship team. I had come through under pressure, and we had won the big games. We had won the NIT, and the good feelings from this triumph and my celebrity should have kept me on top of the world. Instead, I was still weak from the effects of being drugged, still unsure of what had happened to me and what it meant. With the championship in hand, everyone else was ready to forget the drugging incident even happened, but I couldn't.

I soon had more than championship basketball and my kidneys to worry about. I found myself in another kind of game, one equally threatening to my life, or so I thought, because it was the danger of "messin' with a white girl."

I met Jennifer in the spring of my sophomore year, right after receiving an invitation to the 1960 Olympic trials in Denver. I walked out of Coach Orsborn's gym office into a bright spring morning. A girl came up to me and said, "You're Chet, aren't you? I've been trying to figure out a way to meet you for a long time." She said she'd been at my games, and I could tell she had more interest in me than just my playing basketball. To me Jennifer looked like the actress Loretta Young, with classical features and huge eyes set off by an olive, Mediterranean complexion.

The eleven o'clock classes had just let out, and students were approaching us from all directions. At six feet seven inches, black, and a campus hero, I was always visible on campus. And by that time, I had learned the terms of my fame. I'd never before talked this way to a white coed, and I felt as if we were a spectacle. To throw off suspicions, I reached into a notebook and began scribbling as if I were giving her an autograph. I felt silly but thought I had to deflect anyone's perception of the moment. She asked with a sly grin of complicity, "Is that all? How about your phone number?" I wrote it down, and we'd begun.

Older guys in Benton Harbor, my friends, and my brothers' friends had warned me over and over again to stay away from white women. Jennifer was not only white but also rich. She came from Winnetka, Illinois, a suburb on Chicago's north shore, then, as now, one of the richest towns in the country.

After our first meeting, I began noticing Jennifer around campus. She would try to talk to me, but I generally stayed out of her way. But she was persistent and always seemed to be in my line of vision at the student union and along the walks between classes. Finally, Al Saunders persuaded me to give it a chance and take her out. To him, any chance to move on a pretty girl had to be taken. His Chicago confidence overrode my southern caution and actually made me take the dare as a test of my masculine charms.

I was ready to take some chances after the pressures of the last few months. I was still on a roller coaster and needed some new high or other. In the back of my mind was the fact that all year I'd felt helpless and used even as I'd become a nationally known player and the biggest name on campus. The racial horrors of our southern road trips. My being poisoned at the NIT. I was trying to take a risk and get back at somebody for what had happened to me and also to win something of my own to match the public glory. That and a combination of wonder and curiosity led me to risk taking out this beautiful girl and seeing where it would lead. I also felt I'd been on the verge of doing something like this ever since high school when the white girls would crowd the basketball players, just waiting for some signs of interest. Now I was almost an All-American and on my own. Who was to say what was forbidden? Or so I thought.

I was one of the few people on campus with a car, because my brother Fred had given me his old '55 Chevy. It was a real heap, one of those two-toned jobs from back then, a combination of light blue top and dark blue hood and, by then, several other rusty colors. Convinced we couldn't chance being seen together, Jennifer and I concocted a plan. She would sneak out the back of her dorm, jump in my waiting car and lie flat on the floor in the back until we were off campus. She rushed in breathless, and I hit the accelerator. As we sped down the hill, I was terrified and kept asking myself: What am I *thinking* of? On the radio, Ben E. King was leading the Drifters through "There Goes My Baby," and I thought, Here goes everything.

We went to a friend's off-campus apartment, to which he'd given me the key. Jennifer and I went up the stairs, and I remember fumbling with the key in the lock. I was so frightened that I almost had to hold my right hand still with my left. Once inside, we talked for a few minutes. I can't even remember what we talked about I was so scared. It was a small apartment, and the bedroom was visible to both of us from the moment we walked in. Jennifer's big eyes batted at me slowly. She was more gorgeous than I had allowed myself to imagine. I hadn't even had an honest look at her on campus. I hadn't dared to stare. But now I sort of drank her in.

Slowly, she began to undress. So I followed her lead as if this were all happening to someone else. Finally, she had taken off all her clothes except her panties. In a panic, I just sort of gaped at her. This was the 1950s and the first time I had ever been with a naked girl in a bedroom. And here I was in Peoria with a white girl at that! As if in a dream, I walked over to the bed to touch her—her shoulder, maybe her breast, I don't remember. But I knew instantly I couldn't go through with this and snatched my hand back, urging her to put on her clothes. My whole body was quivering in an adrenaline rush of desire and fear.

Believe it or not, we got dressed and began to talk. Another first. Here I was, a sophomore in college, and she was the first white woman with whom I ever had an extended conversation, unless you count my high school guidance counselor. That's how segregated my life had been and still was. We started by talking about mutual and neutral subjects like classes, sports, or friends. In other words, we began to relate normally to one another as one young person to another.

But then we had to get around to the inevitable subject of black and white. To our mutual surprise, Jennifer and I found we had a lot in common. Winnetka had kept her from knowing anyone the least bit different from herself, from knowing black people, from exploring what the world was really about. I told her about my years in Mississippi and in Benton Harbor, about my isolation and shyness, things I couldn't admit to even my roommate or family. She couldn't believe that an All-American basketball player could feel so lonely and awkward.

We both admitted to a deep curiosity about our encounter, but years of warnings and conditioning brought back the fear. The drive back to Bradley was the longest of my life. We hadn't done anything, but every stoplight seemed to be red for about five minutes. I felt as if I were escaping my execution when she finally got out of the car and snuck back into her dorm. I asked myself over and over, How could I be so stupid? Our relationship should have ended right there, but it didn't. And, in a way, I knew it wouldn't because I could see Jennifer was determined that our encounter would be a revelation for her about black-white relations. I was caught in its grip, too.

I lied to Al and told him she'd been great in bed. Mostly, I was glad to get it over with. But Jennifer kept calling, and I didn't say no. We saw each other for the next month. We went to drive-in movies, the "passion pits" for young people of the early 1960s. You could be together for hours in a movable and very uncomfortable bedroom. My fear of discovery kept me on edge. We did make love, ultimately, but it didn't carry the shock of that first night in the apartment when just touching each other seemed like a dream, that first night when we found out we were both human beings. Making love did give rise to a whole new set of fears. We didn't use protection, and I prayed, "Lord, if you help us get past this moment, I swear I'll never get in a situation like this again."

I made up my mind that we just had to stop. The sex made everything even more complicated. I tried to tell Jennifer on the phone that our relationship was over. She begged to see me one more time, sure she could change my mind in a face-to-face meeting, one that I supposed would end with more sex. I said no and tried to beg off a meeting. I didn't want the challenge or the temptation. Phoning in my good-byes wasn't very brave, but I was scared and I'd had enough.

Jennifer convinced me to see her, however. We settled nothing, argued, felt miserable as only sad young lovers can. That night behind her dorm, Jennifer threw herself in front of my car, almost hugging the front tire, and refused to move. I couldn't drive away, and I certainly couldn't leave her there. Finally, I managed to drag her up to the dorm door, and her roommate helped her the rest of the way into the building. I drove back to my room and tried to sleep, hoping against hope that we were finished, over and out. I felt terrible.

At three o'clock in the morning, the sound of a piercing car horn ended my fruitless attempts at sleep. It was Jennifer slamming the horn of my car. She'd snuck out of her dorm and was filthy drunk from what might have been a whole bottle of vodka. Half-afraid, she was suicidal and very worried about exposure. Mack Herndon and I dragged her into our dorm, the athletic dorm for black male students! She vomited in our shower, and it took us forty-five minutes to revive her by washing her face with cold washcloths. I called her roommate to let her know where Jennifer was. I told her that when we'd cleaned her up, I'd call again so that she could let us in the back dorm entrance for the second time that night.

I knew we had to get her back to her room before dawn or else it might be curtains for all of us. Jennifer wasn't rational, and I was frantic. I had to make the decisions, and I was so sorry that this beautiful girl whom I cared about was now a problem threatening to destroy the two of us. Her long brown hair was tangled and matted, her eyes bloodshot and wild. Her scarf and jacket were soiled and half-soaked, her sweater rumpled. She was exhausted, and all our passion and argument were gone—like children who had played hard at a party and now felt near collapse. But we were also afraid of our parents or, in this case, the college. At five o'clock that Saturday morning, we got Jennifer back to her room, and our longest night was over. I stayed tense throughout the next few days awaiting our fate. I couldn't believe something more wouldn't come of all this.

Sure enough, Jennifer had become hysterical and called her father and told him we were having an affair. Luckily, her father called Coach Orsborn, not the university. I think that probably saved me right there because Orsborn wanted Chet Walker to stay in school very badly. He was awfully anxious when he called me in and asked if Jennifer and I had had a sexual relationship. I tried to stare him down, all the while wondering what his angle would be in this business. "No," I lied, with all the conviction I could muster. The coach was so relieved that he looked like a balloon losing air. "Thank God. If you got a white girl pregnant in Peoria, I'd be gone almost as fast as you because I brought you here."

I was surprised a few days later when I picked up the phone and it was Jennifer's father. I couldn't think of anything to say. I didn't know exactly how much he knew or what he was going to do with the information. Actually, he didn't sound angry but rather cool. He asked me if I had dated his daughter, and I said we'd gone to the movies a few times! He said, "Well, she's very upset and said you don't want to see her anymore." He sounded quite happy about this. Then he allowed that Jennifer was boy crazy and he knew it. I couldn't quite figure it out, but it was almost as if he and I were on the same side, and Jennifer was the problem. From worrying about being expelled, I had progressed to listening to a very relieved coach and then to a father griping about his daughter. I began to breathe easier.

The only punishment meted out to anyone was to Jennifer herself. Her father came to take her out of school. I was walking back to Harper Hall one afternoon in May when I saw her in front of her dorm down the street. She was standing next to a long, sleek car, watching a man struggling on the steps of her dormitory with two huge suitcases, which he stowed in the trunk of the car. It had to be her father; he was all business. She looked so sad and downcast. She hugged her roommate, who had often acted as our lookout and go-between, got in the car, and was gone. I was frozen in place, but my mind was racing. I thought back to Mississippi and the days when I'd walked quickly down the road in Bethlehem, daring to look at the little white girl in the yard only after I was safely out of sight. Years later, when I was playing for the Bulls, Jennifer called me up to talk. She'd been married and divorced. The years hadn't brought us any closer; we had little to say.

I returned to more innocent pursuits, within racial boundaries. I dated Joyce, who was a part-time student on campus. Her uncle ran Big John's Barbecue Pit, Peoria's finest and a hangout for black and white students alike. Joyce would always let the black basketball players have free barbecue, and we really loaded up. When I stopped seeing her, Al, Mack, and Tim Robinson came to my room as a delegation one night to inform me of their serious problem. Joyce was stiffing them, no more free eats at Big John's. They told me that Joyce and I just had to get back together because they were starving. They manhandled me, put a little dormitory muscle on me. So Joyce and I resumed our romance for the good of the campus. All in all, this was a kids' affair with no consequences and just what I needed after Jennifer.

My status as a basketball player probably made me immune to the usual repercussions when a black student was caught in a compromising situation. Had I just been another black student or even a less prominent player, Jennifer's father would probably have called the university, not the basketball coach, and pushed to get me expelled from school; and she might have testified. Because of my athletic prominence, I was more important than she was in the Bradley scheme of things. It was an interesting but difficult proposition for me to accept.

I didn't date any other white girls at Bradley on the sly. In later years, I have had brief relationships with white women but nothing lasting. I believe athletes have the same sexual attitudes and values as other people. We probably have more opportunities to fulfill desire because, as sports heroes, we have great power and allure. My value to Bradley was such that I'd almost become immune to sexual scandal. I had power, but I was too scared to understand it. But many players in succeeding generations of college athletes have understood and abused this immunity while coaches, athletic directors, college presidents, and universities have looked the other way.

Jennifer was doing something compulsively. I responded out of curiosity and was able to get away with it. She left school whereas I stayed on. I wasn't completely clear on the meaning of this astonishing fact, but I knew that being a basketball star had saved me. I was more important this time.

8.
Educations

We called my cousin Victor "The Professor." He was about ten years older than I and told everyone in Benton Harbor that he had a Ph.D. from the University of Maryland. Of course, most everyone knew that he had only finished high school and had taken a few college courses while in the army. Nobody called him on the facts for they weren't important. Victor not only read widely but was also a wise man. He told me, "Education and knowledge are the backbone of your soul, Chester." Victor linked education with growth: the more you knew, the stronger your character might become. He became excited for me, that I would be the first person in our family to truly break the pattern of educational denial that plagued our family and other black families. I would be living Victor's dream, too.

I recalled Victor's words many times as I settled down at Bradley. There were to be no more Jennifers and no more NIT championships after my sophomore year. But I matured as a player and as a man and really learned what would be expected of me.

I beat all the odds at college. By working very hard, I not only stayed in school and remained eligible, but also graduated, even making the dean's list my senior year, a fact that made my mother proud. I even surprised myself. Mack Herndon and Tim Robinson had flunked out, and Al Saunders was off the team but finishing his degree and living off campus with me. I had more time to concentrate on my work, and it paid off.

I didn't get the education I should have at Bradley, but much of that was my own fault for taking the options that everyone expected me to accept. When I finally began to take more courses in my history and education majors, I found the work extremely interesting. I always had a keen interest in sociology and human behavior. The more I could learn from educational psychology, the more I applied myself. By the time graduation came around, I wished I could begin again with my new attitude wedded to Victor's advice.

It takes two years in college to find a major. At that point you can get into work that truly interests you without having to take a lot of requirements. So many college athletes never get to that point. They come underprepared from high schools and junior colleges with no intention of finding themselves academically or discovering a calling or a love of learning. They merely go to school to "stay eligible" for basketball, never doing enough work in any subject area to come close to competence. To them, college means playing in nationally televised games where scouts sit up and take notice. Players figure after two years of college heroics, they'll sign for a million plus. All they want to do is chase the NBA.

Some professors meant a great deal to me while others immediately assumed I couldn't or didn't have to do the classwork because I was black and/or an athlete. Mostly, my world expanded at Bradley and so did my confidence. Some readings do stick with me after all these years. I really cared about a paper I wrote in my freshman year on Somerset Maugham's *The Moon and Sixpence*, a novel about the life of the painter Paul Gauguin. Gauguin fascinated me. Here was a man who found his place after years of trying, a man who achieved real success but then found a lot was missing in his life and ran away from that success. Even in college, I was fantasizing about that escape—to run away to paradise. That was my dream. I also wrote a paper on Howard Fast's *Freedom Road*, a novel about slavery and reconstruction, which would become the first movie I worked on as a producer almost twenty years later. In Ralph Ellison's *Invisible Man* I could easily relate to his Battle Royal scene in the first chapter when I recalled boxing as a kid for the men in Mississippi.

I was not very aware of the black political movements in the South when I was in college. The Southern Christian Leadership Conference (SCLC), the Student Non-Violent Coordinating Committee (SNCC) and their great protest strategies, the freedom rides and voter registration projects were not issues on the Bradley campus, which was almost all-white and predominantly conservative. Central Illinois was almost a southern border state. My knowledge came more from the classroom, from teachers such as Dr. Garrett and Professor Lawrence Lew.

In my sophomore year, I had Professor Lew, whose political science class made me keenly aware of the political dimensions to my life. Dr. Lew had been a citizen of the world. He did his undergraduate work at the University of Nanking before World War II and fled during the Japanese occupation. He was then a government researcher in London and Washington. Bradley's most prominent professor in political science, he wrote many of the entries on China in world dictionaries of political science.

I had been used to just getting by in my courses, playing on the faculty expectations for me while I concentrated on basketball. But Dr. Lew gave only essay tests and wrote in the margins of all my papers, "Elaborate, Mr. Walker!" He didn't care for simple, bare-bones statements. He wanted opinions to grow out of them. I had such a hard time expressing myself because of my shyness and wariness. He pushed me to understand what college work and writing were all about and made me believe I could achieve something. He didn't treat me as a basketball player or a special black student but as someone he wanted to teach to think, to express himself. As a foreigner, he didn't have the American prejudices about the potential of certain students.

His gift to me was to push me to develop my reasoning power and learn how to express myself in writing.

I was always afraid that what I had to say was not important. I don't believe that students coming from disadvantaged educational backgrounds should be allowed to play intercollegiate sports as freshmen. Let them practice hard and get their satisfaction in the gym in sweats. But subject them to whatever it takes in the classroom to allow them to enter the general college population by sophomore year. Don't allow them to see themselves as special cases but as people with minds who have to learn to use them because it's a long life after college. Chances are that it won't be the NBA or the National Football League (NFL).

For big-time college athletes at a Division I school, there's never enough time day by day, week by week, to pay attention to both classwork and their sport. I came to college with few study skills, a scant reading background, and little self-confidence. I could have spent all day, every day, at my classwork and still not have caught up with the majority of my classmates.

I also worked at the equivalent of a full-time job in practicing, preparing for, and playing my sport. Great college athletes aren't all naturals with a body sculpted by the Lord. To become a skilled basketball player takes an incredible amount of hard work, time, and sweat. I believe that big-time college athletes certainly put in at least as many hours at their trade as college professors do on their classes.

I would like colleges and universities to take out an insurance policy on each player. In the event of a career-ending injury, a player could stay in school for four years and work for his degree. Of course, there's no guarantee that any player will have a professional career, but colleges should do as much as they can to support the life outside of sports of the student athlete from whom they are reaping such benefits.

A major college athlete must be able to learn, to stay at his craft, to take instruction, to integrate advice with his own inclinations and instincts, to work with others, to subordinate his own

goals to that of a team. That's a curriculum in itself. Such a regimen meant, for example, that I went beyond majoring in basketball. It was more like putting in week after week at a job with
overtime, nights, and weekends. I found myself daydreaming
about games all the time as well; all athletes probably need some
kind of course in mind control or yoga to let us off the sports
hook when we need to do our classwork.

I concentrated on school in whatever time I had left. Yet I
always had enough curiosity and enough eagerness to understand my world that I responded to those teachers who encouraged me to believe I could do the work and could elaborate more
on my answers. By the time I was a senior, learning had become
fun as well as a lifelong challenge. Nothing gave me more confidence to face my future than my success at Bradley *in the classroom.* I found I could learn about history, economics,
psychology, and understand myself and my culture. Beyond
knowing where I came from, nothing was more important to me.

College was, of course, much more than classes and sports
for a young man. It was a rude awakening with my return to the
South and then my romance with Jennifer. It was comprehend-
ing many new social relationships and learning about a widen-
ing world. Growing up in a Michigan town, the music I liked
was rock and roll and country music. Jazz was a whole new experience for me. When I'd go to Chicago with Al Saunders, a lot
of the jazz clubs would let us in because we were so tall although
we were underage. The life and action on the south side in the
1950s still buzzed with every kind of live music. Suddenly, it was
like finding a wondrous black city. I didn't think of it in terms of
segregation patterns or deprivation. It swung!

Chicago had been a mystery to me until that time. You
might think that is crazy since during all my years in Benton
Harbor, Chicago just sat an hour or two away from us like the
Emerald City. But my family was Deep South and mistrustful of
any big city. We almost never went to Chicago except to the Lincoln Park zoo once or twice. In a way, that innocence allowed us

to grow up more peacefully without either the city's sophistication or its temptations.

In my freshman year at Bradley we began to party at The Villa in Peoria, which was an all-black nightclub that catered mostly to white students. It was a honky-tonk joint in an isolated area of town. We were especially welcome there as heroes after our NIT victory. The place was faithfully raided once every three months by police. On the night of a raid, the police chief would call Coach Orsborn to tell him to get us out. Orsborn, pragmatic where his star players were concerned, would call Bobby Joe Mason and tell him that the raid would be, say, at ten-thirty or eleven that night. So after 10 P.M., Bobby Joe, Al Saunders and I would coolly saunter outside and take up positions across the road to watch the fireworks when the cops arrived.

Many people were very kind to me during my years in Peoria. I remember the night I was invited over to the house of a prominent alumnus of Bradley, a businessman who supported the basketball program. He had even given me a few dollars now and then under the table, nothing that today's NCAA bloodhounds would approve of but just enough to tide me over until the next college grant payment. His sons adored me and peppered me with questions about what it was like to play against Oscar Robertson or to play in Madison Square Garden.

I'd never been in the home of a well-to-do white person for dinner. Even though everything was as pleasant as it could be, I wondered why I felt so different and out of place. How could I be this hero and yet feel so isolated, such an outsider? Many times I thought, It must be me. I sat there making conversation and having a good time, but the setting was strange, and the whole time I wondered, Who am I?

We had a delicious dinner and talked freely but exclusively about Bradley basketball. I wished they would have asked me something personal, but they didn't seem to want to know my background, where I came from. I thought I would like to tell them about my mother and sisters and brothers, about Anna Laura.

After dinner, my beaming hostess told me, "Chet, we have

a great surprise for you!'' And from the kitchen she produced one of the biggest watermelons I had ever seen. I didn't know whether to laugh or cry. It was the middle of winter. God knows how much trouble she had gone to in order to find watermelon in winter. This was her treat for me. She innocently felt she was doing something special for me, and she was. I love watermelon! My mother and I would sit on the porch for hours eating the sweet juicy melon and spitting seeds.

But this special surprise watermelon also made me choke. My feeling then, and now, though, was why does all this have to be so difficult. Why must black people constantly have to worry about accepting or denying stereotypes of us? Lord knows, I have deflected enough basketball conversations in my lifetime when people I meet just want to reduce me to their memories of me, or show off their sports knowledge or good feelings for black people.

I had a good time that night when I was twenty years old eating a watermelon with an upper-middle-class family in Peoria. I was also aware of the limitations and boundaries that our backgrounds placed on us. Only basketball gave me the clout to have been invited at all. Without my role, who would I have been to them? How would we have met?

But just as surely, the eagerness of that nice lady to look on me as someone to whom she would give a special treat, the light in the eyes of her sons as they heard me talk about Oscar Robertson—surely these were positive human responses. They didn't change race relations in America or cure my isolation. In that more innocent time, we were civil and hoped for more. They could congratulate themselves on having me to dinner, make me comfortable, perhaps influence me to press other recruits to come to Bradley. I could be impressed with the invitation.

Another experience in socialization was a complete contrast to my watermelon surprise. After my freshman year, Bradley found me a job working on the railroad in Peoria. The white football players got easy jobs driving trucks, but I was awarded a back-breaking job driving spikes and hauling huge railroad ties. I worked with older black guys who were really tough. Some of the men were sixty years old, and the skin on their hands was so rough from all their years on the railroad that it was like alligator skin. Their swollen fingers looked as big as carrots.

The guys on the railroad gang called me "Young Blood" and didn't know whether to be impressed by my celebrity or get on me for it. I worked extra hard right from the start to get them to believe I would pull my weight. Once that happened they sort of adopted me. On Friday after work when we were all paid, they would leave at four-thirty for a bar where they would drink straight liquor until about 7 P.M.; then they would all reel home to their families. We would drink strong stuff that seemed always to have "Old" in front of its name—Old Taylor or Old Harper or something like that. They drank to let off steam, but they were always very protective of me and didn't want me to get in any trouble for being with them, because I was really drunk after one or two shots of their medicine.

The bar always filled with black workingmen from Caterpillar, the Hiram Walker distilleries, and the Schlitz brewing plant. The railroad gang was the dirtiest. We would walk in there just covered with grime but wearing it like a badge of honor. The railroad men enjoyed showing me around. They would say, "Hey, this is Young Blood. We're going to introduce him to real life." But they would say this without rancor, without jealousy. They were proud of their own jobs, their own ability to provide. I felt their strength as older black men who were survivors. I saw them as more than that. They were the fathers I hadn't had since we moved north.

One night one of the men asked me very tentatively, "Chet, will you come to my house?" I could tell it took a lot for him to ask and that he was convinced I would make some excuse to get out of it. But I just said, "Man, I'd be glad to come to your house." He had eight or nine kids, and he was so proud of them and that I'd shared their table with them. It was like being back with the Walker family in Bethlehem. His wife cooked up a storm. It was such good food that I stopped in all summer to get chicken and greens to go.

Monday, when we went back to work, he didn't want me to

do anything, just operate the little sidecar. He would caution me
not to pick up some heavy railroad tie, that I might hurt my back
and not be able to play ball. I had to tell him that he didn't have
to give me any special treatment. None of the men on that railroad crew had ever seen me play. They couldn't afford to go to
the games, nor would they have felt welcome in the Bradley
fieldhouse. Yet I was treated gently, courteously, and fairly by
these proud older men. They didn't want me or need me for anything, but I certainly needed them.

After my sophomore year at Bradley, the university secured
me a construction job in Peoria. I was tearing up pavement in the
downtown area with a jackhammer. I could feel the shocks rippling down my back and legs. The noise was deafening, and the
temperature seemed always to be hovering around one hundred
degrees. The work was so hard that at night I couldn't even take
off my dusty, stinking, wringing-wet clothes but would just fall
asleep in them and shower in the morning. I think I could have
taken even this sort of punishment if it had not been for my boss.

With him it was always "Boy, do this!" and "Boy, do that!"
He really tried to break me whereas the white Bradley football
player working on the same crew drove a gravel truck around all
day. Supposedly, we both had jobs arranged by Bradley; there
was no reason at all that we couldn't have taken turns in the cab
of that truck and with that jackhammer. I angrily interpreted all
this as racist and began to boil like that pavement itself.

The boss would have been a good plantation overseer. I
could imagine him laughing with his friends at night about
how hard he worked that black kid who thought he was an All-
American athlete. Finally, one awful day I just cursed him out
and quit and rode all the way back home to Benton Harbor in my
filthy clothes in my battered Chevy.

That was when Shel Radom gave me that great job driving a
truck for his hardware and supply business. I would deliver
loads of chemicals such as DDT to area farmers to protect their
crops. He showed a lot of confidence in me and even left me in
charge of the store for periods although he would call me a lot to

My mother, Regenia
Walker. She is my
connection to the past
and to the future.

Chester, age 9. My
mother's son.

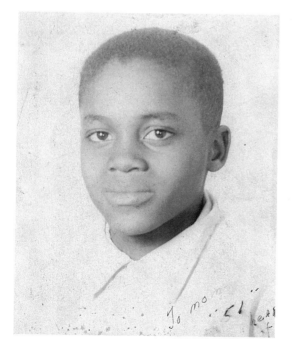

As a high school senior in Benton Harbor with my best friend, Jim Turner. Growing up in the projects, we were all the same size.

Driving the baseline for Bradley against the University of Houston. I dreaded roadtrips to those segregated southern cities. *(Special Collections Center, Bradley University Library)*

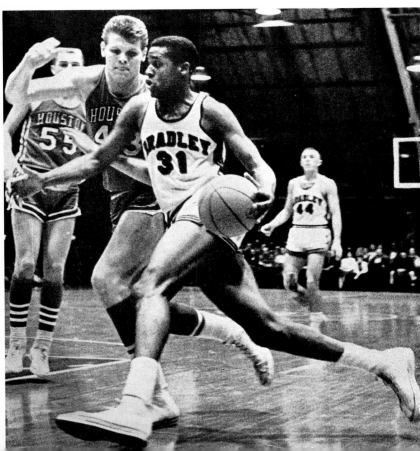

I could really sky for the ball at Bradley until knee and kidney problems made me more earthbound as a player in the NBA. *(Special Collections Center, Bradley University Library)*

NIT Tournament, 1960. The *New York Post*'s question remains unanswered to this day. My Bradley teammate Mack Herndon is the interested reader. *(Special Collections Center, Bradley University Library)*

I downed glass after glass of water at courtside after feeling drugged and dehydrated before the NIT semifinal game. *(Special Collections Center, Bradley University Library)*

I felt as terrible as I
looked during a timeout
in the "juice" game.
*(Special Collections Center,
Bradley University Library)*

The Philadelphia 76ers
were assembling an
awesome team in the
mid-1960s, and I was
proud to be a part of it.

On the move for the Bulls in the old Chicago Stadium. The New York Knicks defender with all the hair is current Bulls coach Phil Jackson. *(Chicago Bulls)*

My offensive game was built on patience. I had many head, eye, and shoulder fakes that I used to make the defender commit himself. Then I'd go up and get the basket or foul shots or both.

Age 35 in Hollywood,
about to begin my new
career.

The night of the Emmy
Awards. How proud
my mother would have
been at this moment!
(Craig T. Mathew)

see how I was doing! It felt wonderful to be part of an operation where I had some responsibility and fair treatment. Shel gave me respect and a chance. I earned the rest.

People say to me all the time that things are so much better now for athletes, for black people, than in the 1950s when I was coming of age. Or they urge me to be patient and remind me that change comes gradually. But if a black kid has a year of freedom taken from him now while he waits for society to change, that's a year of freedom he cannot relive or in which he cannot learn. That's another dream denied for another generation—or two or three. When people are always asked to wait for something, they may not live to see it. My mother didn't. Neither did my sister Anna Laura.

At Bradley, I was black, poor, and an athlete. Some college exams were foreign to me. They might as well have been in Russian. But if some knowledge of life test had been given to a kid from a suburb, he would have flunked. Yet I had to be judged according to the standards set up for him. At Bradley, I was asked to leave part of my past behind. I was told how fortunate I was to be out of the ghetto. But it wasn't the "ghetto" to me; it was my life, my rudder.

People are always saying, "Get out of the ghetto . . . ," but how do you take the strength and leave behind the waste and the anger? You have to make the anger work for you, not drag you down with regret or guilt. And you have to respect yourself in whatever situation you find yourself. Basketball gave me the power to cut to the front of the line. After a life at the back of the bus, such treatment was heady indeed. I had never felt that power before in any other way.

This enormous engine goes chugging on all around a player, and it's easy to feel powerful. The athlete doesn't realize how his future is damaged. He needs basic skills and the discipline, patience, and guidance to develop them. The fact is, he won't make the NBA or the NFL, not in 99 percent of the cases.

He should be thinking, Can I make the cut in that engineering firm, that ad agency, that law office? The conversion of sports power into more lasting leverage in this society is a riddle and a curse to most gifted athletes. It's a cruel rainbow that arcs over them. Nobody has quite the hang time to touch it for long. And it is gone before they know it, leaving embittered, bewildered men.

People often don't take into account how an athlete becomes a cash cow for his school. The NCAA controls thousands of athletes who make millions of dollars for their universities. When I was at Bradley back at the dawn of the sports-media era, the school was able to raise its ticket prices, and its television and radio fees went way up as we became a national power. Bradley's publicity machine built me up when I was a sophomore.

Then for thirteen years in the NBA, night after night, eighty-two games a year, all over the United States, the P.A. announcer would bark, "From Bradley, number twenty-five, Chet Walker!" How can you put a price on that much publicity for the school?

In 1958, I received room, board, books, and fifteen dollars a month for laundry. That was it. I'm not covering up any fancy deals that I've agreed to forget. Many students on campus from the suburbs of Chicago or St. Louis had money to burn. But several times I had to waver between a new pair of shoes and foregoing some meals. I was not allowed to work on campus during the basketball season. I *could* resell my four free tickets to each home game and faithfully did, using the money to buy clothes. As a teenager, I would quickly grow out of clothes like some giant in a fairy tale whose limbs just kept growing longer and longer. Fortunately, my brothers Fred and Moses let me rob their wardrobes or handed down some clothes to me. My sister Alter and her husband would send money to me from Benton Harbor when they could. I would try to save money by cashing in part of the unused meal tickets we got from the athletic departments. We were the "meal tickets" for the program, and here I was using my food money for necessities! Today I suppose the NCAA would swoop down on such "deals" like a hawk.

When I was a junior at Bradley, we had a guy come in from

Washington, D.C., with a real rep preceding him. At six feet four inches, he was a forward who had been all-city, and Orsborn gave him a scholarship on the basis of press clippings and reports. The fact was that in practice this kid, Robert McGuire, just didn't seem that good. He was slow off the ball, couldn't shoot very well, and just didn't seem to have any kind of a game we could figure out. He was friendly enough, almost too gregarious as he tried to get tight with us. He was so personable in fact that, while still a freshman, he had his own radio program on the campus station. But on the court—nothing. He vexed us all.

We thought he might be some kind of plant or ringer but why and for whom? He just seemed older somehow. All the black students became wary of him. He was a sharp dresser, articulate, and pretty conservative. In fact, he was more accepted by the white students than by the brothers.

Before the year was out, Robert McGuire had split, leaving big bills at local stores and no trail. It turned out that he was a con artist, twenty-five years old, an army vet who'd somehow used clippings to forge an application for an athletic scholarship. He wasn't "Robert McGuire" at all. Bradley was plenty embarrassed to find out that in its zeal to sign a top recruit it had really been taken. Remember this was before videotape, ESPN, national visibility of high school players, and media saturation. Today, prize recruits are national televised property. But "Robert McGuire" almost pulled it off at sleepy Bradley in 1960.

My junior and senior seasons on the basketball court at Bradley were somewhat anticlimactic after the excitement of my sophomore year. We continued to have excellent teams but fell a little short each season. In my junior year we were 21–5 and won 12 straight games at the start of the season. I scored 50 points in our first game of the season and averaged 25 points per game. But we lacked the veteran leadership of Mason and Owens. We started to fade and had our 46-game home winning streak broken by Drake. Finally, St. Louis beat us 70–63 at our fieldhouse, which kept us out of the NCAA tournament. Bradley officials were skittish about sending us back to the NIT after the intrigue of 1960, so our season was abruptly finished when the NIT invitation was turned down. To end the season, I was named to three first-team All-America teams, and, of course, District Attorney Hogan invited me to his Manhattan inquisition.

In my senior season at Bradley, we had a 21–7 record and were ranked sixth nationally. Yet our team was erratic and not very sound. Al Saunders was gone. Herndon and Robinson had flunked out. We had exciting new talent in center Joe Strawder and guard Levern "Jelly" Tart and had our moments. We edged Louisville 80–79 in a game in which I scored 40 points and stuffed in a rebound to win at the buzzer. In front of sixteen thousand at Chicago Stadium, we edged Notre Dame 92–87. I had broken every Bradley scoring record by the time I was through and was named to six first-team All-America teams in 1962. Our season stalled that year in the semifinals of the NIT when Duquesne beat us 88–85, and my college career was over. It was time to look toward my future beyond college.

It's hard to remember that in 1960, professional sports weren't that much more lucrative than other professions that certainly had longer and more secure futures. At Bradley, I began thinking of teaching American history in high school as a career. It wasn't until my senior year at Bradley that I realized I might be drafted, not by the army but by the NBA. This sounds incredible today when All-Americans face pressure to leave college from their freshman year on to the tune of several million dollars.

My era in college (1958–1962) was a breakthrough period in the integration of college basketball, and it happened immediately preceding the Civil Rights era. Bill Russell and K. C. Jones had been stars at San Francisco in the mid-1950s but they didn't face the level of racial animosity we did in the Missouri Valley Conference where 50 percent of the valley's schools (Houston, St.

Louis, North Texas State, and Tulsa) did not have integrated teams, and Bradley, Cincinnati, Drake, and Wichita State did. We had the only conference that routinely sent northern schools into the South and deep South to play. The Atlantic Coast Conference (ACC) was all-white at this time as was the Southeastern Conference (SEC).

When Shellie McMillon, who preceded me at Bradley by four years, played a game in New Orleans, the fans sang "Bye Bye, Blackbird" when he fouled out. He was refused service at a restaurant, so his teammates had to bring him food in paper bags out on the sidewalk. Barney Cable, his co-captain at Bradley, told me he was so embarrassed for Shellie that he almost cried. Joe Billy McDade, who was Bradley's senior center when I was a freshman, remembered the first time his grandmother saw him play in Houston, and she had to watch as fans spit at him and called him "nigger."

I terrorized the teams we played on the road in the South in my three years at Bradley. I always made it a point to play my best in those southern cities. It was a mission to grind them down. I could understand some of Jackie Robinson's controlled fury. I let it all out on the court in those years.

Finally some of the discrimination was broken by the University of Cincinnati's Oscar Robertson's refusal to play in Houston if he couldn't stay with his team at their hotel. This occurred in his senior year and my sophomore year, *after* my initial trip down there, which had shocked me into wanting to leave school altogether. Oscar, as a senior All-American and the most famous college player in America, finally had the clout to draw attention to the humiliation we endured.

Black college students isolate themselves on white college campuses even when they would appear to have little reason for doing so. Many assume whites don't want to associate with them. Unfortunately, this assumption is often based on bitter past experience. I remember one night when I went out for a beer at a little bar adjacent to the Bradley campus. I made eye contact with one of my white teammates and was about to nod hello or more when he just put his head down and turned his back on me. This was someone I spent countless hours with Monday through Friday, but away from the court he was afraid to acknowledge me in front of his friends. This was not a onetime incident but a recurring pattern I encountered in social situations.

I remember the next day at practice, this same teammate was all smiles, asking, "Hey, Chet, how are you?" I was furious. Here I was the senior All-American captain of a nationally ranked basketball team; yet I'd let this guy, a third-team scrub, bring me down and make me miserable. Perhaps I should have gone to Orsborn to sort things out. I might have gotten him thrown off the team, but then I would be viewed as uppity or vindictive, a troublemaker, someone to keep an eye on. That never was my desire.

At other junctures in my college career, the team at Bradley seemed real and close to me. Never more so than when my basketball dreams appeared clouded or in doubt. In my senior year we lost at Wichita State 88–86, and I scored 44, more than half our points. After the game, I urinated bright red blood and was very scared. I had no idea what was happening to me. We boarded a midnight train in Wichita to carry us back across the Kansas plains, heading northeast toward Peoria. Again I was confronted with my mortality. I sat there with stabbing back pains and just knew that the bloody urine had something to do with my kidneys being damaged two years before in the drugged orange juice incident during the NIT. I had vivid memories of the poisoning in New York City that day, the coaches frightened that I would not play, the doctors not telling me to sit it out, my fear that if I did not play, my great moment in Madison Square Garden would be lost forever. Now I might be in real physical danger. The game that I played so hard and loved so much was taking its toll on my body.

Through my own reflection in the window, I stared hard out into the darkness as the train passed one small Kansas town after another. Trains had always worked their magic on me. As a young boy on the farm, I listened to the long dying whistles of the rolling trains making their way north through the Mississippi delta. I loved it when we would take road trips out to Drake University, riding the Rock Island line to Des Moines.

But on this trip my reveries were interrupted every half hour as I made my way to the tiny train restroom to try to urinate something that was not blood red, hoping that this nightmare would go away. On one trip back to my seat, I passed the student manager, Bob Carruthers, who put out his hand to ask if I was okay. There was a strange silence on the train, but it did not reflect the loss of the Wichita game; rather, I felt that my teammates were truly concerned about me, my well-being, and it warmed me. A basketball team becomes a family with all that implies. At least the good teams come together at moments of crisis. A player develops relationships that he remembers for the rest of his life. They aren't simply memories of championships or wins and losses. Players live and die a little bit together.

Basketball teams that succeed generally like each other as people. The sport is so intimately timed and calibrated, with five people trying to move as one, that it's very difficult to mesh if personal hostilities get in the way. At Bradley, I'd played with fine people. I thought back to my sophomore year when I'd played with senior leaders such as Mike Owens and Dan Smith, who both were from small Illinois towns. Owens had red hair and a round face and the real fire to go with them. Dan was tall and thin, good-looking and a very smooth player. These were the men I remembered as the pain would seize me up. Back in my seat I dozed off for what must have been an hour before the conductor rattled me awake with "Next stop, Peoria, Illinois!" My heart started pounding. I knew soon I would have a name for what I was experiencing.

I was checked into Methodist Hospital for what turned into a five-day stay while the hospital ran tests on me. My roommate was an eighty-year-old man dying of cancer. In constant pain, he would moan out loud. I would pull the curtain aside, go over and sit down with him, hold his hand, while he mumbled the names of his family. After five or ten minutes, he sensed my presence and calmed down though he remained incoherent. I thought of my own fears and memories of my mother attending my sister Anna Laura. It was so quiet in that room where death had entered. I helped him prepare for his last journey. When he died a few weeks later, his family asked me to sign his memorial announcement.

On that first day at the hospital I was taken to an examination room, where they poked and prodded me and extracted just about every kind of fluid for analysis. The tests went on for hours, and results revealed I had ruptured a blood vessel and severely bruised my left kidney but that it could be treated with proper rest and medication. The condition might have been aggravated by a blow during the Wichita game, but I hadn't been aware of one. The doctors did say that the initial weakened condition was probably a result of being drugged at the NIT two years before when I played two games in a state of severe dehydration after experiencing cramps and nausea. This kidney problem has followed me through life.

In the hospital I received many cards and letters from teammates, opposing players, the governor, and even Senator Everett Dirksen from Pekin, Illinois, the town that boasted it had no black people. Even my old flame Jennifer sent me a get-well card from the Ohio college to which she had transferred.

One night I was lying in bed in the hospital listening to the radio when a guy and girl who were nurses appeared in my room holding hands. The girl was Hawaiian, and the boy was from Pekin. They told me they were about to elope and that I was the first person to know! They were going to Arizona but were afraid to tell his parents. I was so gratified that they had picked me to share their joy and fears. I think it was a combination of my being a celebrity of sorts and also that I was a minority and would understand why they were leaving in secret to escape the prejudice.

I was really touched. When you play college or professional

sports, you constantly wonder who *are* all those people massed in the stands night after night. You never know what they really think of you. Do they simply cheer for your baskets and groan at your mistakes? Do they feel they come to know you as a person by how you carry yourself or how much discipline or courage or drama you bring with your game? Basketball is so naked, so intimate. Yet we who play find those who watch a mystery. Our own attraction to them is just as hard to pin down. I suppose fans see us in so many good and bad times that they think they know us. Yet that twelfth man at the end of the bench whom they chuckle at or clap to come in at the end of a rout might be a bigger man in his personal life than the team's star. He might contribute more to the life of the team in off-court situations or be a staunch friend. Our games are woven into the fabric of our entire lives whereas when we play for you, we are your diversions.

While I was recovering in the hospital, some of the players went to an off-campus party attended primarily by white female and black male students. We called them "sneak" parties. The campus police raided this one on the pretext that they were looking for alcohol. They confiscated a moderate amount of beer. But as a result, seven students were suspended for the year, including two white girls and five black guys, one of whom was our starting center, the sophomore Joe Strawder. Joe was a very hard-working guy, whose suspension was to set an example. I felt for him. He'd traveled an even harder road than I for his chance at Bradley; he came from a broken family, had been a migrant farmworker in Florida. But he wasn't an All-American, and the college came down hard on him.

A few days later when I was released from the hospital, I was pressured by the black student body and by the local NAACP chapter to boycott the remainder of our season to protest the treatment accorded Strawder and the other students. They wanted to make it clear that the suspensions were for interracial dating, not having beer. This was credible because never before had a fraternity party raid resulted in suspension.

The NAACP literally sat on my doorstep for three days try-

ing to persuade me not to play. One night four or five black male
student friends came to my apartment to work on me. I later
learned from one of them that they had even planned to nab me
and take me up to Chicago for a while. Little did they know that
being abducted in conjunction with Bradley basketball was in
my line! I did believe Strawder was being made an example, and
there weren't many black teammates left. Tim Robinson had
been dropped from school. Mack Herndon had flunked out.
Bradley had cut Al Saunders loose for not reporting the offer of a
bribe a year before. I felt like an endangered species. What did I
owe Bradley? What did I expect of myself?

When I received medical clearance to play again, I wasn't
sure what to do. I decided to call the *Peoria Journal Star* and give
them the statement that I would play but under protest of the
Bradley administration's action, that a racially prejudicial punishment had been meted out and had not been redressed. That
story never appeared. A sportswriter told me later that his editor
refused to run it. Basketball was always more important to Peoria than my rights or those of any other person in town. Furthermore, the Peoria paper covered all our games on the road in
the years I was on campus and never once did they comment on
what the black players went through before those hostile southern crowds.

Instead, I remember many quotes from Coach Orsborn, saying "Chet has all the qualities that you hope to develop in your
own son. Everyone on campus looks up to him." I'm thankful to
him if he truly felt that way. I wish he'd expressed it in Houston
or in New York City at the NIT when I really needed the support.

Finally, when all is said and done, I think Bradley was the
right place for me at that time in my life. Bradley was a nice, little
intimate school and Middle America personified. It allowed me
to meet good conservative people who liked me as a person,
within the strictures of racial separation that existed then and the
glare of publicity. I'm sure that I prospered there in a way I
wouldn't have at other schools. A giant campus would have
driven me further into my shell. Perhaps so would a more lib-

eral, more intense small college. As a young man, I was in social confusion. Everybody knew who I was, but nobody knew me. Bradley was a gentle initiation.

I learned more at Bradley than I could have ever learned at a southern school. Bradley opened more doors and gave me more chances than I could have dreamed of. A lot were still closed, but I'd become a man, stuck it out, graduated on time, made my family proud, developed my skills to the utmost. Not a bad four years for a kid spirited into town on a small plane, scared out of his shoes and sick to his stomach. I was on my way to a larger America. My world had expanded and so had my choices.

9.
A Rookie Again

In 1962, I went back to being a rookie but one rung up the ladder, this time in professional sports with the NBA Syracuse Nationals. I wanted the Boston Celtics to draft me. Who wouldn't? But the NBA's perennial champions chose John Havlicek of Ohio State on the first round. Syracuse chose me in round two after taking Len Chappell of Wake Forest in the first round. Initially, I was worried to be going to Syracuse, which seemed like another Peoria to me and a long way from my family. Yet my first season with the Nationals was a genuine success, one I enjoyed in every way.

I signed my first professional contract for $12,000, which was sweetened with a $2,000 bonus. I gave the bonus money to two of my brothers to refurnish their homes and to say thanks in some small way for all they had done for me. With the rest, I started saving toward a down payment for a home for my mother, and I bought myself my first new car, a Chevrolet Impala, a hot model in 1962. So Coach Alex Hannum made me, the rookie, drive some of his veterans to practice all season long. My job was to pick up Al Bianchi and Johnny Kerr and provide them with their standing order for a cold six-pack waiting in the backseat. Al and John razzed me some, but they were really terrific to me and helped build my confidence on the court.

There wasn't much hazing of rookies on the Syracuse team but more general exuberance and confidence. With Kerr and Bianchi, I had found the first men in my basketball life who were totally supportive of me and accepted me without reservation. John and Al were extremely close but opposites. Big Red Kerr was merry and red-haired Chicago Irish whereas "Blinky," as we called Bianchi, was an Italian whose dark good looks and tough-guy image made him a perfect comic partner to Red, for whom he functioned as the straight man. They almost adopted me as their trainee. I was chosen to be "their" rookie: it wasn't as their "boy"—there's such a difference in spirit, and young black men can always tell the difference. I never thought of my gofer status as anything but fun. I was learning all the time from them on and off the court.

Red Kerr made me believe I could play ahead of Syracuse veterans such as Lee Shaffer and Dave Gambee. He was perhaps the best-passing center in the history of basketball, and we ran a majority of our plays off him at the high post. He had an amazing give-and-go pass, where he would actually bounce the ball back between his legs blind to a streaking cutter for a lay-up. That play would always bring down the house. Red was still working on that play in old timers' games twenty-five years later when it had become a lost art like glassblowing. Red also helped me to relax, to realize after a loss that there would always be tomorrow to give it another shot. It was his perennial fate to play in a four-team Eastern Division where two of the centers were Wilt Chamberlain and Bill Russell. But his own unique game always kept him competitive.

The Syracuse organization had a lot of good people, starting with the owner, Danny Biasone, one of the NBA's most colorful early owners, and I felt lucky to have him take me under his wing. He was grizzled and tough, and it somehow fit that he'd made his money with a string of bowling alleys. He was a man with a big heart and a small purse who lived for his players. When I first visited Syracuse, he picked me up at the airport, his great big overcoat pulled up over his ears like a mobster. In an

Edward G. Robinson voice, he growled, "How are ya, kid? Welcome to Sireecuse!"

Danny was an operator who always had a twinkle in his eye. He introduced me around town, and from the start I knew I would be treated like a son. The Syracuse franchise was for working people. Danny had come up through the ranks and was a success in his town, in his place. We played at small Onondaga Memorial Coliseum in Syracuse, one of the league's legendary home courts. Our loud fans were so close to the action that they practically sat on the court. They made life miserable for our longtime opponents such as the Celtics and Warriors, and no one wanted to play us at home. I liked Syracuse, but I suspect I would have exhausted its best features if the team hadn't moved to Philadelphia a year later. Syracuse had a smaller black community than Peoria. I lived in an apartment up near Syracuse University and got to know Syracuse sports stars Dave Bing, who became an all-NBA guard for the Pistons, and tight end John Mackey, later of the Baltimore Colts.

Biasone's handpicked coach for the Nats was Alex Hannum. I couldn't have been luckier than to play for Alex my first year in the league. Alex was a marine veteran who'd been around the league forever. He could dish it out and have you come back in his face and then buy you a beer after the game. It's a rare coach who'll treat his players like men. To me, he was color-blind and sensed how much support I needed as a young black player, especially when I would be vying for time on a team with so many front-court veterans like Dolph Schayes, Dave Gambee, Lee Shaffer, and Johnny Kerr—all white. But Hannum convinced me that I could play with anyone in the league.

The Nats were a seasoned outfit with a brilliant passing game and a core of veterans who really knew how to play. Year after year they finished a solid third in the NBA's Eastern Division behind the Celtics and the Wilt Chamberlain–led Philadelphia Warriors. I adjusted to the pro game pretty easily, thanks to the fact that at Bradley we mostly played a man-to-man defense. I notice a lot of NBA rookies are lost on defense because in college they played only zone.

I was just so relieved and happy to be out of the Missouri Valley and away from Confederate flags and Dixie bands. I didn't expect to get much playing time that first year but rather to learn the system slowly and to spell the veterans. Things didn't turn out that way because Schayes, our veteran star at forward, was injured so I got my minutes. I hadn't dreamed I would be starting. I expected to concentrate on learning my trade. That was thirty years ago, of course, but I still feel the right approach for a rookie is to ease into the system. Syracuse didn't have that luxury that year, so for me it was baptism by fire. Luckily, I loved it.

I didn't have many major adjustments to the way the NBA game was played. Certainly, the players were older, a bit stronger and rougher. But in 1962 college and pro basketball did not differ as substantially as they do now. There were fewer zone defenses in college ball and none of the clear-out one-on-one stuff in the pros. Both college and pro games were more up-tempo with shots taken on the run.

My first NBA game was against the Lakers and Elgin Baylor, a superstar and a physically punishing player. Sure enough, Dolph Schayes was hurt, and I was thrown in to guard him at the outset. He scored over 40 points on me, and no one had ever done that before, not anywhere. Elg went around, over, and through me. I was bounced off picks, left in my tracks, and had my head spun around. But the Syracuse old pros just took it in stride, which helped me a lot. There weren't any network cameras recording this debut of mine. None of the media glare surrounding some orchestrated event. Besides, as somebody told me, Baylor was going to get his 40 points a lot of nights when we weren't even in town. I just picked myself up and kept going and found my pro rhythm very quickly. You must do that as a professional athlete. Everyone is so damned good that you just aren't going to dominate the way you've done at other levels of the sport. But you can survive, get on an even keel emotionally and mentally. Not get too high or low over anything that happens in the long, long season. And gear yourself up for the playoffs when you summon up all your will and every little edge you've found.

I came a long way before those million-dollar, multiyear,

no-cut contracts of today. Twelve thousand dollars was a very decent salary in 1962 for a young college graduate, but it didn't suddenly boost me into the upper tax brackets. It was a comfortable, middle-class wage and one I didn't expect to change much in the next few years. In the days before the reserve clause was challenged, a player's salary might remain static for years. And long-term contracts? They didn't exist. From my point of view, NBA careers were risky and short. That's why I went back to Bradley after my rookie year to work on a master's degree in educational counseling, so I would have a profession to fall back on. In some ways, I have to admit it was good for us that our salaries weren't so out of whack with the rest of society, that we knew we had to prepare for our years following pro basketball. That sense of proportion allowed us to retain some sense of who we were and what real problems existed for the rest of society.

If I had been in graduate school preparing to be a lawyer or a doctor, I could have looked forward to substantial earning power once I hit age thirty or thirty-five. But everything about an athlete's job is ephemeral. Just when the doctor or lawyer is beginning to hit his stride, the athlete is losing a step here and there. Soon his sports career is over, and he must begin again with something else. He never catches up, especially since his undergraduate preparation is probably scattered among various courses that kept him eligible to play but didn't educate him.

The best things he can take with him from his playing days to his new career are knowing how to perform under pressure, knowing how to fit into a team, knowing when to step forward, and, if he's been smart, a college degree and a nest egg that can get him started and act as a cushion as he begins his second career.

Of course, it wasn't just the lower NBA salaries that set those years apart from today. In 1962, the league had nine teams. That meant night in, night out the competition was tougher because every team was so rich in talent.

No European leagues existed to drain American talent although the Eastern League and Harlem Globetrotters still attracted some top-notch players. Besides Syracuse, the NBA in 1961–62 had teams in New York, Boston, St. Louis, Detroit, Chicago, Cincinnati, Los Angeles, and San Francisco. As recently as 1949–50, after the National Basketball League's (NBL) merger with the BAA, the forerunner of the present NBA, there was a confusing, bloated, fledgling NBA of seventeen teams, including franchises in Sheboygan, Wisconsin, and Anderson, Indiana. But then the newly formed NBA shrank to eleven teams in 1950–51, ten in 1951–52, and nine in 1952–53 until it stabilized at eight in 1953–54. The shrinking league prompted Danny Biasone to come up with the idea that a 24-second clock would prevent stalling, force the offense, and create a running game the fans would enjoy for the whole 48 minutes. He was right and persuaded the other owners to adopt the rule for the 1954–55 season, the year Syracuse won the World Championship, an apt reward for Danny. The 24-second clock radically changed the league and breathed new life into it.

In 1961–62, a Chicago franchise was born, bringing the league back to nine teams, where it stayed until 1966. The Warriors had just moved west to San Francisco, following the lead of the Lakers' move to Los Angeles two years before. Team travel was completely different from today. Until the West Coast teams were formed, requiring long-distance air travel, the NBA had always traveled in bizarre fashion. At Syracuse when I was a rookie, Danny Biasone chartered a DC-3 for us. Seats were too cramped for our long legs, and trips were endless and tedious. But that DC-3 seemed to be one of the safest planes I've ever flown in. You could land that baby on a tennis court. At times, I swear, the DC-3 flew so low and slow that I actually watched traffic lights on town streets turn from green to red. One night en route to St. Louis we were to stop for refuelling in Chicago, and I thought I spotted my home in Benton Harbor as the DC-3 lazed noisily toward Lake Michigan.

When we got where we were going, hotel rooms didn't have television sets, and meal money was limited, eight dollars a day my first year with the Nats. We ate at a lot of White Castle restaurants, about the only places that stayed open to players keeping NBA hours. I consumed hundreds of those little square burgers laced with onions. They stayed in your stomach for about three days. In New York City, we ate at the Garden Cafeteria right across the street from Madison Square Garden and went through the line with trays just like everyone else.

My first roommate on the road was Porter Merriwether, a black rookie from Tennessee State who was cut in midseason. We certainly didn't have to hide in our rooms because of the nuisance of publicity as today's stars do. We practiced in armories and community centers, and we played preseason games in high school gyms. We were tall, but we were not larger than life. We didn't have anything like an equipment manager. We lugged our own sneakers. We took our wet, stinking uniforms back to the hotel to dry them in the bathroom. On a three-game road trip, we got so smelly that we could hardly stand each other during team huddles and time-outs. Trainers taped ankles, and when we had an injury, they would freeze the skin with a strange, cold spray. That passed for sports medicine in 1962. Often we were encouraged to play through muscle and joint pain, often with a shot to numb the affected area.

In 1962, the scale of the NBA was local and very intense. Rivalries were fierce in a nine-team league where we would play each other ten to twelve times per year even before the playoffs got started. We really got to know each other's moves and games, and this familiarity didn't exactly breed good fellowship. Competition in the Eastern Division then was very lopsided with the Knicks the perennial doormat. In the early 1960s, each team would play 72 games, which would eliminate the lowly Knicks, so that Boston, the Philadelphia Warriors, and the Nats could go at it in the play-offs. When the four teams played a double-header, the arena marquee would read NBA EASTERN DIVISION HERE TONIGHT. In my only year in Syracuse, we split 12 games with the Celtics in Bob Cousy's last year and John Havlicek's rookie year. In the two preceding years, the Celtics had whipped the Nationals 20–5 in the regular season, so we knew we were developing a strong nucleus for a future team. Those Boston teams set the league standard.

The Celtics' Cousy and Russell were a perfectly matched pair for the 24-second clock. Russ could rebound, hit Cousy, the open-court magician, with the ball on the dead run, and we would be off to the races. Tom Heinsohn and Sam Jones would spot up and fire away on the perimeter. Or Cousy would sail straight down the middle with his incredibly long arms on tiny, sloping shoulders. He would move as if he were flowing through water with the ball on a string. We dazzled with our attack, too. We had a lot of motion in our offense, a lot of cutting off the post, in which Kerr was a master at bounce passes, blind passes, "give-and-go" plays. We played exciting ball.

In fact, I would say that current NBA fans don't know what they missed back in 1962. We didn't have many dunks per game except off rebounds or by Russell and Chamberlain. Coaches still discouraged it as hotdogging. Instead, our style of play featured more ballhandling in the open court, more swift passing, not all the isolation stuff you see today. None of the incessant backing in, one man with the ball while four others watch a superstar go to work on some poor victim. We put up many more shots on the run, and that's why rebound totals were so much higher then.

For example, the World Champion Celtics of 1962–63 took 110 shots per game whereas the 1985–86 World Champion Celtics took only 90 per game. The number of shots per game has continued to decrease in the 1990s. The Celtics never had the highest shooting percentage, but they always corralled the most rebounds. Guys like Tom Heinsohn, Sam Jones, Frank Ramsey, and John Havlicek would just fire from anywhere and depend on Russell, Tom Sanders, and Heinsohn to get the ball back for second and third shots. I think it was more of a fan's game in the early 1960s than it is today. At its best, it was racehorse style and almost as fast as end-to-end hockey. Everyone on the court had to be able to handle the ball. The point-guard, off-guard designation hadn't evolved yet, nor had that of small forward, power-forward. The center could camp out in the middle and prevent people from barreling down the lane. Everyone had to be a sharpshooter from medium range. Now with the illegal-defense rules, the NBA has shrewdly made the center follow his man out to the top of the floor, clearing the lane for the Michael Jordans and Dominique Wilkinses to fly in for the slam. The NBA wants nothing less than acrobatics now. That's how they sell the game.

We actually outscored the Celtics by 3 points per game in my rookie year (121–118) but finished ten games behind them because our defense just couldn't match up to what the Celtics threw at us with an all-time defensive player at each of three positions: Tom Sanders (forward), Russell (center), and K. C. Jones (guard). We were also a younger team in transition. Dolph Schayes who'd been an All-Star to rival Bob Pettit at the forward position during the 1950s had now worn down and was a part-time player for us. Besides the rock of John Kerr at center, we had many young frontcourt players (myself, Lee Shaffer, Dave Gambee, Len Chappell) just learning the NBA. We had the speed and the smarts with Hal Greer, Larry Costello, and Bianchi at guard. We just didn't have Boston's size, defense, and strength.

The fans in our small Memorial Coliseum would have gone through a wall for us as we would have for them. Referees were part of the action, too. We had histrionic, tough little screaming guys like Sid Borgia, who was as big as a minute, a bald, screeching part of the show. When he danced around Wilt Chamberlain after calling a foul, I thought of Rumpelstiltskin hopping and stamping his feet in the fairy tale. When Wilt would get on Sid, it was as if he were pursuing some mole around the court, bending to get to ear level. And Sid would shout right back at him things like "If you were six inches shorter, no one would have heard of you" and "I've put more into this league in eighteen years than you have." Or he would ride Wilt about his poor foul shooting.

Another original was the classic Mendy Rudolph, whose hand motions were as graceful as those of an orchestra leader. He was lordly, almost above the fray but as tough as Sid, with the ego of an opera star. Then there was Earl Strom, whose iron jaw and inflexible toughness made him a target of fans and players. But Earl gave as good as he got and always stood up to any abuse.

In the pros, you can never take it for granted that you'll beat a player on a given night. Everyone's just too good. I had the hardest time against Tom Sanders, Gus Johnson, and Dave DeBusschere—players who were smart enough to try and take away part of my game and not go for all my moves. I had played against DeBusschere ever since we were in high school, so I suppose we knew each other all too well.

I was in the second wave of what I call the NBA pioneers. We were the players, predominantly black, who broke into the league after the 24-second clock was introduced. It was a time of superior basketball and incredible individual players. Today's writers and fans don't appreciate our generation. They act as if the players in the 1990s were the only ones who matter at all. This is nonsense. The court moves I saw by Maurice Stokes, Elgin Baylor, Earl Monroe, and Gus Johnson were astonishing.

Stokes was a player who combined the moves of Oscar Robertson *and* Elgin Baylor, the first absolutely complete NBA player who could do everything every night. Baylor himself had enormous power and a thrust off the ground around the basket that allowed him to literally stay up in the air after he'd pushed another player aside, sort of lord of all he surveyed, before shooting or passing off. He had a nervous twitch that made his head bob in the open court, a built-in head fake that made him resemble a wild, prancing stallion. Monroe was only six feet two inches and couldn't jump, but he had a series of choreographed hesitating spins and fakes in the paint that left larger defenders looking foolish. Gus Johnson was one of the original NBA musclemen who also had a complete game. He would batter an opponent on one play and fly over him the next—all with that gold star flashing in his front tooth.

People tell me that today's NBA players are vastly superior to my generation in physical ability. Well, I would like to see one of today's highfliers try and do all those fancy dunks wearing a pair of Chuck Taylor Converse All-Stars from 1960. Those shoes had only a thin sole and hardly any cushioning. If a player could

jump back then, it was all in his own legs. Today the shoes
are aeronautically engineered. They come with cushions and
pumps. It's like having springs or tiny trampolines attached to
his feet. Couple that with Nautilus training for his legs from his
early years, and he is quite a physical specimen. Tiny Spud
Webb's and guard Dee Brown's winning the slam dunk titles at
recent NBA All-Star games are proof that almost anyone can ele-
vate today, regardless of height or natural jumping ability.

I can draw the lines of succession in the NBA from Stokes to
Baylor to Gus Johnson to Julius Erving and move from the 1950s
to the 1980s without even getting to the era of Jordan and Magic
and Bird and Charles Barkley, where many current fans and
players complacently think the NBA began.

At the 1993 NBA All-Star game, for example, players were
asked who was the first black player to play in an All-Star game?
Not one current player knew. When they were asked if they had
ever heard of Don Barksdale, not one could answer yes. Barksdale represented the Boston Celtics in the 1953–54 All-Star game.
When asked about that game, he said that he'd been effectively
frozen out, that Coach Joe Lapchick of the East squad had told
him not to shoot, just to rebound and play defense. He didn't feel
welcome at that game, and he didn't feel part of the team. Barksdale's experiences as a *professional* player are similar to mine in
college: traveling in the early and mid-1950s and not being allowed to stay in the team's hotel or eat at restaurants. He died of
cancer on March 9, 1993. His lasting contribution was a sports
foundation for kids that he set up in San Francisco. In an interview for ESPN two weeks before his death, he pleaded, "Give
everybody the same chance you'd like to have."

School kids today can't name their own ethnic and racial
leaders, they don't know their country's presidents, they don't
know much at all about this country. I like to put achievements
in context, to know history and what led to what. Today's athletes arrive in the big leagues thinking they've got it made and
never bother to learn their trade. They're built up so high by the
media before they've even played a minute in the NBA that they

think they define the league; yet, they're ignorant of what has gone before. They think basketball began with them. I'm here to tell you they didn't invent the game or the moves, and even all the shaved heads on the court today had a precursor in that beautiful bald dome of my onetime teammate Hal Greer.

In the 1960s, players felt we were part of something new. We felt the same about our stunning new opportunities in American society. There wasn't all this emphasis on trash talking and barking in each other's faces all the time. We were cool, not hot, taking our cue from jazz and hipsters. Never let your opponents know they're getting to you. Kill them quietly and efficiently. In the summers we might really let loose in playground battles, but in NBA games on the court in the 1950s and early 1960s, we felt our status was too precarious to jeopardize it by being too creative.

The times forced us to respect each other more, because of the moral and social weight we carried. First, most of us were exempt from the military draft because of height or student deferments. Campus demonstrations were going on all over the country, first about Civil Rights, then to protest the Vietnam War. Since so many of the young men who died were black, we had to acknowledge that they were dying in our place. Not just in Vietnam but in Alabama, in Mississippi. Few of us were making much money, so economically we were roughly on a par with other young black men in that regard. We were all trying to make the NBA major league in the public eye.

Every era has its own philosophy and its own idiosyncrasies. In my time in the pros I saw the amount of trash talking greatly increase as playground culture became more the norm. Sometimes the combination of talk and rough play would lead to general melees on the court, in which combatants would be all mixed up. M. L. Carr of the Pistons and later the Celtics tells of taking a swing at Tom Boerwinkle, the Bulls' enormous center, during a Pistons-Bulls scuffle in the late 1970s. M.L. missed Tom with a roundhouse swing, but Tom didn't see the punch. M.L. said, "He didn't see it or he would have killed me. So I slapped him on the butt and said, 'Come on, big guy, let's go break it up.' "

Today's jawing players want to make a statement, too. They want to assert their will against their opponent. That's always the goal in basketball. And who turned out to be the biggest trash talker? Larry Bird, perhaps the greatest white player of all time. Bird provided a running, almost announcerlike commentary as he backed his man down low, all the while describing the play that was coming and how helpless the defender would be. Once, after destroying Mark Aquirre, he threw his wristband to him as they left the court. Aguirre went ballistic. Such intimidation comes from competitiveness and sheer instinct for court survival.

Another reason for today's more expressive style is that black culture is now much better known through televised sports and a variety of blues and rap music. Verbal challenges through signifyin' and playin' the dozens is now everywhere known to white society. It is used to sell shoes, beer—all sorts of products—as well as to provide a running dialogue in a movie such as *White Men Can't Jump.* In short, coaches can't stop the jive now that it's been sold to the public. It's part of the entertainment.

In my time we had a quieter respect for seniority. With my father's pain and the struggle of six older brothers in the North, I felt pulled to those who had trod a path before me. I believed in guys who had paid their dues, and I still do. Now as then, it's not the size or strength you bring to your endeavors that counts, as much as the size of your heart, and that's true in any workplace, including the basketball arena. There are simply more or less flamboyant and overt ways of proving yourself. The athletic goal is the same, but the path may be different than the one our basketball forefathers took.

Surely, one of those forefathers was the great Maurice Stokes, a terrific player whose pro career in the mid-1950s I followed closely. Mo Stokes was my idol when I was in high school. At a strong six feet seven inches, he was a complete player who

averaged 17 points, 17 rebounds and 5 assists a game for Rochester, and later the Cincinnati Royals from 1955 to 1958. Here was a
young black man who was so swift, so sure, such a leader. Mo
seemed to have made a firm break in the color line when he was
named NBA Rookie of the Year in 1955–56, the year *before* Bill
Russell joined the Celtics. But in 1958, late in his third season, Mo
collapsed after a play-off game and went into a coma. A form of
encephalitis was diagnosed; a fever had burned through his
brain, destroying many of his normal functions. Doctors also
thought he might have suffered a head injury from a bad fall in a
previous game; no one was ever sure. When he regained consciousness, Mo was cruelly handicapped, unable to function normally or form understandable words to communicate. Jack
Twyman, Mo's teammate on the Royals, became his legal guard-
ian for the next twelve years in one of sports' more amazing ex-
amples of black-white brotherhood. For many years the NBA
stars ran a summer benefit game for Mo at Kutsher's Country
Club in the Catskills, a fabled place for summertime competition
back in the fifties and sixties.

Alex Hannum knew I admired Stokes, that he was one of
my heroes. Once during my first year with the Nationals when
we were playing in Cincinnati, Alex generously offered to take
me up to Christ Hospital to see him. Alex led me over to Mo's
bedside, saying, "Big Mo, this is Chet Walker." Mo looked agi-
tated and excited, happy for the visit but able only to grunt, "Uh,
uh." After that, I broke down and cried for the incredibly talented young man Mo had been and in realization of just how
lucky I was. Maurice Stokes died at age thirty-seven in 1970.

Just as my second year in the NBA got under way in the fall
of 1963, my mother had a stroke and went into a coma. She
would pass away that November. She had had a serious heart
problem complicated by diabetes and lifelong high blood pressure. Regenia Walker was sixty-five and had reared ten children.
Life had been hard on her as she struggled to keep us all together

and on the straight and narrow. Her eyes were always on her
family and the Lord.

I left the team and hurried home to Benton Harbor. Seeing
her in the hospital room with my brothers and sisters at her bedside, I hoped she somehow knew I was there, that we were all
there. As I sat beside her, I had a vivid flashback to the night I
watched her at Anna Laura's deathbed in Mississippi. I thought
of her days and nights in Benton Harbor working as a maid or
picking fruit in the orchards. She had sacrificed her whole life to
make things better for her family, including the absolute break
with my father and the South, the only worlds that she had
known. To me, my mother, Regenia Walker, was a great black
warrior queen who led her children out of the wilderness.

Wise and intelligent as she was, she was born in a society
that prevented her from accomplishing all of which she was ca-
pable. She was a serious woman of great piety, whose religion
and children were of the utmost importance to her. None of us,
my mother included, really got to know all there was to Regenia
Walker.

My mother never went to one of my games, never saw the
crowd cheering her boy, never saw me run a fast break or make a
jump shot. But I know she listened to my games on the radio. It
never bothered me that she wasn't in the bleachers, because
sports didn't play an important part in my relationship with her.
There's no doubt sports set me apart, but at home I was still
Chester, Regenia's youngest son who was making her proud. I
basked in her love and acceptance. What had really been important to my mother was for me to finish high school and college.
She saw me become the first Walker to accomplish that, and I
was thankful.

Several days later at the funeral, the church overflowed
with friends and family. It was my turn to walk down the aisle to
see my mother for the last time. I looked down on her in the casket and sensed that she had attained a final peace. Until then, I
hadn't cried. But going back up the aisle to leave the church, I
overheard a woman tell her little boy, "That's Chester. That's
Chester." That was the trigger that released my tears, and they

kept coming and coming. I never realized until that moment how important a success like mine would be to my people, especially to young kids. My mother would have felt that that was worth all the struggle and sacrifice because her life had made the difference in my life and in the lives of my brothers and sisters. So I was a someone to give further meaning to her life.

With tears still streaming down my face, I heard my mother's voice when the preacher came up to me outside and said, "God bless you, son." I too found some peace that day as well as a new resolve to keep on going. As I watched her casket placed in the hearse outside, a little girl shyly tugged at my sleeve to ask me for an autograph.

I think I'm a lot like my father as well as my mother. When my temper emerges, I'm frightened by this legacy from my father. I've always tried to conceal this part of my personality as much as possible. I've controlled my temper with the patience, understanding, and sweetness that my mother gave me. Yet I think that if I had stayed on the farm in Bethlehem, sooner or later my father and I would have had it out over his treatment of my mother. In fact, it's possible that when we were older, my brother Robert or I might have killed him. It's a terrible thought to carry around with you.

A big part of my life has been spent in fleeing from my father's image. It's probably one of the main reasons I haven't gotten married. I worry about treating women the way he treated my mother. The worst intimation I had of my temper was in Chicago after a fight with a girlfriend. I told her to call a cab. While we were waiting, she asked for a glass of water and then threw the water in my face. The next thing I knew I'd lifted her off the ground by the throat. I'd seen red, blinding red in front of my eyes. I released my grip on her after I saw her eyes begin to roll up in her head. I could hardly believe I'd just done this to another human being. I was stunned and she was terrified. She'd never seen this side of me before.

Why don't I want to pass on my mother's wonderful qualities to children of my own? Why bet against her in my nature? Wouldn't she have wanted me to have my own family? These are very difficult questions for me to answer. I think about the way America might treat my children. I wouldn't want a child of mine to have to struggle the way I did. I was lucky, extremely lucky. I didn't run into a bullet with my name on it. I made it through high school and college, the first in my family to do either. I've had two satisfying careers. I come from a large family and I have fifteen nieces and nephews I care about deeply. This book is my contribution to black children. It's what I want to say to the sons and daughters I do not have.

My family life was complex and difficult. Most black families are large collections of relatives in different places, but the effects of slavery and poverty and separation have made our lineage a tangled record.

I had an eerie experience of family entanglement in the fall of 1963. During the exhibition season of my second year in the NBA, we played a game in Memphis, Tennessee, which is only about one hundred miles north of Bethlehem, Mississippi. After the game, I was getting dressed to leave the locker room when an old white man came up and sat beside me. His name was Lester Greer, and he said, "Boy, you don't know me, but I know you. I'm from Bethlehem, and I know your daddy and granddaddy. I knew all of them. In fact, you never knew it, boy, but I'm your kin."

Lester Greer went on to tell me that his grandfather had a child with a black woman, and that child was my great-grandmother. It turns out he was one of the men in town who paid my friend Henry and me to box with each other when we were kids! He told me even at that time he could see I had athletic talent. I thought he was trying in some way to take credit for some of my success. "We're awfully proud of you down in Bethlehem," he drawled.

I was stunned. In a way that both angered me and made my flesh crawl, Lester Greer wanted to have a piece of my heroism, my celebrity. It was okay to admit he was the relative of a successful, well-paid athlete. Before then, I was just another nigger, a nobody, definitely not someone he could admit as a relation.

Now I felt as if this man had just gone down to the slave quarters and summoned me. The Greers were one of the leading families in Bethlehem. They were our greatest enemies, I suppose. Here was the white man whom old Wyatt from the poolroom said I should never trust. He was intruding on my family and then sucking out the very accomplishment I was so proud of. He was an old, old man. Perhaps he was simply hoping to connect with his past. But I certainly didn't need this.

I don't know why Lester Greer finally chose this time and place to tell me about my family and his. Was it simply the confessions of an old man, something like "Nearer My God to Thee"? When I told my cousin Bertie of this amazing encounter, she said that everybody in our family in Bethlehem knew about the Greer connection. But I'd only been ten years old when we left. How could I have known?

Years after our meeting in Memphis, I would learn that Lester Greer had had a bigger hand in the Walker family's survival than I knew. After we left Mississippi for Michigan, my father got into trouble with the local Ku Klux Klan over his angry calls for better educational facilities for blacks in Bethlehem. The Klan abducted him and took him ten miles north to Potts Camp, where they might have lynched him. But one message from old Lester Greer was enough to set my father free. For a while afterwards neighboring men were protecting him with shotguns. So our relationship with the Greers indeed prolonged my father's life.

My sorrow for my father is profound. After we left Mississippi, he never again cared about me or anything I did, but I understand what drove him to extremes. On the cold November day in 1950 when we all left the farm, he had nothing left. His family was lost to him. My father loved the land so much that in his heart he thought he could still make it work for him in the South. My mother could not believe in him any longer. She thought the oppression we all lived under would never allow us to reach our potential, that the South and people like the Greers would stunt us, make us wither and die like a ruined crop, like my sister Anna Laura.

My father never really gave up his dream for the land. He married again and had a whole second step-family to work the farm, like some biblical patriarch. He died in September 1992 in a nursing home in Mississippi at age ninety-three. I don't know what he thought of my college degree or basketball success. He lost us and we lost him.

I kept my mother's faith in education alive. I planned to complete a master of arts degree in educational counseling at Bradley. In the summer after my rookie season I returned to school to begin work on a graduate degree in counseling, so that I would have some profession to fall back on after basketball. No two million dollar contracts were cushioning my future. And for black students, the only real choices that seemed to have career possibilities in the early 1960s were education and social work.

Back in Peoria, I again realized the difference between the court and the classroom. Basketball players must have *quick* minds. The decisions on the court are split second in nature: whether to pull up, pass off, take it to the hole, switch on defense. Concentration in basketball takes place on the run. It was always hard for me to gear down to the pace of the classroom and make adjustments to study and participate. I think many people who believe athletes are just dumb should consider the different modes of thinking that athletes need to be successful. There's no instant correlation between intelligence in sports and academic success. For me, it became almost an act of will to make my mind slow down for the classroom. Doctors cautiously consider many factors before making a diagnosis. Professors never want to come to decisions; they just want to ask more and better questions! Athletes think in patterns related to their occupations as well.

After years of using my basketball intelligence, when I went to work in the film business, my daily round just seemed so slow. People took forever deciding on a story property or casting part. I couldn't adjust to that, people covering their back, or figuring out how to take credit or lay blame. On the court what you see is what you get. What happens is what you make happen. The decision is final. I know life can't be lived as if we were all on a basketball court. I wouldn't want that sort of racehorse existence in my life all the time. Off the court is where we all live most of the time. There, problems are too complex for quick decisions although quick decisions are still sometimes the best.

One of my best quick decisions did come in a classroom that summer at Bradley in a philosophy of education class that was lazing along one bright morning. A white male student was offering his opinion that black people were trying to move too fast, the conventional wisdom of the day about Dr. King and the Civil Rights movement in their targeted areas of voter registration and integration of public facilities. I began to seethe but typically held my tongue. Suddenly, the student next to me, a white nun in full habit, rose from her seat to say, "That's bullshit!" Everyone froze, convinced they hadn't heard correctly. But she left no doubt, repeating "That's bullshit!" Before I could think, I found myself on my feet looking the first speaker straight in the eye and exclaiming, "She's right. She's right."

I had shocked myself, speaking out like that. Never before had I dared to utter an opinion about anything as controversial as racism in a public place, let alone a classroom full of white people. Then another student, a nun sitting on my other side, stood up to add her two cents. Later it dawned on me how strange we must have looked: these two tiny women, like bookends, at either side of this huge young man—in unison, supporting Dr. King.

I went to the student union with the two nuns after class, the first of several such get-togethers. I wondered how old they were, probably in their late thirties, but it was hard to tell because of their habits. From the standpoint of a southern Baptist boy, I thought nuns were squeaky-clean angels of mercy, low-key and always humble. But these women were gutsy and ready for battle, and I was in awe of them. My mother had always told me that the Bible was a "progressive" book. That was her word. She said the Bible had liberated her with its many stories of people fighting for freedom. She would have been frightened of being called "radical," but she would have stood shoulder to shoulder with these two nuns.

The two sisters had grown up in Peoria and worked in St. Francis Hospital there. They were able to take courses only in the summer. We talked about the state of revolution in black Africa. They used the word "apartheid" in our discussion, which I'd never heard before. But as we talked, I began to understand how apartheid applied to the United States and to my own life. Here I was in the Bradley cafeteria getting my real university education.

Funny how from this day on, that summer-school class seemed to open up for everyone. People made statements, were challenged, and responded. I said many things about my early days in Mississippi that I'd never told anyone. I described my eye-opening trips to Houston and St. Louis. That class and its frank discussions prepared me to go on to Philadelphia and the next phase of my career and to take a greater interest in black people's position in the larger society. I went back to Bradley again in the summer of 1964 for course work but finished two credits and a master's thesis short of my graduate degree.

I think it was the new responsibility I felt for my family's legacy that made me get to my feet in that classroom. That summer of 1963, heroic young Civil Rights workers, both black and white, were risking their lives, especially in Mississippi. I was certainly not on the front lines, but I was gaining confidence. Although I had accepted the privileged but restricted role of a professional athlete, I knew I would have to find a way to live with myself. I was beginning to see just how far I had come and how far I had to go.

10.
The Making
of a Dynasty

In 1963–64, when Danny Biasone could no longer afford to run the Nationals in Syracuse, we came down to Philadelphia as the 76ers. The NBA was a growing business that was too competitive to allow a team to remain in the small-market cities that had once cradled the entire league. Team owners followed the money trail. Fred Zollner moved the Pistons from Fort Wayne to Detroit in 1957. Lester Harrison sold the Rochester Royals in 1957 to a Cincinnati group of investors. In 1960, the Minneapolis Lakers moved to Los Angeles, and in 1962 the Philadelphia Warriors moved to San Francisco, following the sports expansion of the baseball Dodgers and Giants.

Eddie Gottlieb, the Warrior owner, was an older Danny Biasone, and his whole life had been in basketball. Gottlieb went back to the early days of organized basketball in the East. He was called "The Mogul" for his deal making. He had organized and played for the Philadelphia Sphas (the South Philadelphia Hebrew Association) in the 1920s. He never thought Philadelphia was a professional sports town but rather a high school and college town. So the Warriors and Wilt Chamberlain went west.

In 1961, the league's first new team since 1950 was added in Chicago, but the Chicago Packers, renamed the Zephyrs, found it tough going and lasted only two years before moving on to become the Baltimore Bullets. Pro basketball was on the move and hasn't stood still since.

Of all these shifts, our move from Syracuse to Philadelphia in 1963 was the hardest for the players because we didn't move into virgin territory for the NBA but to that of the enemy. The Syracuse Nationals were the hated rivals of the Philadelphia Warriors from the 1940s until 1962. Players such as Schayes, Costello, Bianchi, and Greer were mortal enemies to Philadelphia fans. Who were we kidding? Just moving to Philly and calling ourselves the 76ers wasn't going to fool any of the Philadelphia faithful. The only team the Philly fans hated more than the Syracuse Nationals was the Celtics.

The Philadelphia fans not only didn't take to us but also ignored us. They could afford to because the Philadelphia area was a hotbed of basketball. Fans there had built up allegiances to the long-established teams of the minor-league Eastern League, which had a franchise in Camden, New Jersey, and in smaller industrial cities in eastern Pennsylvania. They also had their Big Five college teams. Temple, Villanova, Penn, La Salle, and St. Joseph's had long-standing rivalries and routinely outdrew the fledgling 76ers in college doubleheaders. Whereas the 76ers had trouble clearing five thousand at the gate with the greatest players in the world, the Big Five's Quaker City Tournament right after Christmas drew fifteen thousand to a day-night doubleheader.

The NBA was still seen as a shaky operation in 1962. No one thought anything when Wilt Chamberlain joined the Globetrotters after his junior year at Kansas. Or when Bobby Joe Mason became a Trotter. When I played for the 76ers, Hal Lear, the ex-Temple star, was a guard in the Eastern League who habitually scored 20 points per game. He could have played NBA ball all through the early and mid-1960s. But he chose to stay in the Eastern League, essentially a weekend league, so he could keep the security of his high school teaching job. The two jobs together earned him just about the same amount as an NBA salary. The disparity was just not that wide.

The 76ers were heading for trouble. Fans are usually behind expansion teams because they're so happy to have a team placed in their cities but not in Philadelphia. The fans weren't stupid. They knew we were the same guys they used to hate in Syracuse uniforms. So we faced a sullenness as well as a fight for a share of the basketball market. Philly fans were demanding and could turn on you very quickly. Philly was a cliquish town; and I felt that if you didn't hail from there, you didn't stand a chance of assimilation. That's why Wilt Chamberlain, Earl Monroe, Guy Rodgers, Wali Jones, and Walt Hazzard were always Philadelphia players no matter where their college and professional careers took them. If you'd been a schoolboy star in the city, that defined you as surely as anything did, at least to the Philly fan.

With only nine NBA teams, plenty of talent was left over to man the Eastern League. This was long before European teams were an option for players. In fact, two of my Bradley teammates played in the Eastern League in 1964–65: Levern Tart, who became a high scorer a few years later in the ABA, and Joe Strawder, who played an aggressive center for a few years with the Pistons. Philly players such as Lear and Bobby McNeill (St. Joseph's) played for the Camden Bullets. Old Paul Arizin (Villanova), a perennial All-Star and two-time NBA scoring champion for the Warriors in the 1950s, chose to retire from the NBA, rather than follow the Warriors to San Francisco. Arizin was already in his midthirties when he played for Camden from 1962–65, but his team routinely drew crowds almost as big as ours.

Hal Greer and I helped win over some of the Philadelphia fans. In the summer of 1964, after our first year in Philadelphia, Hal and I began to play in the Sonny Hill League at the Baptist church of Reverend Leon Sullivan in north Philadelphia. We played before the black working class in a rough neighborhood. We got the fans to accept us right there. These people were hard to please, sort of like the hard-core entertainment critics at the Apollo Theatre in New York. As younger black players, we found that our reputations were not as sullied by our Syracuse years as those of the veterans. Just by staying around that summer and showing we weren't above getting to know the neighborhoods won us a lot of credit. Hal and I did this on our own. We weren't part of a team community outreach program like the NBA showcases today. Nobody paid us any promotional fees. We just wanted to play some good ball.

Sonny Hill was a Philly guy who worked with the labor unions in the city. He'd grown up with Wilt, Guy Rodgers, and Hal Lear; and he was a successful playground player though not a college star. The summer league was his baby. Our team was called the Kent Taverneers, and we had some local legends to round out the squad: Jay Norman (Temple) and John Chaney (Bethune-Cookman). Chaney, now Temple's fine head coach, was our player-coach. He was smart enough to surround us with home talent to keep the hostile fans at bay. We also had a guy named Alonzo and a kid named "John Boy" whom we literally recruited from the street. A few years later we heard he died of a drug overdose on a basketball court.

The church gym seated about 500 people, but about 1,500 fans tried to get in every night. We were the bad guys, the outsiders, the pros and college boys; but for three years running we won the league championship. That gym was sweaty, funky, and loud. The fans wore big hats and loud pants and shirts. They would talk to us throughout the games, and we would give it right back. People would pass bottles and joints in a real carnival atmosphere. There wasn't much betting because nobody had any money.

Earl Monroe was a Philly playground legend who was playing at Winston-Salem State College in North Carolina at the time. He would make dramatic entrances into the gym, usually arriving in the middle of the first half like some rock star. The game would stop, and people would stand and chant, "Jesus, . . . Black Jesus." Earl would then do his thing—all that marvelous whirling and wheeling down low to get loose for impossible twisting shots. He was the James Brown of basketball. Ducky Burks, who owned a clothing store in the north Philly neighborhood that sold the latest in black fashions, was so desperate to beat us that he put in a call to Bill Bradley at Princeton. Bill became the only white player in the Sonny Hill League. After one game, he got hooked and began driving down twice a week to play. That's what always marked him and made him a fan favorite, even in Reverend Sullivan's church gym. People in that neighborhood weren't inherently violent. They weren't out to hurt anyone. If you respected them enough to come and play in their house, they respected you back.

But they loved to tell you about it, one way or the other. Trash talking was for a specific purpose. It was a form of intimidation to get that special edge, but it was used selectively. "In your face" was common in the black community many years ago. Now it's said for its own sake and is even part of ESPN's loudest commercial about pro-football telecasts though what "in your face" means in football with those birdcage helmets the players wear is beyond me. Television used to be years behind in its use of street language, but rap music closes that gap with lightning speed today. You can see it all on MTV.

In 1963–64, my first year in Philadelphia, I was thrilled to be chosen to the East squad for the NBA All-Star game. I hadn't dreamed that I would achieve such recognition in only my second year in the league. I would go on to play in six more All-Star games, but this experience was singular because it was my first time and I was as wide-eyed as any kid might have been. But it looked like we wouldn't play at all.

I came to Boston eager to play with my peers, many of whom were still my heroes. I expected to concentrate on the game but found out I was to be part of more important history. I think that night propelled me toward my subsequent role as a players' spokesperson. It opened my eyes and forced me to recognize how little freedom or control NBA players had. Using the only leverage we had to press our point with the NBA owners, we threatened to boycott the All-Star game.

The struggle that came to a head that January had been brewing for years. The players had tried again and again to convince the NBA owners to recognize a players association that could bargain on such issues as contracts, playing conditions, and a pension plan. In 1957, before another All-Star game in Boston Garden, the players, led by Bob Cousy, had threatened not to play the game unless the NBA formally recognized the Players' Association. Commissioner Maurice Podoloff met with the players. Pension planning was begun, and the game went on. However, as the years rolled by, the owners practiced a delaying action that seemed calculated to drag the whole issue of pensions down into legal double-talk and nonaction.

Through the years players would meet periodically and wrestle with the question of how to pressure the owners into formal recognition. The moving spirit of the Players' Association was the Celtic Tom Heinsohn. He dealt with the owners' representative on pensions, the Detroit Pistons' Fred Zollner. However, no progress was being made. In the fall of 1963, the NBA had a new commissioner, Walter Kennedy. By then, the players had a new lawyer, Lawrence Fleisher, a young guy from Harvard whom Heinsohn had met in Boston. They'd begun to talk about underwriting the players' meager pension fund. Heinsohn had a professional interest in such a potential windfall because he was already rising in the insurance business.

Heinsohn and Fleisher told Kennedy in the fall of 1963 that they wanted to speak with the owners about pensions when the owners met at the All-Star game. So Walter Kennedy and Fred Zollner sat down with four players—Heinsohn, Kerr, Tom Gola, Guy Rodgers—on the morning of the game to hash out the proposed plans. It was agreed there that if the players would accept the plans on the table, the implementation of the plans would be "taken up" at the next league meeting, perhaps in February, perhaps in May. Kennedy and Zollner signed this agreement, and the four players accepted it in principle.

Everything that happened that day and evening was provisional because the NBA Players' Association was more like a loose confederation of veterans. We had no official elected representatives team by team at that time. We thus had no collective bargaining agreement and no right to strike. Fleisher couldn't be the legal representative of an informal group. Nonetheless, we pushed ahead to accomplish what we could in the moment.

Everybody left: the owners to discuss changes in the league constitution, the players to participate in an afternoon practice before the game. But in the afternoon, the players began to have second thoughts. Larry Fleisher urged us to take a stand before the game, that pressure exerted by threatening not to play that evening's game, one to be televised nationally, was our only weapon. Three times, Kennedy was given a note to "call Fleisher." Each time he chose not to.

Game time grew closer and closer. Heinsohn and Pettit met with Kennedy about 6 P.M. and insisted he meet with Fleisher. Kennedy did, with Pettit, Heinsohn, Bill Russell, and Lenny Wilkens in tow. They demanded a meeting with all the owners before game time to put the pension plan into effect *immediately.* No more deferrals. Kennedy then went back to canvass the owners, who by this time were furious at us, their employees. Their reaction boiled down to "How dare these wage earners spoil our party? How dare they act as if they had any control over their labor?" In effect, they told us, play or else. We'd agreed to what Kennedy and Zollner had signed in the morning, and that was that.

The clock kept ticking toward the 9 P.M. game time. Boston Garden began to fill up. I imagined the owners somewhere in the building cursing the field hands and muttering about who was going to pick the cotton. At about 8:25 P.M., Kennedy appeared in our dressing room, reported the owners' refusal and made a speech about the background of the case. He promised us that if we agreed to play the game, a pension fund would be initiated. On Fleisher's recommendation we then voted unanimously to play. We heard reports that the Laker owner Bob Short threatened to fire his stars, Jerry West and Elgin Baylor, if they didn't take the court. Can you imagine that happening to players today at thirty or forty million dollars per superstar contract? Now, with each established player a minicorporation, the owners no longer have that arbitrary power. At 8:55 P.M., Pettit informed the owners that the game would go on.

The tension went out of us like a balloon but our adrenaline stopped as well. We came out and began the game about twenty minutes late. My first All-Star game was an anticlimax to all the locker-room excitement, and it was a sleepwalkers' affair. I played twelve minutes and scored 4 points. Our East team won 111–107 with Oscar taking over when none of us had much energy. That night, I would say, the NBA Old Timers game was probably more entertaining than the All-Star contest. We dragged along as if we had weights on our ankles.

Celtics President Walter Brown was furious with the players and especially his own guy, Heinsohn, for busting up his All-Star party. He called Heinsohn in the next day and just tore into him, telling the press "Heinsohn is the Number One heel in my long association with sports." There is nothing like an owner challenged to bring out all the latent power ploys in his or her arsenal. Nonetheless, the deal was done, and the Players' Association was on its way. Our pension-plan proposal differed from those of baseball and football. It called for thirty-year-endowment life insurance policies of $2,000 face value and $1,000 annual premiums, with the player and owner contributing $500 for each year the player was in the league. This money doesn't sound like much today, but in 1964 dollars it was a start toward our security.

From this one shaky start, the NBA Players' Association grew into the strongest players' group in sports; the biggest notch in its belt is taking down of the reserve clause for all sports in the mid-1970s. Until then, the reserve clause bound players to one team for life, preventing any freedom of movement and prohibiting players from selling their skills to the highest bidder. Our Players' Association victory in 1964 was the beginning of the end for owners' total control. It would take many years and many battles, but the subservient relation of players to management was on its way out. After the All-Star confrontation, the NBA Players' Association was formalized. Larry Fleisher be-

came our general counsel. He grew into one of the most powerful men in basketball as the NBA went far ahead of other professional sports in securing players' rights over the next two
decades. Dave Gambee became the first elected player representative from the 76ers in 1964–65, and I succeeded him in 1967–68.
When I was traded to the Bulls in 1969, I became the Bulls' player
rep, a position I held for all six years I played in Chicago.

I learned another lesson about power that night in 1964 that
I had never known before. These negotiations had me standing
shoulder-to-shoulder with white people as part of the same ad-
vocacy group. That was a first! It was an amazing new experience, the owners versus the players, both black and white. I
watched almost openmouthed as owners tried to bully their superstars into playing a basketball game. I had never before felt an
affiliation outside the black community, not in Benton Harbor,
not at Bradley. That night I could see how power constitutes itself not only in racial but also in economic terms that have nothing to do with race. Oppression and ownership are not a simple
matter of white over black as I had believed.

Those Philly fans who were skeptical about us had legiti-
mate complaints. In 1963–64, our first year as the 76ers, we went
34–46 and were eliminated in the first round of the play-offs. We
were a team in transition. The older Syracuse players—Schayes,
Kerr, Costello, Bianchi—were still competitive, but we needed
new blood. We started to put the pieces together in 1964–65, and
one of the big additions was the rookie Lucious Jackson from
Pan American University and Beaumont, Texas. Luke was rock
hard and agile at six feet nine inches and 250 pounds. He began
the season at center and by year's end was in double figures in
both rebounds and points, making the all-rookie team. Luke just
about invented the power-forward position, and, had it not been
for a serious achilles tendon injury in 1968–69, he would have
had a great career.

The fans were not exactly pouring in as we stumbled along

in the first half of the 1964–65 season. One night in November the Warriors came into town, and we beat them 128–117 before all of 3,800 people at Convention Hall. Wilt put on a show for his home folks, taking 58 shots, scoring 63 points, and grabbing 32 rebounds. My old mentor, Alex Hannum, was now the Warrior coach. He was ejected from the game, but all of us could see him peering through the curtains on the stage at one end of the hall. It was about this time that Hugh Hefner began providing us with Playboy bunnies as our mascots at every league stop. Our "home" bunnies came from the New York Playboy club. One night Johnny Kerr presented them with a bunch of carrots. Announcer Dave Zinkoff had to come on the P.A. system to plead with the fans not to steal the bunnies' banners. They were lucky that was all the fans grabbed for.

In the early days with a nine-team league, we became very familiar with opposing teams' strategies and the strengths of individual players because we came against each other so often. By Christmas 1964, we'd already had it out with the Celtics four times. Just before Christmas, in a wild game with the Celtics at Convention Hall, Luke Jackson got into a fight with Boston's Satch Sanders and scored 23 points with 26 rebounds against Russell. At halftime, one fan pulled Celtics coach Red Auerbach's tie in an effort to choke him. Another fan fought with the officials. We lost the game 118–109, but Luke was an enraged bull, shedding Celtic players as if they were bad bronco busters.

Even with all kinds of promotions we had small crowds. The NBA was still in its doubleheader phase, trying to pump up interest with two-for-one deals for the fans. Most club owners honestly weren't sure that fans would buy just one NBA game. So we had our share of so-called neutral court games where two road teams would be the first game on the card, like a wrestling or boxing night. It wasn't until the mid-1970s that the doubleheaders disappeared and that owners felt confident enough to sell their teams in a one-game package or had enough clout to rent the major arenas in various cities. When we really came on as a team in Philly, our neutral court dates magically and gradually decreased from 25 in 1964 to 8 by 1968. In 1964–65, we played 25 of our 80 games on neutral courts whereas the league average was 12. The owners kept us out of our own town, a sure sign of franchise instability. Not surprisingly, we went 18–7 in those neutral court games but even worse, only 13–12 in our tiny number of home games. We didn't feel at home *at home*, and it showed.

As the 1964–65 season reached its midpoint, we had a lot of problems. Even with Luke Jackson, our rebounding was poor. At midseason we were 20–21. Even our shooting had gone bad. Kerr, Greer, and I were all way down in shooting percentage. I just didn't have a feel for what we were doing on the court. Not to mention the fact that at the All-Star break, we'd played exactly 13 home games.

However, if we were in trouble, the San Francisco Warriors were in a nightmare of their own. They'd made the NBA Championship Finals against the Celtics in 1963–64 behind Wilt and a young Nate Thurmond but then had fallen apart due to injuries and illness. The Warriors were about to free-fall to a 17–63 record in 1964–65 and had lost 12 straight games at the All-Star break. Their attendance was even worse than ours.

We began hearing trade rumors about Wilt even before Christmas. But at what cost? We couldn't break up the nucleus of our team to acquire him. How could we get Wilt without giving up any of our starting five? At the same time rumors were afloat that the Los Angeles Lakers would pay up to a million dollars in cash to get Wilt. I felt we had the upper hand on any deal because of the strong Philadelphia connection in the ownership of both the 76ers and the Warriors. Ike Richman, co-owner of the 76ers, was not only Wilt's friend but his financial adviser. Ike and Eddie Gottlieb, owner of the Warriors, had been friends for years and involved in many business deals around the Philadelphia area. All this sounds very close to tampering today, but at that time the NBA was clubbier in atmosphere, and the owners were a small, close society.

Sports fans always remember the Celtics-76ers matchup as

that of the two giant centers with the goatees squaring off against one another in the middle. Bill Russell against Wilt Chamberlain was the greatest individual rivalry in the history of the NBA. But the Boston-Philadelphia feud went back to the Warrior-Celtic battles of the 1950s where Boston always came out on top. Ike Richman and Irv Kosloff, the 76ers' co-owners, had watched Boston kick Philadelphia teams around for a long time. Ike's dream was to bring down the hated Celtics. It was personal with him. His ego was as large as that of Red Auerbach. He wasn't a basketball man, but he was a sharp operator. He knew where to find the missing piece in his puzzle, and he knew it was Wilt. Someone who could battle Russell and who could rally the reluctant Philly fans.

Ike was a volatile guy and very impatient with our play. He was always coming down into the dressing room at home and speaking his mind to us. Often Coach Dolph Schayes would just stand back and listen. Right after Christmas 1964, after we lost to the Royals before five thousand on a night when Ike gave away free basketballs to swell the crowd, he barreled in and berated us: "Aren't you hungry enough for points anymore? You didn't see the other team stop. I'm not worried about money. Just give me a good game. I'm not kidding you, any more of this stuff and I'm going to shuffle the deck."

Following the All-Star game in St. Louis on January 13, 1965, Wilt Chamberlain became a 76er. The deal was finalized at Stan Musial's restaurant and was one of the great steals of all time. Wilt came to the 76ers for Lee Shaffer, Paul Neumann, Connie Dierking, and $300,000. Lee's knee was bad, and he hadn't even reported to us in 1964–65 but chose to stay in North Carolina with his trucking business when the 76ers wouldn't increase his salary. Lee never played a minute for San Francisco. Dierking and Neumann were fine pros but not All-Stars. Our 76ers nucleus stayed intact, which let me breathe because earlier speculation was that the player going west in the deal might be me. At those moments, an athlete realizes how little control he has over his career.

As Wilt's lawyer, Ike Richman drew up all the papers and secretly promised Wilt a piece of the 76ers if he would agree to the trade. A rule existed at that time, and still does, that a player is not permitted to own any part of an NBA team. So an agreement was made on a handshake between Ike and Wilt that when Wilt eventually retired or when the team was sold, he would have a piece of the action.

With that agreement in place, Wilt reluctantly agreed to come home. Dolph Schayes began at the outset to placate Wilt and let him call the shots. He let Wilt set his own schedule, let him take a week off to handle business and personal affairs in California. The joke was, of course, that Schayes had hardly been a Chamberlain fan as an opposing player and coach. He had gone on record that Wilt was a poor team player and that high school boys could shoot fouls better. Now, coexistence was the order of the day. But Dolph never had the force of personality or the coaching strategy to gain Wilt's or our team's respect.

The first few weeks after Wilt's arrival, we could feel the growing tension, particularly between Wilt and Hal Greer. Hal was our team leader, a tremendous competitor, a great shooter. Hal held the 76ers together for many years through many coaches, a franchise shift, and personnel changes. A quiet guy, he was a fierce player. He was one of the finest open-court shooters I ever saw, for he could race down court, stop on a dime twenty feet out on the dead run and bury the shot. More than anyone else, the 76ers were his team, and he wasn't about to give up that role without insisting on more respect from everyone, including Wilt and Dolph.

The most drastic change with Wilt aboard was the attention he received. No matter whether he sought it or not, he became the focal point. Greer didn't adjust too well at first to Wilt in the middle, for Hal liked to tear down on a break and have the lane to operate. Wilt took up a lot of space on the blocks. I adjusted easily enough, and so did Wilt. Coming to Philadelphia at this point in his career was actually perfect for him. He'd scored so many points in his first five years that scoring had actually become a bore to him, something tedious. Wilt had *averaged* 50 points a game in 1961–62. What was there left to prove in that department? The league had demanded it, the fans had expected it. He was ready to throw off a lot of the burden, and he became the passer and team player that he would remain for the second half of his career. The 76ers allowed him to shift to that role because of our multiple offensive weapons.

Playing with Wilt meant finding his rhythm every night. You had to get him the ball exactly where he wanted it in the post. Some nights he was a dominant scorer. Other nights, when he didn't feel it, he would dish off. Wilt was a streak player who didn't want to be fouled because his already-weak foul shooting was getting worse from the time he joined us. Yet night in, night out, he was a towering force. His rebounding and defensive presence alone made us more of a threat. Even so, we remained streaky with little sense that we could put a move on the Celtics. We finished the regular season at 40–40, only one game better than the first half of the season without Wilt.

We knew we had the potential, but we hadn't put the team together on the court. Everyone's game adjusted. John Kerr lost a lot of his playing time. Luke Jackson moved to forward after a brilliant start as a center. I put in six hundred fewer minutes in 1964–65, and my scoring average dropped from 17 to 13 points per game. Attendance hadn't exactly soared. We reached our lowest ebb in March when the Warriors won their sixteenth game of the year against us in Convention Hall before about 1,600 people. I could have counted the house with a pencil and paper. Everything sounds hollow in an empty building—the bouncing ball, the public address system, the fans' noise. Phillies' exhibition games took over the lead stories in the Philadelphia sports pages as reporters and fans alike figured we were going to play out the string and regroup for next year. Wilt briefly entered a hospital with pancreatitis. We squeaked into the play-offs but didn't expect to go very far.

Our first-round opponents were the Cincinnati Royals of Oscar Robertson and Jerry Lucas. They came in with 10 wins more than we had, but we stole the first game at Cincinnati 119–117 with Wilt making two free throws to clinch it, making him 6–18 for the game. It was strange, but I bet if you totaled up the foul shots Wilt took with the game on the line, you would find him shooting around 75 percent. I got hot with an 18-point second half but wore myself out taking my turn at guarding Oscar.

The next day a sickening event occurred in Alabama. Mrs. Viola Liuzzo, a mother of five from Detroit and a Civil Rights worker, was shot and killed in her car in Selma, Alabama. Her death occurred after Dr. Martin Luther King, Jr., led 25,000 people to the Alabama capital of Montgomery to climax a five-day, fifty-mile voters' rights march. A delegation of twenty marchers tried to present a voting rights petition to Governor George Wallace but was stopped by seventy-five state troopers with nightsticks. The marchers were told the governor's office was closed. In a speech King called for a massive economic boycott against Alabama by organized labor and consumers and for federal funds to be withheld.

Daily stories such as this one continually made me wonder how important our games were in the greater scheme of things. But what did I do day by day? I primarily blocked out the thought like most of us do as we denounce someone else's misfortunes in another place. The black players discussed race all the time in private. We were concerned about our roles but saw no way to translate concern into action.

In game two of the play-offs back home at the ancient Arena in Philadelphia, Oscar scored 40 points, and the Royals stole the game 121–120. I had 22 but had to dog Oscar the second half, an exhausting job. When he had the ball, he was constantly pushing forward in stops and starts. Or he would post up down low. He had a feathery-soft release point for his shot, up around his right ear. And with the strong body of a forward, he was a handful. Then we had a real scare when both teams took the same plane back to Cincinnati for game three and landed there with the left engine in flames. Just another day for us!

We polished off the Royals 3–1 in that series and now faced

the Celtics in Boston Garden, where we had lost 8 straight games. Our team fared no better in the opener, which we lost 108–98. Boston's press was fierce, breaking down our ballhandling. Yet we bounced back to win game two in Philly 109–103 by bringing our corner men back to screen and throwing longer passes up court. Satch Sanders was a main disrupter, the best defensive forward in the league. Boston went up 2–1 in the series; and then we tied it back in Philly with a 134–131 victory in which Hal Greer hit a miracle 30-foot shot at the buzzer to force an overtime. Today it would have been a three-point winner and would have brought down the house. Kerr insisted Hal was fouled and should have won the game right there with a free throw. Auerbach almost had a stroke arguing the shot came after the buzzer. Wilt had 34 points and 34 rebounds. I chipped in with 31 points and hit some tough jumpers over Sanders in overtime.

We split games five and six in Boston and Philly, bringing our string of losses in Boston to 10; we hadn't won there since moving down from Syracuse. This was surely the most bitter, hard-fought series I had ever played in. Our win in Philly tied the series at 3–3 and brought us to a decisive seventh game in Boston.

The 76ers weren't really together yet as a team. During the play-off with Boston, *Sports Illustrated* came out with Wilt's first-person account titled "My Life in a Bush League," in which he slammed practically every aspect of the NBA as a major-league sports operation. This didn't endear him to anyone though what he said rang true to me. In self-defense, Wilt claimed it was all distorted, that he would sue the magazine. But the distraction didn't help our cohesiveness as a unit. Wilt was grumbling; Schayes was trying to keep his job; and we faced another mountain to climb in Boston. Wilt called Auerbach a "bush operator" in the article and said that Dolph was "too nice" to coach a bunch of hardened professionals. We all slunk away from reporters eager for our reactions. Al Bianchi put it best: "I don't want to comment because we're fighting for the Eastern Division title. Money is what interests me now."

We caught the Eastern Airlines shuttle to Boston in an evening drizzle that seemed typical for mid-April. Flying into Boston was always like going down into Dante's inferno. The whole experience was intimidating, starting with the airport cab drivers. They would bait us: "Who's gonna stop Havlicek?" "Satch has Walker's number." "Russell is still better than Wilt . . . You guys will be lucky to get out of this place alive." The whole city had an edge on. We always felt it in restaurants, on television. In the ride from the hotel to Boston Garden, it seemed the streets were always covered with slush as if the city was waiting for us to leave town before cleaning up. As we proceeded down the long walkway from the bus to the Garden, people gawked at us and jeered as if we were aliens from another planet.

Once we were inside Boston Garden, it was no haven, not for Celtic opponents anyway. The locker rooms were always cold, damp, and dirty. Noise came up from the plumbing to drown out the coach's pregame talk. Rats and roaches lurked in that ancient building as if they'd signed a long-term lease. Often we had to scatter them off the benches just so we could get into uniform. Running out of the locker room to the floor between the banked bleachers to the court felt like taking Daniel's final steps before the lion's den. Hostility was palpable. Boston fans threw everything at us—from toilet paper to rotten eggs.

At least the Boston fans hated us as players, all of us, black or white. As a group, we were the enemy. Going to Boston Garden was rough, but it was like encountering something you love to hate, a masochistic pleasure because we knew the fury of the Celtic fans made us dig a little deeper come game time.

Even the warm-up drills at Boston Garden turned into a contest. Havlicek was very superstitious and always wanted to make sure he made the Celtics' last warm-up shot before the start of the game, any game; he simply had to be the last man on the court. But we would keep an extra ball and send out one of our reserves to make another basket. Then one of the Celtic ball boys would grab our ball to allow John to make another shot. But now we were determined to end the belief that most dogged us—that the 76ers couldn't win in Boston.

This grueling series had to end this night, one way or the other. As we broke the huddle, we spoke about not being intimidated. This game would end the Celtic domination. We had never put together a complete game at Boston Garden, and now we had one last chance. Hal Greer got Wilt's opening tip and came down the left side while Luke Jackson set a pick for me coming up from the bottom to the top of the foul circle. Bailey Howell and Satch Sanders got caught in a switch. Hal hit me coming across the key and my 22-footer hit nothing but net. We got it on.

But near the end of the first period we dug ourselves a huge hole by going down 18 points. Then Wilt, Dave Gambee, and I led a charge and finally shot us in front 45–44. Gambee had 19 points in the first half. He and Wilt offset some brilliant jump shooting by Havlicek, and we left the court at halftime leading 62–61. Hal and I each hit to open the second half, but Havlicek and Sam Jones came back to lead the Celts to a 90–82 margin after three quarters. We spent the last twelve minutes battling a proud champion team and its furious fans. We kept inching back to within 3 or 4 points. With four minutes left, I made a three-point play, Wilt dunked, and Hal made a jump shot to bring us within 1 point at 104–103. But Sam Jones, who scored 37, hit a jumper off a screen, and Boston stayed ahead. I tell you, when Sam scored on those banked jump shots from the left side, I could almost smell the rubber burn as the ball rocketed through the net. When Wilt hit two free throws and rammed one in over Russell in the last nerve-wracking minute, we trailed by one point with five seconds left at 110–109.

Then came an incredible break for us. Russell's inbounds pass directly under our basket was deflected back off him. Amazingly, it was our ball at that very spot. "TIME OUT!" screamed Dolph. Fourteen thousand Celtic fans were on their feet spitting "Defense . . . defense!" at their heroes as we went back to our bench. I saw Schayes's face as we approached him. Anxiety and uncertainty were written all over him. It was obvious he didn't know what play to call. In desperation he just said,

"Get the ball to Wilt." But Wilt screamed over the crowd noise, "No, they're going to foul me." Wilt didn't want the ball because of his poor foul shooting although he was a much better foul shooter with games on the line for some reason. So the play was set up for Hal to throw the ball in to me; Kerr would set the screen for my return pass to Hal for a jump shot to win the title.

I don't think anyone thought the play would work; I certainly didn't. Two passes was one too many with five seconds left in a pressure situation like this one. I made up my mind that this was to be my moment to pull us through to glory. If the pass came to me, I was going to take the shot. I felt a strange certainty about that. As the referee handed the ball to Hal on the baseline, the whole crowd rose to its feet in sections like a writhing animal. I'm not sure how that dank old building stayed on its foundations. All the elements that players and fans spend their lives waiting and hoping for were right here. And I was ready.

But I never got the ball. It was tipped away on the inbounds pass. Once again it was a quirk of Boston Garden that made the difference. The Garden had a wire that angled down from the backboard to the floor to keep the basket steady. The wire was so low where Hal stood that it was impossible for him to get the proper arc on the pass to me. He was to the right of the basket, and I was on the right side, about 18 feet out. Havlicek was guarding me with his back to the ball, but he threw his hands up over his head. Half-looking, half-flailing, he deflected the ball before it ever got to me. It rolled across the midcourt line, where Sam Jones grabbed it as the buzzer sounded. The taped phrase "Havlicek stole the ball!" growling from the gravel throat of Celtics' broadcaster Johnny Most, became the basketball equivalent of baseball's Bobby Thompson home run in 1951, after which the Giants' broadcaster kept screaming, "The Giants won the pennant!" The Giants won the pennant!"

Indeed, Havlicek stole the ball, and the Celtics were champions still. A sea of Celtics' fans came onto the floor, mobbing Russell and Auerbach, who thrust his hated victory cigar over his head. Dolph later said that as soon as he saw the pass, he

knew it would be intercepted. He explained to the press that we
had Wilt underneath to guide in Hal's shot. Well, we needed to
paper over our confusion and rationalize our last hectic moments in the huddle.

In any event, although the swift collapse of our dream left
us numb, we knew something really good had started with the
76ers. It wasn't our turn quite yet, but we could see it coming.
Wilt had been with us for only a half-season, and we needed
more youth, speed, and ballhandling. I suppose we came within
sight of the mountaintop before we were actually ready for the
climb. The NBA is funny that way. More than any other sport, it
seems that a group of players has to know how it feels to compete for the title and lose before they can really summon up the
will and consistency to become a championship team. There
have never been any shortcuts in the NBA.

Players have a difficult time remaining close because of the
intervention of the press in all our relationships. The press has its
job to do; I respected that and still do. But what happens is that
reporters are constantly asking for our comments after we win or
lose, about our teammates, our opponents. Whatever we tell
them gets sharpened to the most sensational point. Depending
on the context, it could sound like we're blowing our own horn,
slamming an opponent, or just being arrogant. It's hard to go
from city to city just reading the newspapers. You might not see
an old friend for weeks or months but you feel the sting of his
comments about you or your team in the papers or on TV.

I have watched the relationship between Wilt Chamberlain
and Bill Russell unravel over the years precisely because of their
created legends. In those hard-fought play-offs, Wilt and Bill
went at it like pit bulls until the stress-filled, artificial relationship came to replace the real one.

I first saw Wilt and Bill together at Kutsher's Country Club
in the Catskills in the summer of 1964 after my first year in Philadelphia. I was there to play in the annual Maurice Stokes benefit

game, which I considered a privilege. Wilt and Bill were insepa-
rable at Kutsher's before the Stokes game. They ate together,
jogged together, hung out and around together. You couldn't believe that these guys locked horns like two giant rams season
after season. But as the seasons wore on, the public rivalry took
its toll, especially after Wilt joined the 76ers in 1965, and the play-
offs began to mount up. Everything culminated in 1968–69 when
a thirty-five-year-old Russell led the Celtics to a victory over the
Chamberlain-West-Baylor Los Angeles Lakers in the seventh
game, in which Wilt left with a minor ankle injury. The Lakers
rallied from way back, and the coach Butch Van Breda Kolff
wouldn't let Wilt back in during a crucial fourth quarter rally.
After the game Russell said that he would never have come out
of a game like that no matter how much he was hurting.

That was the last straw for Wilt and wedged the two men
further and further apart. Bill left basketball as the eternal winner, and Wilt became the greatest player who would find a way
to lose. This image was unfair, of course, but the press repeated
the stereotype year after year, long after Russell retired, even
after Wilt's Laker team won 33 straight games and an NBA title
in 1971–72.

The press has to shoulder some of the blame for driving the
wedge between these two giants. For one thing, the media was
not comfortable with Wilt and Bill as friendly rivals. It had to
make them antagonists. To me, it was the same "divide-and-con-
quer" strategy used against black people for centuries. I'm not
calling it a plot. I simply mean that America is hardly ever capa-
ble of looking at black people as anything but rivals for the few
pedestals available to us. I know the NBA's marketing strategy
for television has always been to focus on individuals, not on the
game itself. It was always "Wilt against Russell," "Magic against
Bird"; then "Michael against Charles Barkley"; now it's "Shaq
versus 'Zo." What starts as a commercial investment in names
becomes a way to divide and conquer.

Black people recognize how harmful this tactic can be. It re-
lates to something much deeper, though. Black people are

chronically set against one another by the larger society, but it is our own fault that we do not push past this strategy. At the same time it's so understandable. If sports is the one territory we've got, we'll fight over it. But there's no reason to kill ourselves over space we don't own. When you come right down to it, gangs don't realize how fruitless their protection of turf is. This battling is one way we become our own enemies. Black people scuffle with each other on the basketball court for a few slots; we battle for schooling, affirmative action jobs, the token position, a bit of the battleground.

Since we haven't achieved equality in America, we try to be superior to *somebody*, in this case to the brother next door, whom we'll fight for the crumbs. The house nigger crowed over his superiority over the field nigger. The man in the row house is most hostile toward those left in the projects. The suburban black tries to convince his white neighbors that *he's* the toughest S.O.B. on crime they ever met.

I first saw black heroes pitted against each other on the courts and have followed it off the field for most of my adult life in America. I hope Bill Russell and Wilt Chamberlain bury the hatchet. They were and are great, strong black men, who deserve to be lionized as individuals and to be respected as friends at the same time.

11.
"The Greatest Team of All Time"

Bill Russell was named coach of the Celtics in 1966. I heard the news with pride, but my emotions were mixed. He became the first black coach in the history of the NBA or any major sports league. But we would have to go all out to beat him.

The Boston-Philadelphia rivalry always meant more to me than just a basketball battlefield. Much of what I learned about American history as a schoolboy in Benton Harbor was bound up with the images of these two cities. To me Philadelphia meant the Liberty Bell and the cradle of freedom, Ben Franklin and Independence Hall, where the Declaration had been signed that set Americans free. The Philadelphia I knew in the mid-1960s also was home to Frank Rizzo, the city's racist police chief and future mayor, who was, to black people, like some nightmare sheriff who'd followed them from Mississippi or Alabama.

Boston has always been depicted as a tough town for black athletes to work and live in. I knew all about South Boston, violent school-integration battles, and various incidents between players, police, and the public. But Boston also had a ringing liberal legacy in my mind: the Boston Tea Party, the Battle of Concord, Paul Revere, the Abolitionists, and Crispus Attucks, a black soldier in the Revolutionary War and one of its first casualties, the only black man in American history I'd ever heard of in high school. To me Boston also meant the Kennedys and liberal legislation in my own time.

I'd always hated Red Auerbach's arrogance and flamboyance. I also knew he had made Russell head coach in part because Bill had forced his hand by threatening to retire unless he was made coach. But I had to give Auerbach his due. He was the first coach in NBA history to play five blacks at one time on the court for the Celtics in the early 1960s. In 1950, he signed the NBA's first black player, Chuck Cooper. So, in spite of everything, in sports history Boston placed itself in the vanguard by its inclusion of black athletes.

People today think NBA basketball is the great liberal professional sport in America, but it has not always held that distinction. Changes were gradual throughout my playing career. In a preseason briefing to the 76ers on the league's rule changes before the 1966 season, referee Mendy Rudolph was droning on and concluded by asking if there were any questions. Wilt shot back, "Yes, there certainly are: what about getting the NBA some black referees?" Wilt and Mendy went off in a corner to talk about it, and before the season was out, the NBA's referee corps was integrated.

Even today, black players who come in with a more radical point of view or who are very controversial do not become coaches. I couldn't begin to conceive of a strong college coach such as John Thompson or a Bobby Knight in professional basketball. I think Thompson and Knight would be driven out by players who want to really run their own show nowadays and by a nervous management that can't control the players. A black figure comparable to baseball's Leo Durocher or Billy Martin would be impossible. Frank Robinson as manager was too much for the Orioles, Giants, and Indians to handle. All managers and coaches exist to be fired. I know there are both black and white timeservers in pro sports, but too few black men ever get a chance to even be that.

As of September 1994, there were *four* black head coaches

out of twenty-seven in the NBA: Lenny Wilkens who has been around for years, John Lucas, Butch Beard, and Don Chaney—*twenty-six years* after Bill Russell. Four black coaches—K. C. Jones, Chaney, Stu Jackson, and Gene Littles—were fired in 1990–92. Chaney received a second job at Detroit in 1993–94 whereas Sidney Lowe, Fred Carter, and Quinn Buckner had recent short coaching runs with losing teams before being let go in 1994. Magic Johnson returned to coach the 1993–94 season with the Lakers to great fanfare but found it a discouraging business and hard on his health. Since 1990, over fifteen new white head coaches have been hired. The league is now almost 80 percent black on the court but a white preserve everywhere else, especially in the front office although there is an encouraging trend with new, young front-office talent such as M. L. Carr, Billy McKinney, and Stu Jackson. Elgin Baylor and Willis Reed remain general managers, and Wes Unseld has been kicked upstairs by the Bullets. We'll see if gains can be consolidated, but we've been down this road before.

A pro basketball player's hours are strange. The afternoon is spent resting up so you can expend an enormous amount of energy at a time of night when most adult human bodies are winding down toward bedtime. After a game you're either bushed or so wired that you don't settle your body back into a cycle of hunger and sleep until close to dawn. Soon it's early morning calls for airports or practices, and then the cycle repeats itself.

I guess that's why I always enjoyed talking on the phone late at night when I was a player. It gave me a chance to unwind. A friend of mine in New York had wanted to fix me up with a dancer in Broadway shows named Barbara. I got her phone number, and we started to talk way into the night after her shows or my games, sometimes until two or three o'clock in the morning. She had this Marlene Dietrich–like voice that could drop a couple of notes into baritone sexy and bring me out of the

dumps. We would talk about love, sex, friendships, careers, relationships. Sometimes she caught my games on T.V. and *she*, a
Broadway dancer, would compliment *me* on my nice legs! I
counseled her through two difficult relationships with guys, but
still we never met.

One Sunday night I was back in Philly after an afternoon
game in New York, and Barbara called to say that I'd walked
right by her at Madison Square Garden as we were coming out.
"Why didn't you say something to me?" I asked. "I didn't want
to reveal myself yet," she said. We finally agreed to meet in a
coffee shop in New York, and, as you might expect, there was no
Hollywood ending. It wasn't that easy to talk in person. Her
physique didn't match her voice or the fantasy I had of her; she
was short and rather plain, and I think she knew I was thinking
that she wasn't the person I'd imagined. No one was at fault. She
was still lovely Barbara. Meeting her wasn't the issue. Our
friendship was, and that's what has always mattered to me. I was
a shy young man, and the phone was often where I could be my
truest self.

After the 1964–65 season and our devastating loss to the
Celtics, I found myself back in Philadelphia trying to erase the
series finale from my mind. I very much needed someone to escape with, and I looked forward to spending a lot of time with a
young New York City schoolteacher named Charlene, whom I
was dating at that time. We probably weren't in love, but we
cared for each other a great deal.

I had met Charlene in New York through a friend of mine
from Syracuse. We'd exchanged phone numbers but didn't
begin a relationship until the team moved to Philadelphia. Charlene was an independent, aggressive young woman who was a
feminist even before there was a movement. She wore her hair in
an Afro, and we talked politics a lot. She introduced me to the
New York theater scene, and I remember we went to see *Golden
Boy* with Sammy Davis, Jr., in the title role.

I'd called her up and invited her down for the weekend in
Philadelphia. She didn't seem at all herself when I picked her up
at the train station, sort of grim and preoccupied. I couldn't snap

her out of it. Before we got out of the car, she told me she was pregnant. I was absolutely stunned.

I had a welter of conflicting feelings. I didn't want to be a father. I didn't even want to be married. In the 1950s, if you'd gotten a girl in trouble in Benton Harbor, you did the honorable thing and married her. Some of my high school friends had so-called shotgun weddings. The experiences of these teenagers with few opportunities and a baby on the way scared me as I watched them struggle to make ends meet. As I got older, I saw guys drop out of college to get married. As a player, I had also always tried to avoid this situation for I thought it could destroy an athletic career.

Charlene and I were facing a traumatic situation. We didn't go in my apartment but drove down by the Schuylkill River to talk honestly about what to do. We discussed our dilemma for a very long time, mostly going in circles. It was her suggestion to consider abortion; she wasn't ready for a child. She told me she hadn't wanted to tell me until after the Boston series for fear I would be unable to keep my mind on the games. My heart was really breaking. She was carrying this child and the burden by herself because of me and my basketball games. She was looking out for me! Going through her school year, wondering if she would be back in the classroom that fall, or ever. I didn't know how to react. We talked about how we felt, about where we both wanted to go with our careers. About how we weren't really in love, not in all the right ways. After a long drawn-out conversation and many tears born of strong emotions, we decided on an abortion.

Abortion rights have been perhaps the most politicized subject of the 1980s and 1990s. Charlene and I were attempting to deal with the situation in the decade *before Roe* v. *Wade* when anything to do with abortion was tainted by criminality, sordidness, and shame. We both knew of clothes-hanger abortions, botched abortions. I was scared, Charlene even more so. She didn't want to be a mother at that time, but she didn't want to be sterile or dead either.

I didn't really know where to begin, how to even find an

abortionist. I did know a guy named Woody who had been around the neighborhood. He always dressed in a suit and tie, and the gold on his hands and around his neck glistened; he carried a lot of money and made sure I knew it. Woody was the kind of all-purpose gofer who is always hanging around athletes. Guys like Woody make you walk the other way if you're an athlete and smart. I never quite knew what he did nor did I want to know, but I guessed he wasn't putting in a full day at the office.

I called Woody and asked if he could stop by my apartment early that evening. Sitting in the lobby of my apartment building, I told Woody only what I thought he needed to know. He said that he did know someone who would perform the procedure. He walked across the street, made a phone call, came back, and told me that it could be done at nine that night and would cost three hundred dollars. I said, "I have the three hundred dollars, but what am I going to have to pay *you*?" He said, "Don't worry about it. I know you. You're a friend. I'll just forego my fee." Knowing Woody, I didn't believe him and felt sure the price included a cut for him. But money wasn't the issue; he had the mentality of a street hustler, and I accepted that.

So Charlene, Woody, and I drove to a place in west Philadelphia. It was in a lower-middle-class neighborhood near the University of Pennsylvania. When we pulled up in front of the house, we decided that I wouldn't go inside. If the woman who was to perform the abortion was under surveillance and the police came, there would be no way for Charlene or me to keep this quiet if I was caught in a police raid. So Charlene and Woody went in while I remained in the car frightened, concerned, and ashamed. Frightened of what could happen to Charlene, of the neighborhood, the police, and the possibility of my exposure. Concerned that something might go wrong and that she might be injured and have to be hospitalized. And ashamed. Deep down, I knew I should be by her side right at that moment. I thought of my mother and of the ten children she had born in pain and had raised to be women and men. Was this action worthy of all she had taught me? Was she looking down on me as I sat huddled in that car?

I flipped on the radio. It was Ben E. King singing lead with the Drifters, and it was one of my favorite songs about magic moments that were different and new and summer nights sweeter than wine.

God, it was nice to have that music. The song was about a magic night, and that's what I wanted to remember about Charlene and myself. Now she was in danger, and the mellowness of our time was in the song. *She* was in that house. She was the one who had to undergo that abortion for two hours. And all I did was count the minutes. She had been counting the days until her period, then fretted when it didn't come. Then finding out for sure why not. Then coming to Philly to tell me everything in the uncertainty about what would happen next. All the courage was on her side.

After more than two hours, Charlene came out of the house supported by Woody and another woman. She inched her way forward, taking each step very carefully as if she was afraid that the slightest wrong move might cause her more pain or injury. I quickly got out and helped Charlene ease herself onto the seat while Woody walked around to the other side of the car. I caught a look at the woman who had escorted Charlene from the house, but she avoided my eyes. I didn't know whether she had performed the abortion or not, but each of us recognized an unspoken agreement not to recognize each other.

In silence I drove us back to my apartment. Woody quickly went to his own car and disappeared into the night. I helped Charlene upstairs. We still didn't speak. We couldn't find the words that might bring us together. She wanted to keep her dignity, and it didn't seem fair that it had been all her burden. Finally, in a barely audible voice, I asked, "Are you okay?" She didn't answer immediately. "I'm fine . . ." "Are you hungry?" Again, a pause. "No, I just want to lie down here."

I watched Charlene lying on my couch, trying to relax her wounded body into a comfortable position. I knew I couldn't relax. I didn't believe in abortion. All the church teachings that my mother cared about were against this act. But here we were. We'd gone ahead and done it. It's strange how all sorts of propo-

sitions in the abstract seem so clear until you find yourself sharing someone's pain in your own life. It was a long, empty night
between us as I kept vigil over her. Finally, we both fell asleep.
The next morning Charlene said she wanted to catch the eleven
o'clock train back to New York rather than stay with me any longer. I asked if she shouldn't stay and rest to make sure there
weren't complications, but my heart wasn't really in it. She insisted. I knew she wanted to leave this apartment, the city—everything associated with this abortion, and that meant getting
away from me.

I took her to the Thirtieth Street train station and walked her
to the lonely track where she caught the train to New York. We
gave each other an empty hug, hardly a symbol of the affection
we had shared. Then she stiffly made her way down the ramp to
the train, and we were out of each other's lives. Back in my apartment I prayed for us both that we would not have to suffer further for what had happened. I was unable to share her pain, or
ease my mind or hers. To this day I am ashamed of my role that
evening and haunted by its emptiness. Even if we did the right
thing it was a cold comfort.

The 76ers loaded up for the 1965–66 season. Instead of
going for a territorial choice as expected and selecting Jim Washington from Villanova, they drafted Billy Cunningham from
North Carolina, who instantly gave us a dynamic sixth man in
the mold of John Havlicek. Then veteran Johnny Kerr, a stalwart
on our team since the mid-1950s, was traded to Baltimore, and
we secured young Wali Jones, a flamboyant guard who'd made
the all-rookie team in 1964–65. Suddenly, we were mobile as well
as very big and strong. It was evident from training camp on that
we had the horses although Wilt and Dolph still couldn't communicate and Wilt did pretty much what he wanted to on and
off the court. When Wilt's pancreatitis acted up and he was gulp-
ing pills like candy, he wanted more rest time. When he was feeling fine and Dolph yanked him for a normal blow, Wilt

complained to the press. Some nights he would shoot, some nights he would pass. We adjusted to his moods since either way the 76ers were too much for other teams to handle. Cunningham was an immediate star, and, though he cut into my playing time, I couldn't complain too much since we started so strongly. Some teams gave us fits. Old John Kerr had a good laugh when his lowly Bullets walloped us twice in November 1965, partly because John always played Wilt very well.

We went up to Boston in early December 1965 for what promised to be another of our sacrificial visits. Why would we think otherwise when our losing streak there had reached 19 games and was beyond rational explanation? We played the Celtics on December 3, the day Mrs. Liuzzo's killers were convicted in Montgomery. The 76ers owner Ike Richman went with us to Boston and sat right by our bench. Early in the second quarter Ike stood up and toppled over where Al Bianchi caught him and cradled his body gently to the floor. Ike was pronounced dead of a massive heart attack at the hospital less than an hour later. He was fifty-two years old. Eerily, his wife Claire telephoned our dressing room at halftime to urge us to win this game for Ike. Back home in Philadelphia she had watched on television as her husband slumped over in front of her eyes. What a horrific sight! We *did* go on to break the streak in Boston that night. Our Saturday-Sunday games with the Knicks were postponed, a feeble tribute to a man who had meant a lot to us as a team and as individuals.

Ike was the real architect of the 76ers but didn't live to see us win the championship. He had negotiated the sale of the Warriors and had brought the Syracuse franchise to Philadelphia. Wilt, who lost a trusted friend and adviser in Ike, admitted, "I owe the man all I have today," although all the handshake deals Wilt made with Ike regarding future ownership of the 76ers would go up in smoke as Ike's partner, Irv Kosloff, assumed major control of the team.

Oddly enough, after Ike died, the 76ers really put it together as a team. We rolled into March neck and neck with the Celtics for the lead in the Eastern Division; then we stepped up the pace. Boston won its last six games, but we took the Eastern Division by winning our last 12, putting us at 55–25 over Boston at 54–26. Then we sat and waited and waited while second-place Boston played a ten-day, five-game series against the Cincinnati Royals for the right to play us. The bye that the regular season Division Champions used to get never helped unless a team had players trying to heal from injuries. The Celtics won their series and were battle hardened. We sat around and lost our edge.

Sure enough, the Celtics roared into the play-offs and beat us by 19 and 21 points in the first two games. Our shooting was horrible. Billy Cunningham had the jitters in his first play-off series. Hal, Wali, and I shot around 33 percent. We bounced back to win game three in Philadelphia and went ahead 13 points in the fourth game only to have the Celtics roar back and win in overtime. We committed enough mistakes to lose an entire play-off series with at least 25 turnovers, an estimate since box scores didn't yet track such things. We put ourselves in a huge hole, down three games to one with the only relief in sight offered by the fact that the fifth game was back in Philadelphia.

As if we didn't already have our work cut out for us, Wilt and Dolph began a controversy in the newspapers. We had an hour-long practice on Monday at Convention Hall, but Wilt stayed in his Manhattan apartment. Dolph explained that Wilt had worked so hard on Sunday in Boston and had played such a great game that he didn't have to attend what Dolph called a "loosening-up drill." Poor Dolph, always picking up for Wilt after the fact. Wilt, of course, had missed practices all year. He would go through his own routines at other times, arriving independently of the team before games or going through private workouts. Irv Kosloff had tried unsuccessfully to get Wilt to move to Philly. It is a fact of professional sports life that superstars have their own "Chamberlain Rules" or "Jordan Rules." Most other players understand and accept this.

Boston won the fifth game and the series 120–112 despite Wilt's massive 46 points and 34 rebounds. We made just three abortive runs at the Celtics during the game. Russell had 31 re-bounds and provided his team with what we just didn't have yet: court leadership. Now all the reporters just wanted to get at Dolph, who insisted, "This team was one hundred percent to-gether, understand?" But nobody listened. This season, our best so far, ended abruptly with the Celtics still on top. It was clear that Dolph could not communicate with us and that he wasn't a good-enough game coach to pull us through against a team like Boston. Dolph was a perfectionist but in a place of his own with his own training regimen. He couldn't transfer his knowledge. We needed a strong taskmaster who would snarl us into line and not make excuses for anyone.

We got our man when Alex Hannum replaced Dolph Schayes in the summer of 1966. Needless to say, I could hardly wait. Alex had shepherded me through my rookie year at Syra-cuse and had been a winner everywhere he coached—St. Louis, Syracuse, San Francisco. Our fall training camp on the Jersey shore showed us how tough Alex was prepared to be. Wilt ar-rived in his new Bentley singing Bob Dylan's "Like a Rolling Stone," but there wasn't anything free and easy about Hannum's boot camp. Alex ran us so hard right from the outset that I lost twenty pounds. We were feisty. In our first exhibition game with the Atlanta Hawks in Knoxville, Wilt got into a fight with Zelmo Beaty. I took that as a good sign. We had a young team. Cunning-ham had a year of experience. Wali was now a team leader on the court. I was in my prime. Wilt still had something to prove to everyone who said he couldn't win the big games. Alex told Wilt that if he wanted to win like Russell, he had to become a total team player. The two of them had knock-down-drag-out battles where we had to pull them apart.

Alex was an amazing blend of toughness and understand-ing. Once he really rode me hard at a halftime in Boston Garden, challenging me to show him some guts in the second half. At Logan Airport after the game, Alex pulled me over to a bar and bought me a few beers to show it had been nothing personal. That was his style: say it, get it over with, and get on with it. He treated us like men and expected such treatment in return.

We tore through the league and for a while it appeared as if we wouldn't lose 10 games. And what do you know, we finally began to draw crowds to Convention Hall. We finished at 68–13, eight games ahead of Boston, which remained a brilliant team at 60–21. We were 28–2 at home, losing only to Boston twice. We averaged 125 points a game and won by an average margin of 10 points. No team would average that many points again until the run-and-gun Denver teams of Doug Moe in the early 1980s, and they gave up more points than they scored. We were a devastating offensive team and a dominant defensive team. Wilt led the league in field-goal percentage and rebounding, and he was third in scoring and assists. Hal Greer averaged 22 points, I averaged 19, and Cunningham 18. We shot 48 percent from the field as a team, which was 4 percent higher than any NBA team had ever shot over an entire season.

I'm convinced that the 1966–67 76ers would be a dominant team in the NBA today, more than twenty-five years later. With Wilt, Luke Jackson, and me, we would still have a size advantage over other teams. We had a great sixth man in athletic Billy Cunningham. Our guards Greer and Jones could run the break as well as shoot from deep. Larry Costello and Dave Gambee were great veteran subs who could change the complexion of any game. Matty Guokas and Bill Melchionni were heady backcourt youngsters. Finally, Alex Hannum was as resourceful and tough a coach as the NBA has ever seen, a man's man and a player's coach.

We really let down on a late season western swing and lost in San Diego, Phoenix, and Los Angeles. Alex was livid at halftime in our final game in San Francisco and got into a screaming match with players that we were afraid would come to blows. Fortunately, it didn't happen, but when we got back to Philly, we had lost our momentum and even practices didn't revive it. Alex was a maniac because he knew we'd been coasting, and he was determined there would be no play-off let down. We'd done too much partying in San Diego and Tijuana. Now it was time to get back to work, but I wasn't sure we hadn't forgotten how.

Just before the play-offs, the NBA Players' Association demanded a six hundred dollar pension per month for ten-year men, resulting in Commissioner Kennedy's threat to cancel the play-offs, a standard ploy for any sports mogul when players get uppity. By March 15, the players and owners had agreed "in principle" to the agreement. Irv Kosloff sounded off that he had decided to fire Dolph Schayes even before last year's play-offs, that letdowns within games against contending teams had led to the decision. So we promptly went out and lost our home opener against Cincinnati. Two minutes into the opening period, referee Earl Strom had to warn Hannum and the Royals coach Jack McMahon to cut out the rough stuff. Fans pelted Strom with paper and orange-juice cartons. Meanwhile, in the other first-round play-off series, the Celtics began their quest for their ninth title in a row by whipping the Knicks by 30 points. Reality was upon us. Were we on the verge of blowing our chance at a championship after our great season? We woke up and swept the last three games from the Royals to advance and meet Boston.

NBA fans concentrated on the battle between Wilt and Russell, but every second in the Boston-Philadelphia matchups there was much more going on. Every big game has many little games within it. Sanders and I dueled for years, scrapping for position at both ends of the court. He would drape himself on me like a spider. All elbows, knees, and sharp angles, he was very difficult to shake. Luke Jackson could just bowl over Bailey Howell. We had a huge advantage there. K. C. Jones tried to slow Greer down and make him give up the ball. K. C. was squat and built like a football halfback but could move laterally so well. Two wild cards were Wali Jones and Sam Jones. If either shot the lights out, the other team was in trouble. They were streak shooters: Sam a smooth, quiet assassin; Wali a pumping pinwheel, legs and arms flying out at odd angles. Then there were perhaps the best sixth men in the history of the game, Cunningham and

Havlicek, relentless runners and scorers who could change a game just by checking in.

You play hundreds and hundreds of games in your career from playground ball on up, but there is nothing like the preparation for a crucial game at any level of competition. Every moment before the game is charged with one emotion or another. In the pros the strategy has all been worked out in practice or from looking at films and reviewing scouting reports and tendencies. Mentally you try to image the times you've played your opponent in the past. You can't quite bring him into focus until you really body up against him after the game begins, but you try.

Then you get the coach's last speech in the locker room, which can be very rah-rah or low-key, depending on the coach. The desired result is the same however: to break the last huddle in the locker room together high and ready to do what it takes. There's always a dead zone as you make your way out of the locker room and up through the labyrinth of tunnels and corridors threading between the stands.

You burst into the light and the low hum of the rapidly filling arena and begin to warm up. The crowd starts to get into it, shouting encouragement or insults at the home and road teams. Either way your adrenaline really begins to pump and build as you loosen up, dunk the ball, drop some long shots, feel the excitement amongst your own teammates. I never even noticed the opposing team at this point. It's as if you were in your own pressure cooker with the steam rising.

We are down there on a court which, even in a huge stadium with four or five decks and twenty thousand people, looks like an ordinary basketball court, the same court that you've been playing on since you were a kid. The rim is round, the net is hung, the floor is marked. The other nine guys are there. It's surprising how, when you need to, you can either block the fans out or use them to get you up. Sometimes I felt as if they were painted faces in immovable chairs, like the background in a painting, and we on the court were the graceful or powerful brush strokes filling in the foreground figures. At other times, the fans were very alive, like sections of a loosely connected, segmented snake, all hums and anticipation.

A horn sounds taking you back to the bench for the national anthem, the shedding of warm-up suits, the little rituals of preparation that players go through. Some players slap everyone's hand, worried that if they miss one guy, it could be bad luck. Others insist on standing in the same place in line during the national anthem or sitting on the same seat on the bench. The anthem itself, even though you've heard it a thousand times, puts you in a martial mood, preparing you to go to war against the enemy. The only thing you can think of at this point is attack.

The coach's final words are few but you break the huddle as the crowd anticipates the battle. Only then did I ever allow myself a look at an opposing team such as the Celtics. The funny thing was that I would only see the uniform—Celtics green or some other color. I would stare right through their chests until the opening tip, never acknowledging my opponent except as the enemy.

Satch Sanders of the Celtics was my arch rival. I was the country boy, he was the city boy from New York. Later on, when I got to know him, I found him a wonderful person. When I was inside an arena and on the court, everyone on the other team was anonymous and to be destroyed. It didn't matter if we had gone to high school or grade school together, whether we'd shared good times in the off-season, whether we'd known an opponent's family. We didn't even recognize that person for forty-eight minutes. That's the definition of a professional athlete. Today you see a much more clubby, chummy atmosphere. Guys play golf together, organize benefit games in the off-season. Even all the trash talking on the court makes it seem as if there's more personal communication between players. They play just as hard, but the socialization seems very different to me.

On April Fools' Day 1967, we whipped the Celtics, winning the opener of our series 127–113. Greer had 39 points, and Wilt had a quadruple double before any of us had ever heard of such things (24 points, 32 rebounds, 13 assists, and 12 blocked shots). I almost got into a fight with wide Wayne Embry. Wali hooked up with Larry Siegfried. About midway in quarter one, I was faking Bill Russell on the baseline and drove my shoulder deep into his chest. He almost collapsed on the court with his breath knocked out of him. I was called for charging on the play and left him curled like a pretzel. He staggered to the bench and vomited into a towel. He came back in the second quarter, but Wilt dominated him.

Game two was at our old nightmare arena, Boston Garden. We won 107–102, the first victory for our team in a postseason game in Boston since 1960. I led all scorers with 23 points. This great, proud, veteran Boston team seemed finally to have met its match. Back in Philadelphia for game three we had a record thirteen thousand fans in old Convention Hall, and they roared as if they were cheering all of the Philly Big Five college teams at once. Wali Jones was down with the flu but got out of a bed to play. Wilt pulled down 41 rebounds. I'd never seen Russell work any harder, but nothing was clicking for Boston. Our club was younger and stronger, and we knew it.

The cool, pressure-tested Celtics were beginning to unravel. Red Auerbach tried to bait us and manipulate the referees by complaining we called "fake" injury time-outs. He called our tactics a "disgrace" and "bush league." Since Commissioner Kennedy practically worked out of Red's office, it didn't surprise us when our trainer, Al Domenico, was summoned to meet Kennedy before Sunday's game three in Boston to discuss the injury issue. Wilt and I agreed this game was one of the fastest-paced we'd ever played. My legs cramped, and I needed dextrose tablets and massage to keep going. Wali Jones was indeed "Wally Wonder" as he outplayed the two other Jones boys, Sam and K. C., all by himself. Red wasn't about to let the Celtics die gracefully. He growled and fumed, "Just wait until they win eight years in a row. Then we'll talk." Sam Jones said that he'd never seen Wilt play so damn hard, that he was everywhere.

Boston salvaged some respect by winning game four in Boston 121–117. We had come up there in bad physical shape. Wilt had inflamed knee-joint capsules and couldn't walk up or down stairs without going sideways. Wali had tonsillitis, and Hal appeared to have caught it, too. Our old friends, the Garden fans, greeted us in their usual fashion, pelting us with eggs and coins when we ran on and off the court to the dressing room. It was an all-out barrage. With only twenty seconds left, we had a general brawl triggered when Matty Guokas fouled Sam Jones hard. Wilt pulled Sam off Matty; then Embry pulled Wilt off Sam. Havlicek and Sam had shot brilliantly with 31 and 32 points respectively. Just another Boston game. But we weren't discouraged. We'd come back several times in this game and were still up 3–1 and going home for the clincher.

Tuesday, April 12, 1967, was *the* night. Alex told us, "There's only one thing I'd rather do than win the series in Boston and that's win it in Philadelphia." Alex was coming full circle in his battles with the Celtics. As a young player-coach with the St. Louis Hawks, he had battled the Celtics in 1956–57, meeting them in the most exciting NBA final series of all time. Bill Russell was capping his rookie year, changing defense in the NBA forever with his shot blocking. The Hawks were led by the great forward Bob Pettit. Four of the seven games were decided by two points and the seventh game went into a second overtime period in Boston. So many Hawks fouled out that Alex had no one left to put in but himself. With the score 125–123 in Boston's favor and few seconds on the clock, Alex threw a three-quarter length-of-the-court inbounds pass to Pettit, who caught it and went up for a jump shot that rolled around the rim and out. Boston had won its first championship. That game was a nationally televised Saturday afternoon affair and jumped the NBA toward major-league status.

Here we were, a decade later with Alex bringing us home to finally topple the dynasty that had started with that Hawk loss. Philadelphia was ready. Even the standing-room tickets were sold out by early Monday morning. As a team, we were very tired but ready. I'd played forty minutes per game in the first four games. Wilt was averaging 20 points, 30 rebounds, and 9 assists. Boston broke from the gate like greyhounds and led 8–0 and 37–26 after one quarter. Russell out-rebounded Wilt 10–3 in the opening period, but for the rest of the game, Wilt out-rebounded him 33–11.

We spotted the Celtics a 16-point lead in the second quarter but then roared back. Wilt and I came alive offensively and sent Bailey Howell and Russell to the bench with three fouls each. We shaved the lead to 70–65 at the half. Deep into the third quarter I played the best minutes I'd ever played in a Boston series. I felt as if I could do anything, move to the ball, take my man, see the court. With about four minutes left in the third quarter, I hooked one in over Don Nelson to give us a lead we never relinquished.

Then came the game's most spectacular play. Luke Jackson leaped like a lion to block a Bailey Howell shot at the top of the circle, then raced down the loose ball and rumbled in for a dunk that almost tore down the rafters of the old hall. The applause was deafening, and we were up 75–72. When Wali Jones made eight baskets in the last six minutes of the third quarter, we pulled ahead 100–94. Alex noticed the older Celtics were tiring, so he put in Guokas and Cunningham to push the ball. We ran the Celtics into the ground with our speed, building the lead to 15 points. With about five minutes left, I hit a 20-foot jumper to give us a 20-point lead and raced back up the court waving my arms. I'm not sure I ever got that excited again on a court. It certainly turned on the fans once more. With three minutes to go, a fan lit a ridiculously long cigar mocking Auerbach's victory stogies over all the years.

I was happy for Hal Greer, who had spent a decade chasing this moment. Wilt was vindicated finally as a player who could win the big game. We simply poured it on. We outscored the Celtics 97–57 over the last thirty minutes of the game. Alex had helped us put everything together and had pushed the 76ers over the final hurdle that took us to the 1966–67 championship series.

After taking the Eastern Division series from our Boston nemesis, the NBA finals in 1966–67 were almost an anticlimax.

For Alex, it meant coming up against the team he had coached the year before. The San Francisco Warriors were led by the center Nate Thurmond, who always gave Wilt a run and by the mercurial Rick Barry, in his second year already the most dangerous scoring machine in basketball. We had to focus hard after the euphoria of our victory over Boston and almost let game one get away from us. We prevailed in overtime, 141–135, with Wilt and Nate each playing fifty-three minutes in the pivot. The big controversy came late in regulation time with the score tied. Barry drove to the right baseline against me and threw a backward pass to Thurmond, whose last-second lay-up was blocked by Wilt. The Warriors screamed, "Foul!" but we went into overtime for the win. We won game two easily but lost game three at the Cow Palace in San Francisco when Barry scored 55 points. He shot 22–48 from the field, and his arm was so tired he couldn't lift it for a last foul shot. I scored 33 points and Hal 38 to win game four in San Francisco.

We hoped to win the title in game five on Sunday, April 23, in Philadelphia, but we were humbled 117–109 when we blew a 13-point lead. In the fourth quarter we scored all of 13 points and committed 9 turnovers. The papers began to work us over about not getting the ball into Wilt, but we'd won all year with the outside game. Besides, Wilt's foul shooting was at a low ebb, and he'd played himself ragged in the Boston series. Barry was pouting every time Bill Sharman lifted him from the Warrior lineup. So it was back to San Francisco for game six. We hadn't wanted to leave our fans without the title, but we dug our own hole.

Game six came down to me on the foul line with two seconds to go to seal an NBA World Championship. The first quarter of game six had been an 800-meter race, which ended with us ahead 43–41. The game seesawed at this fierce clip. Thurmond was playing brilliant defense against Wilt. We were down by 12 points late in the third quarter, but Wali bailed us out with 16 points in that period. Alex was leaping up, protesting call after call to try to get the referees to call more fouls on Thurmond. We were up 123–122 with four seconds left when the season narrowed to a jump ball between Luke Jackson and Tom Meschery near the Warriors' basket. The ball was tipped to me, and I was fouled by Thurmond. We took the long walk to the other end of the court. I saw before me the culmination of every player's dream. You're standing alone with everything on the line, with all eyes on you. I made both shots, and our long brilliant season had ended. We were the champions!

Alex went around the roaring locker room shaking everyone's hand, saying "We made it, baby. We made it!" He even kissed Hal Greer on top of his shaved head. Hal didn't stop dancing until hours later. Wilt was his old self, speculating to reporters for the umpteenth time that he might quit basketball, this time to fight Muhammad Ali or challenge Craig Breedlove in his new speedboat. Alex gave Wilt the game ball, telling him that he'd given of himself all year so we could all get to this moment. Wilt was still carrying the game ball the next day at the airport in Philadelphia and would present it to Claire Richman, Ike's widow. We moved our party operations in San Francisco to Nate Thurmond's restaurant, where we continued far into the night. Alex told the press that we were perhaps the greatest team ever assembled, and Bill Sharman, a proud old Celtic, allowed that Alex might be right. Fred Schaus, the veteran Laker coach, said that this final game was the greatest basketball game he had ever seen.

The night in San Francisco ended with me at dawn on the balcony of my room in the Jack Tarr Hotel in San Francisco. I could hear a woman's cries of pleasure coming from the room of a teammate. But I felt something both magic and ominous about San Francisco at 6 A.M. I looked out at the sun rising above San Francisco Bay and enjoyed a peace we all should feel more often in our lives. The city looked beautiful, like a Mediterranean town of white villas tucked into the hillsides. Yet the contradictions in the view were clear. On one side of me was the Golden Gate Bridge. I could also make out the penitentiary hulking there on Alcatraz in the morning fog. I knew San Quentin was to the north in Marin County.

From this glorious city you could see two of America's most famous prisons, incarcerating thousands of young black men who'd dreamed of basketball as their savior. I remembered the two days I'd spent in jail in Benton Harbor. I'd been so lucky. I'd worked so hard; yet, it wasn't difficult to imagine my life having taken a different twist and my having wound up in jail. Great athletes populate our prisons, many as good or better than the players who've made it in professional sports. But having real chances and avoiding the snares were not their destinies.

To counter the depression I felt, I recalled all my winning moments from Benton Harbor through Bradley and knew that the 76ers' championship was the sweetest, the best. I knew if I could finally drop off to sleep for a few hours that it would be untroubled and secure. Off the court the world held, as it always did, too many contradictions for me. There was, quite simply, nothing left for me to prove on the court.

12.
Setting Priorities

The 1960s were the most interesting period in my lifetime. During those turbulent times we all learned a lot about ourselves as Americans, both black and white. You didn't need a Ph.D. to be educated to American realities. You could grow up on the streets, go to Vietnam, get your head busted in a riot, demonstrate in the South against Bull Connor, or protest against the war on college campuses. Young black people today may have more opportunities than most of us did in 1960, but they also have more despair. What we had back then was more suppressed anger coupled with a tremendous sense of hope.

The 76ers' 1967 NBA championship came in the middle of a very volatile era. America was in the middle of a Civil Rights revolution as well as a war in Vietnam. Black groups in the revolutionary struggle began to approach black athletes for assistance because we were public figures who could influence the public and because we had money to support the movement. Many black athletes adopted the Black Muslim faith, and many more considered the idea.

Both whites and blacks became suspicious of the Nation of Islam's power to organize the black working class and the poor. Civil Rights leaders began to speak against the Nation: Roy Wilkins on behalf of the NAACP, James Farmer speaking for the Congress on Racial Equality (CORE). Farmer charged that "the Nation is utterly impractical and dangerous." He added that, in his opinion, the Black Muslims aided and abetted segregation. Malcolm X responded that "an integrated cup of coffee is not sufficient for 300 years of segregation in America." What was needed was human dignity, he preached, not integration.

Malcolm's rhetoric was hypnotic. I saw him only once and that was in Harlem by chance in the early 1960s when he was surrounded by Black Muslim guards who, frankly, were pretty scary. Malcolm was a revolutionary teacher with an oppressed and sordid past. He'd learned the value of education and given himself one in the streets, in prison, in the movement, from books. Malcolm became too hot for the Black Muslims, who put him under wraps. But I liked his ability to keep changing and growing.

I was seriously considering adopting a Muslim name and perhaps participating in the movement. I was urged to attend a meeting at Muslim Mosque 5 in north Philadelphia to speak about racism in sports and the exploitation of the black athlete and to attend the rest of the meeting as an observer.

All the men were soberly dressed in conservative black suits. The women wore long, dignified dresses. I was introduced to tremendous applause and gave my talk. I thanked them for the invitation, saying that I was personally investigating the philosophy of the Muslim movement and hoping to learn more. At the close of the meeting, one of the men was further explaining some points of Muslim doctrine to me and he said, "Brother, one of the advantages of this organization is that you are allowed to have more than one wife." He thought he was describing a selling point to me, but his remark really put me off. How could I be part of such a faith when I was raised by a woman who struggled to raise ten children by herself? I knew too much about husbands who abused wives, about fathers who wanted their children to be beasts of burden on the farm. I couldn't see how a man, any man, who had to struggle in this society could provide for many wives and many children. What would they take from him? What would he have to give?

So that night, even though I did agree with a lot of what the Muslims had to say, I decided I could not join them and still keep faith with what I knew in my heart about how my mother had lived her life. The author Richard Wright said, after a long alliance with the Communist party, that in the end he couldn't agree with their inhumanity, that in principle the justice they advocated was compelling to him, but that there were too many inconsistencies and too much propaganda and that they used black people for their own ends. He wrote, "I'll be for them, even though they're not for me." That about summed up my view of the Black Muslims.

I was also approached by the Black Panther party. We talked, and I decided once again that I couldn't afford to become an active, visible part of a radical political organization. I did agree to help them with donations for some of their community service programs that provided meals and services for kids in the ghetto, causes I considered extremely worthwhile. I couldn't slight these programs simply because I disagreed politically with the Panthers' threats of violence. But I was afraid to come out in public as a supporter.

Like most public figures who have experienced racism in their lives, I found that my insecurities about what I had achieved and the tenuous nature of my place in society wouldn't allow me to risk everything in a public forum. I think many middle- and upper-middle-class blacks are paralyzed in a curious fashion. We often give money anonymously to a host of causes. On one hand, we don't want to publicly support radical political groups for fear of losing whatever we've attained. On the other hand, we are loathe to criticize spokespeople whom we *know* speak for us, whom we see fighting back and naming all the evils that we curse in private.

My political activity was predictably mainstream. In 1968, I worked to elect Hubert Humphrey in his race against Richard Nixon. Irv Kosloff was scheduled to go to Washington, D.C., with some business associates to meet Humphrey, but he became ill and asked me to go in his place. To me, this was quite an honor. I flew to Washington to meet with Humphrey and his wife in their home at the Watergate Apartments complex. I sensed the power that one man might have in his grasp. Because of my association with Humphrey, my name was added to an FBI watch list.

I campaigned with Humphrey up and down the east coast in Philadelphia, Maryland, Washington, D.C., upstate New York, and in parts of Virginia and West Virginia. We rode in a campaign bus with press, financial contributors, and staff members. After Humphrey gave his talk, we would urge people to get out the vote. It was quite an experience speaking to groups of black college and high school kids. I was criticized by friends in more radical organizations for giving Humphrey time I should have given black politicians. One night in New York, when I was getting on the bus for the next stop, a black guy shouted at me, "Hey, brother, which way is up," meaning he had his suspicions about my priorities and wanted to know why I was spending time with a white politician. I found Humphrey a very fine man and regret that he didn't win the election.

That same campaign year I was speaking for David Berger in north Philadelphia when he was running for district attorney against Arlen Specter when a black woman stood up and asked, "What the fuck you doin' up here, Chet?" Her angry question burned right through me. She was absolutely right from her point of view. I told her I couldn't tell people how to vote or what to do, but I hoped that somehow I could help make a difference. That's what I said up front. But I began to suspect I might be turning into one of those celebrities who back politicians offering nothing but promises. I soon left Berger's campaign, having had enough politics for a while.

On the court the 1967–68 regular season was more of the same success for us. We won our third straight Eastern Division title by eight games over Boston with a 62–20 record. We were bounced around playing in different "home" arenas after the brand-new Spectrum's roof partially blew off on February 17. The only tension during the season was about Alex Hannum and whether he would return in 1968–69. Alex had a construction business he ran on the West Coast, and Kosloff wanted him to be more of a presence during the off-season. If Alex left, the whole house of cards might come tumbling down because Wilt was telling everyone he was getting too old to teach a new coach his old tricks.

We started the play-off round by splitting two games with the young New York Knicks and then winning game three 138–132 in double overtime. But a more disastrous victory could not be imagined. Billy Cunningham broke his right wrist crashing into Phil Jackson on the first play in overtime. He was gone for the year. Luke Jackson partially tore a hamstring and limped through the rest of the play-offs. All our vaunted depth was gone, not to mention our complete package of speed plus power. We were suddenly a very mortal, very vulnerable team. And Boston, under player-coach Bill Russell, was hungry for revenge. We took a 3–2 lead in the Knick series on hot shooting by Wali Jones, who played with a partially torn right-knee ligament, and gutty relief work by veteran forward Johnny Green.

But there was a spookiness in the air that Sunday that had nothing to do with basketball. That night, March 31, 1968, President Johnson told a stunned nation that he would not seek reelection in November but would devote all his time to ending the Vietnam War. He also announced that he was sending 13,000 more troops there, bringing the number of American soldiers in Vietnam to 549,000. These numbers were unreal. I always felt a sense of shame that so many young men, black and white, were risking their lives while I was playing a kid's game and acclaimed a hero. I thought of my brother James wounded at Guam in World War II and my brother Fred who had served in Korea.

The political activity during February and March of 1968

had heated up with primary challenges to Johnson by Senator Eugene McCarthy of Minnesota and a belated entry by Robert Kennedy into the presidential sweepstakes. What would happen now was anyone's guess with Johnson cutting out.

A lesser-known event on that Sunday, March 31, was a speech that Martin Luther King, Jr., gave in Washington's National Cathedral, where he predicted a right-wing fascist state in this country by 1970 if racial justice was not secured and Congress did not do more for the poor. Dr. King vowed that he would go ahead with a poor people's crusade in the nation's capital, bringing thousands of destitute persons to camp out for weeks and possibly months.

Dr. King was speaking specifically in the context of the rioting in Memphis, Tennessee, where a sixteen-year-old black boy, Larry Payne, had been killed by a white policeman on the preceding Thursday night. Dr. King had been in Memphis at the time organizing support for the black sanitation workers' strike against that city. He finished his Sunday sermon by announcing he would return to Memphis for the funeral of the dead boy.

On Monday, April 1, Robert Kennedy began a two-day campaign tour in the Philadelphia area. He was mobbed by enthusiastic crowds. Some of the frenzy that was to come in the last few months of Kennedy's campaign was already in evidence. More than nine thousand students jammed the Palestra to hear him criticize the bombing in North Vietnam above the demilitarized zone. People just seemed to want to touch him. They grabbed at his outstretched hands, his clothes. One woman escaped with his shoe. On Tuesday, two days after Johnson, in effect, abdicated, Eugene McCarthy won the Wisconsin Democratic primary with 56 percent of the vote.

That same Tuesday night we finally beat back the Knicks for good, 113–97, in game six in Madison Square Garden. Our first game with Boston was scheduled for Friday night, April 5, at the Spectrum, where we would go after our second straight Eastern Division championship. The headlines on Thursday, April 4, 1968, were all about Kennedy's and McCarthy's races for the presidential nomination or about the fact that in Vietnam, American and United Nations troops had pushed within three miles of the besieged marine fortress at Khe Sanh.

Meanwhile, a federal judge had issued an order barring Dr. King from holding a massive march in Memphis, but King said he would go ahead with the march. Back in Memphis for the funeral of Larry Payne, Dr. King came out of his motel room about six o'clock central time on Thursday evening and leaned over the railing of the second-floor balcony to talk to Jesse Jackson and Andrew Young down below in the parking lot. He wanted to make sure that "Precious Lord, Take My Hand" would be played at a protest meeting that night. There was to be no later for Dr. King. The shots rang out and he was dead.

I always find it easier to listen to the radio than to watch television. I can concentrate better when I try to visualize pictures in my mind. But I didn't want to visualize Dr. King splayed on that motel balcony, with all the commotion and fury swirling around him. Dr. King himself had talked candidly about his chances of living out his years. He'd been stabbed in Harlem, stoned in Chicago, and threatened in Selma and a host of other towns. It seemed to me that we were getting all too used to assassination as another American sport. We were beginning to recognize its moves, how the grief would be organized, how commissions would be formed, editorials written, investigations started. John Kennedy, Medgar Evers, Malcolm X, now Dr. King, and more to come. I sat stunned, listening to various commentators describe what had happened in Memphis, and for once I didn't want the pictures to come into my mind.

What did float back was a memory from when I was six or seven years old. I was riding in the back of my father's old truck on a family trip to Memphis. Going there was like going to another, larger world of sounds, sights, and danger. I remember barely eluding an oncoming car when I crossed the street against a red light while running back to my father's parked truck. I got a good scolding and scared everyone to death, but I'd never even seen a traffic light before and didn't know what the red and green lights meant. Bethlehem, Mississippi, had no stop lights, just corners and bends in the road.

Still held by that memory, I heard the phone ring. It was my friend Barbara. Tonight we talked about sadness and anger, how the two emotions go together and what could come out of them. I think I finally got to sleep around three in the morning. Playing the Celtics on Friday night was the farthest thing from my mind.

When I woke up on Friday morning, I was stung to realize I hadn't been dreaming, that Dr. King was really dead. I hung around my apartment, still absorbing the shock. No one connected with the 76ers called me about the game that night. I did call Hal Greer, but he knew as little as I did. On my way to the Spectrum that afternoon, a thick fog engulfed the streets, slowing traffic to a crawl. Marvin Gaye was singing on the radio about saving children, about who really cares enough to do so. I suppose that's what Dr. King was thinking about in Memphis when he took a hand in the garbage workers' strike. Save the children by allowing their families to put enough food on the table.

Usually when I got to an arena for a game, I was all business, zeroed in, focused. But that Friday afternoon at the Spectrum, I felt vague and purposeless, disconnected from everyone. I walked down the runway into the empty stadium and thought to myself, wouldn't it be wonderful if nobody showed up tonight? No players, no fans. Just a spontaneous honoring of Dr. King. Each person deciding in his own heart to honor Dr. King's memory.

All day long I'd been wondering what my teammates would say about the game and how the Celtics would feel. It turned out the Celtics had met with Auerbach and Russell in Boston before coming down to Philly, and after much frank discussion, they had agreed to play. So they arrived in grief but united and ready to go. The 76ers came straggling in. We never called a meeting although Wilt and Russell talked informally sometime Friday afternoon. Thus, late in the afternoon, when both teams finally got together to talk it over, the Celtics had a position (let's play) whereas the 76ers had mostly unfocused feelings.

I will never forget the Celtics' Bailey Howell, a white veteran from Mississippi State, asking, "Who was Martin Luther King? He wasn't president, you know? Why was he so important that we should cancel the game?"

Dr. King wasn't president, but I felt that he was my voice and the voice of my people in this country. Dr. King had fought for me as a person, for my rights, my worth. He fought to bring humanity and dignity to me and to all people. When the majority of the Celtics and 76ers voted to go along with what the owners and fans wanted—to play this game—I went along and participated against my will in the game. But I wanted to take Bailey Howell to school and show him a thing or two. If I had chosen not to play, I would have been in violation of my contract and would have been stepping over the boundaries of my role.

Before the game, Wilt closed the dressing-room door so we could have a ballot. But now it was too late to have our say. To vote against playing with the fans already in the Spectrum might have triggered a riot. I didn't think this game would get our minds off the tragedy of Dr. King's death, but I didn't want to take a chance on contributing to more rioting by not playing, by turning out thousands of disgruntled fans into the streets of Philadelphia.

When the 76ers took their vote, Wilt and Wali Jones voted against playing. Greer said he didn't want to play either but felt that it was too late to call the game off. I abstained. I couldn't bring myself to participate in this dreary charade. Everyone knew where I stood. We voted 7–2 to play, but I'm convinced if we'd met earlier in the day and voted then, the results might have been reversed. At about 2:30 P.M. Wilt had told general manager Jack Ramsay that he didn't want to play, and Ramsay had invoked contracts, fan safety, the city's volatile mood. As far as I was concerned, it was a done deal. The owners wanted us to play, and so we would. They maneuvered us into an untenable position, holding off the vote until there was no choice as far as I was concerned. No one wanted another riot to break out if the game was canceled. I was trying to balance my social conscience with my job as a professional and the reality of thousands of people waiting for a game that night. It's true that you only have split seconds to make your choice in a situation like that, one that might stay with you for decades. We got ready to play.

At game time, the locker room remained silent and gloomy. Wilt wasn't feasting on fried chicken. Wali wasn't playing his music. I walked out of the dressing room staring straight ahead but seeing nothing, not the crowd, not the court. As we approached the floor, the fans came to their feet and gave us a standing ovation, for what I don't know. Probably, they were cheering us for making the decision to play. We went through all the usual warm-ups. A moment of silent prayer was then offered for Dr. King. Such token moments are frequent before games and have become mere formalities. The "silence" can be for anyone and anything from honoring a dead former player to reverence for a military invasion. What could be the appropriate prayer for the dead dream of millions of people? Maybe silence was appropriate because I felt damned sure that black people in this country had lost their truest voice.

During the national anthem Wali sprinted off to the bathroom as he usually did. As usual, I stood there with bowed head. Alex Hannum always said I took Dr. King's death harder than anyone, but there I was, going ahead with business as usual. I wish I could have done something symbolic right then and there to signify both my freedom and the sorrow of other black people. Only a few months later, Tommie Smith and John Carlos would stun and anger America at the Mexico City Olympics when they stood, each with a black-gloved fist clenched and raised high, their heads bowed on the victory stand after the 200-meter race. I admired them for that. They found a beautiful and dignified way to express their anger and pride. I did not.

***

The 76ers were never really in that game on Friday night. Our indecision whether to play was reflected on the court. The Celtics won 127–118. Neither team had the intensity you expect in a Boston-Philadelphia game. My concentration was so off that I made only 9 of 20 foul shots though I scored 31 points.

The NBA finally got its act together after Friday night and canceled all the Sunday play-off games. Of course, that was after the White House declared Sunday a national day of mourning for Dr. King. After our Friday loss, I bought a bottle of wine and went to see my friend, Laine Howell, an offensive lineman for the Eagles. We sat up most of the night watching television and staring sadly at pictures of the riots from Washington, north Philadelphia, Detroit, and Chicago. So much footage of black rage. We kept going over old familiar ground. Why weren't we as professional athletes able to speak our minds about politics or race? Were athletes prohibited from being complete citizens? Were all athletes in a sense "black" because, like blacks, athletes couldn't speak up?

I suppose all people at some point in their lives gauge how honest or outspoken they can be in terms of their jobs and security. But athletes are hostages of a system that wants to hear nothing from them except product endorsement. In sports a player has to remain almost neutral, become a nonperson, so that *all* the fans can identify with him. For example, it will be interesting to see if Michael Jordan will become more his father's son and the brother of so many dead black men, women, and children, and speak out against handguns.

Athletes have a second problem. If they come out and strongly support a Ross Perot or a Jesse Jackson or a Louis Farrakhan, the American people will take sides about the athletes *themselves*. More important owners and management, companies represented by pro athletes would begin to quake and check their sales figures. Even back in 1968, we wondered if the professional game was worth compromising our personal commitments. As athletes, we were perhaps the most famous group of black people in America. But we were entertainers and supposed to stay in our place. I felt as if I'd already been doing that all my life.

The helpless rage I felt after Dr. King's death still deeply affects me. I was unable to stop a basketball game from being played on a night when black America was mourning and screaming in pain.

In April 1968, I told a *Philadelphia Inquirer* reporter I would like to have seen the Eastern Division championship games postponed, especially the first one. I said, "I've been in a state of shock. I didn't sleep last night. Usually, before a Boston game, I get myself up for the game, but when I heard that Dr. King had been shot, I forgot all about the game. It just doesn't seem important to me anymore." Wilt said, "I personally would not like to play tonight. But I can only go along with what the majority of the team feels."

A few weeks before, Wali Jones and I had signed a petition to prevent South African Airlines from landing at Kennedy Airport. Harvey Pollack, the 76ers' publicity director, asked if we had actually signed it and was obviously distressed when we answered yes. That's why I think the owners were wary about a *real* vote being taken on whether to play the Friday night game or not. Nothing scared team owners more than the sense that their players were becoming political. This was the owners' nightmare in the 1960s. As far as they were concerned, we were paid good money to keep our mouths shut.

On Friday, April 5, the 76ers fell apart on the court, and then all weekend we sat watching America come apart. Cities that hadn't burned in 1964, 1965, and 1967 went up in flames in 1968. Philadelphia stayed relatively calm after Mayor Tate and Police Chief Rizzo clamped down a "state of limited emergency" order, much as they had done in July 1967, closing all the bars and state liquor stores, banning groups of more than twelve people except at bus and train stations or at recreational events. Weddings had to be canceled, as did funeral services. Countless minor incidents, threats, flash points flared up, but North Philadelphia remained quiet, mostly sustaining only shattered display windows. Police cars moved slowly through the area. Palm Sunday weekend, the media focused on the destruction of property in American cities, backed by symbolic shots of Washington, D.C., neighborhoods in flames within sight of the White House or soldiers with rifles on the steps of the Capitol Building: "Rioting Stuns Washington. . . . GI's in Action. . . . Negro Sections Ablaze." The way I saw it, the media, as usual, quickly transformed black people into the problem. Here we were, victims mourning Dr. King's death, but in short order, we were seen as a threat to the very survival of the nation's order, an order that excluded us.

Sunday, the national day of mourning for Dr. King, was also Palm Sunday and the beginning of Easter week. With all the NBA play-off games canceled, the papers replaced box scores of sporting events with the day's riot statistics, city by city, how many dead, wounded, arrested, how many troops brought in, how many millions of dollars in damages. Major-league baseball canceled openers on Monday and Tuesday although the Dodgers argued to play the Phillies Tuesday night since Dr. King would already be in the ground. Bill White, later to become the first black National League president but then a first baseman for the Phillies, was aghast. "This from the team of Jackie Robinson!" he declared. When the Phillies owner Bob Carpenter told the National League the Phillies would forfeit rather than play, the Dodgers caved in.

Wilt and Russell flew to Atlanta for the funeral. Robert Kennedy chartered a plane to bring Dr. King's body back to his home state of Georgia. On Monday a mule-drawn wagon carried the body through the streets of Atlanta. Dr. King was laid to rest on Tuesday. In Philadelphia, I remember Mayor Tate closing all city services for the funeral, canceling trash collection for that day. To think that all this violence and tragedy had begun with the sanitation workers' strike in Memphis.

My teammates and I were still bitter about having played on Friday night, angry that the league had not canceled the play-off openers. Five years before, Pete Rozelle didn't call off the NFL schedule for Sunday, November 24, 1963, two days after President Kennedy was assassinated. The nation was still in shock and the president of the United States had not yet been buried, but the games went on. These contests weren't televised because the networks recognized they had a bigger story that Sunday than sports: murder itself. Try imagining the NFL today carrying on and playing games without network approval.

Viewers found a new spectator sport on television on that Sunday in 1963. After hours of reviewing the assassination of the president, the audience got to see Lee Harvey Oswald shot to death *live* as he was taken through a basement entrance in the Dallas jail. Networks showed the scene over and over again in one of the first extended uses of the instant replay, an invention that ABC had begun using on football telecasts in 1961. So instant replay, the very tool that now sells the NBA as a group of highfliers who stay up forever in a ballet of gravity-defying beauty, was used repeatedly in a way that showed how low a nation could sink.

Our play-off series resumed in Boston on Wednesday, April 10. The first-game loss seemed a distant memory. Again, most of us had a hard time gearing up for this game, drained as we were from the emotional events of the last week. Wilt and Russell were wiped out from attending the funeral the day before and scored 15 and 11 points, but Melchionni, Guokas, and Green carried the 76ers to a 115–106 victory. Back in Philadelphia on Good Friday evening, we won game three 121–114, but Wilt tore a calf muscle and was limping badly.

On Good Friday, three days after the King funeral, a broad Civil Rights bill on housing discrimination passed the House of Representatives. That was the only good news. Philadelphia still had extra police shifts. You could see them everywhere. I saw no signs of a resurrection at the end of this Holy Week.

We took the next two games in the play-offs, for three straight wins, taking what seemed like a commanding 3–1 lead.

The newspapers insisted the Celtics were as good as dead, but we didn't believe it. We were severely hampered by the loss of Luke Jackson and Billy Cunningham in the series. They represented a lot of our diversified firepower, and their absence put much more pressure on the remaining shooters, Hal, Wali, and me. But Wilt and Wali were limping, and I had a nagging groin pull. With a diminished bench, gimpy starters, and our general exhaustion, it was as if the 3–1 lead in games was not really ours.

Sure enough, Boston's tired old men came snarling back Monday night in Philadelphia in a display of guts. We were equally amazing in our futility, never truly in the fifth game, losing 122–104. I shot 3–14, Wali 2–10, and Hal 6–20. We made only 2 of 20 shots in the first ten minutes of the fourth quarter. It was a ridiculous collapse. Somehow, we never got our shooting touch back. Boston took game six at home 114–106, then beat us in a seventh game in the Spectrum 100–96.

Both teams in the final game were weird, almost spasmodic. It felt as if we were mechanical toys in slow motion. Events, injuries, and loss of purpose had caught up with us. We could muster only 40 first-half points on our home court. Wilt got 34 rebounds but took only 2 shots in the second half. His torn calf muscle and pulled thigh tendon hampered any lateral movement. Though our outside shooting went from bad to worse, Wilt continued to kick it out to us on the perimeter. Our inside and outside options were gone, and we went totally out of sync. I had a chance to tie the score at 97 with a minute to play. I drove on Don Nelson and flipped up an off-balance shot from about five feet. The ball bounced three times on the rim, then fell off with Russell grabbing the rebound. That was the ball game and the season. This series was as bizarre and frustrating as the 1966–67 series had been rewarding.

We were all sorely disappointed, including Alex who was convinced the best team did not win. Boston had come all the way back from a 3–1 deficit during a ten-day period when none of the games had seemed real to me. America asked us to go right on amusing it on the court, so that it could forget about riots at home or wars in Asia. Black and white players alike. And we did.

Players today try to stay within boundaries as much as we did or more. Management was afraid of the outspoken black players of my era such as Joe Caldwell, John Brisker, and Frank Russell. But Phil Jackson, a former flower child, is now the coach of a three-time World Champion Chicago Bulls team. Bill Walton could protest the war and wear his hair in a ponytail, take drugs, and finally be accepted as part of the basketball establishment. Now he's a television commentator who criticizes players like the Michigan "Fab Five" as too undisciplined. Kareem Abdul-Jabbar had his share of controversial associations with the Black Muslims, and a gruesome murder took place in a Washington, D.C., home he owned. I guess the moral is if a player is white or he's good enough, people look the other way for a long time at his off-court activities. But for the general run of black players, any sort of political activism or social criticism is not possible without repercussions.

All the violent political deaths in the 1960s made me wonder about the lives I had missed leading, about how I could have been a better man. I knew there were heroic Freedom Riders in the South, who would get on a bus to integrate it, knowing their fate was to be beaten and dragged off to jail time after time. Dr. King made us think about how our own lives could matter. It was personal. If Dr. King had been a political force in the 1940s, my sister Anna Laura might have lived, for she would have been admitted to the all-white hospital. My mother could perhaps have voted in the South. In college I might have been emboldened to do more for my people.

The 1967–68 season wore out in grief and sadness. We lost because the Celtics were healthier, and they focused better after the King assassination. That didn't make the 76ers better people.

It was just the way it was. A one-year championship reign is not much of a reign, and we knew it.

The 76ers should have remained intact for years to come. We were all relatively young and in our prime. Yet in the off-season, long-simmering internal disputes boiled over. We faced all sorts of nagging questions. Would Alex be back as coach in 1968–69? Did he want to return? Did Wilt? Would Kosloff do what was needed to keep them both?

After the 1968 play-offs, rumors flew that the 76ers had dumped the series since we'd been ahead 3–1 when our shooting touch inexplicably disappeared. Wilt took only one shot in the second half of game seven. The rumors were ridiculous, of course. All our injuries had finally caught up with us, and the Celtics' great veteran team had risen to the occasion. A *Sacramento Bee* reporter called to ask about the 76ers' midseason stay at Caesar's Palace on an off day during a western road trip. I couldn't give him any answers although it was implicit in his questions that he was thinking "fix." He was asking questions about Ash Resnick, a casino boss in Vegas and a friend of Joe Louis's. But none of these rumors was ever substantiated. I wasn't involved in any fix during the series; I just couldn't shoot straight and was hampered by the groin pull. Beyond the national tragedies and the distractions, I had experienced a mysterious shortness of breath on and off the court that I attributed to stress. But it recurred from time to time in Chicago with the Bulls. I never did get a reliable diagnosis until I retired and moved to California. Five years later I found out I had a form of asthma.

Ike Richman was the thread that had held the whole dream of the Philadelphia dynasty together. He was the only man who could pacify everyone, get Philadelphia fans on our side, and keep Wilt happy. We lost our chance for a 76ers dynasty largely because Ike Richman died the year before we came together as a team. Ike was our reigning monarch, both a con artist and a very shrewd judge of people. He brought Wilt home to Philadelphia. He had a knack of beating you in a negotiation without really making you sore about it. In my first year in Philadelphia, he promised me a bonus if we went to the play-offs; but when I went in to collect, he convinced me that what he'd really said was that I'd have a bonus if we made it to the *second* round of the play-offs.

Ike was a mover and shaker; he could keep everybody content. Irv Kosloff could not. Irv was a more low-key, laid-back businessman though he was an honorable man. He and Ike played bad cop-good cop during negotiations. Without Ike's drive and ability with people, Irv couldn't make it work. Wilt drifted further away from the idea of remaining in Philadelphia. He'd come to love the West Coast and its freedoms. Without Ike's promise to get him a piece of the 76ers, Wilt lost interest in remaining in the East.

No one on the team was surprised when the 76ers lost Alex and Wilt over the summer. Would their departure put us back to square one? I knew I was heading for trouble before the 1968–69 season. I had the distinct impression that I was on the trading block. It was clear to me that Jack Ramsay, now coach as well as general manager, wanted to build the team around Billy Cunningham. The Cunningham situation had been difficult for me after Billy joined the team in 1965 since we played the same position.

Although I tried to keep it down, my anxiety was tremendous when Cunningham joined the 76ers. He was a great player. At my best, I would never be twice as good as he was on the court. So I suspected it was a matter of time before they worked him in and showed me the way out.

Owners always feel they have to control players and pick the coach who will make sure everyone blends into the system. Why are there only two black head coaches in the NFL? Football players are so physically aggressive and strong that they threaten the owners by their very presence. Therefore, they don't get the chance to lead. General Colin Powell was a company man at the Pentagon. If Powell had spoken on civil rights, minorities, or abortion, he might not have made it to the top of the military pyramid. When Dr. King came out against the Vietnam War, he was criticized by the NAACP and Roy Wilkins for breaking out of the black-issues box. But Dr. King clearly saw how the war was hurting black people at home and killing them on the battle-field.

Most white players didn't come from poverty. The white athlete was playing in *his* world, the one he believed in and belonged to. He didn't have to make adjustments. White players had options in their lives outside of sports. But black players didn't back then. We saw management holding a hammer over our heads. The message today still seems to be, "If you say something, we'll take your ball from you. We'll send you home." So black players don't speak up. To speak up is to cut your own throat.

Take Senator Bill Bradley, whom I admire a great deal. Basketball was only part of a larger world for him. When he came down from Princeton to play in the Sonny Hill summer league, he had a place to go back to. A young black kid doesn't have the luxury of choosing to take that route. We had an NBA players' representatives meeting in Monte Carlo one summer. Bill and I rented a car and drove to Paris. While we were in a taxi touring the city, he gave me an overview of how the world economy functioned! I understood only a little of the grand design but understood thoroughly the concept of the larger world Bradley was preparing himself to join after basketball. It was a world where he would never have to question that he'd be taken in if he worked hard enough. America would and could work for him.

Black players constantly talked about racism as the problem that keeps them from advancing into management positions. I would guess we had more discussions about that than we had about women or basketball games.

I remember going into Jimmy Milan's, a south Philadelphia place with great Italian food, frequented by players but supposedly off-limits because it was known to be a favorite hangout of gamblers with mob connections. Sam Fleischman would take me there. He was a good friend and a heavy wagerer, but he would never ask me anything about our team, about who was hurt or down. We would always go through the backdoor so that I wouldn't be noticed.

One night I ran into Emlen Tunnell at the bar. Em was an old New York Giant defensive back who had played through the 1950s with great Giant defensive teams. He spent thirteen years in the NFL and retired in 1961 with 79 interceptions. Em was very drunk, and he was disenchanted with the NFL. He was angry and frustrated because he badly wanted to be an assistant coach, but he was afraid to pursue it, afraid to make waves. He had played alongside Tom Landry for years in the Giants' defensive backfield, and now Landry was becoming a legend as head coach of the Cowboys whereas Em had nothing. He felt he knew as much as Landry and should have a future in the game.

Hell, he *was* the game; that's what all of us warriors feel. Players think the game belongs to us, but the owners see us as the equipment or a tax write-off. Also, Em didn't know how to "network," as we say today. Where could he begin? Why didn't Elston Howard, Monte Irvin, and Jim Gilliam become major-league baseball managers? Why was Hal Greer never given a chance to run the 76ers when he retired? Hal played as many years for the franchise as Dolph Schayes and could have done a better job as coach. When Hal retired in 1973, the 76ers first turned to an obscure college coach, Roy Rubin, then to Kevin Loughery, who had no coaching experience at the time. Rubin and Loughery "led" the team, if that's the word, to the worst record in NBA history, 9–73.

Later the 76ers went for another white career coach in Gene Shue, who tried to tame the wild group assembled in the mid-1970s—George McGinnis, Lloyd Free, Darryl Dawkins, Terry Furlow, Joe Bryant—before Billy Cunningham took over late in 1977–78 to reap the fruits of the Julius Erving era and win a championship for the 76ers in 1982–83. Not one black player who had a hand in the 1966–67 World Championship team ever got a chance to become part of management in Philadelphia. When we took off our 76er uniforms, we became invisible. In 1985–86, Matty Guokas succeeded Cunningham as coach of the 76ers.

After playing for him in Chicago, Bob Weiss followed coach

Dick Motta's star around the league before getting three head-coach opportunities at San Antonio and Atlanta and with the Los Angeles Clippers. Larry Costello became a resident coaching genius for Milwaukee when he had Jabbar and Oscar in the early to mid-1970s but faded out of coaching after Jabbar was traded to the Lakers.

I never saw Em Tunnell again but thought to myself, is this how I am going to feel when I retire? I was in my prime in Philadelphia, but would basketball have a place for me when my time on the court ended?

The Philadelphia press always played up the contributions of a few of the 76ers to the detriment of others. Wilt Chamberlain was its favorite subject, larger than life, homegrown, the prodigal son who had returned with his superhuman feats, his constant commentary on the league, his ailments, his battles with coaches. Wali Jones—flamboyant, intense—was a local son from Villanova. Our backcourt reserves, the youngsters Matty Guokas from St. Joseph's and Bill Melchionni from Temple, were Philly college stars. Billy Cunningham was adored by the press as a powerful scorer with the jumping ability of a black player. Hal Greer and I never had the Philadelphia connection. We were always the holdovers from Syracuse.

The press, the fans, the front office—all clearly wanted to start Billy Cunningham in my place. We had the only all-black starting lineup in the league in 1966–67 and 1967–68; and to the black community in Philadelphia, to use Cunningham instead of me would look racist. To keep me motivated and get me going, several times Alex even showed me negative letters from fans pushing for Billy. I didn't make it easy for the 76ers to get rid of me, because I was a model citizen and player. Billy and I remained friends throughout this period, but it was tough. We went out of our way not to let the situation drive us apart. Billy had come up playing ball in some rough urban neighborhoods in Brooklyn.

On the day in summer 1969 when Pat Williams called to tell me I had been traded to Chicago, he wanted to set up a press conference for me on the following day. But first I called my friend Sonny Hopson with the news, and he asked if I would come on his late-night radio show and give an exclusive interview. I did and had a wonderful time.

Sonny Hopson was one of my favorite Philly people and a real character. Sonny was one of Philadelphia's most popular black disc jockeys and a neighbor of mine in west Philadelphia. His radio name was "The Mighty Burner." When Sonny left his hometown of Ambler, a small town outside Philadelphia, he told his friends that some day he would come back home "in a chauffered limousine in the company of superstars." One night I was flattered to learn I fit Sonny's definition of a superstar. Sonny called to tell me, in his most dramatic voice, that "the time had come" and that I should meet him outside. When I came down, I saw a sleek limo and Sonny in his finest outfit. Slugger Dick Allen of the Phillies was already on board. Together we had a ball sharing in Sonny's triumphant return to Ambler. We rolled right up to a nightclub and were treated like kings, not celebrities, by everyone. Sonny had his night, and so did we.

Anyway, I gave my side of the story about my trade to Chicago on the air in between Sonny's rap, the top forty, and phone calls. I spoke my mind about how I thought I had become expendable, that the 76ers had developed a situation where Cunningham was the star and I was in the way. It was therapeutic to talk directly to the real fans and more important than any rigged news conference. Many fans called to express anger at my being pushed out of town by management. I knew that many people in Sonny's audience had been watching me since those summer-league days in the Baptist church in north Philly. They were the people I wanted to leave town remembering.

13.
New Start
with the Bulls

In the fall of 1968, the ball never swung to my side. Wali Jones told me those were Ramsay's instructions, never swing it to the right side. I think I was too self-controlled on the court for Ramsay. He wanted more of a rah-rah guy. After one frustrating season with Ramsay as my coach, I was traded to the Bulls, fulfilling my premonition that Alex and Wilt wouldn't be the only ones the 76ers were waving off. My departure just took an extra season.

Some NBA coaches hinder the development of a winning attitude. The most common mistake made by coaches is to over-coach their teams. It's just not necessary. Everyone at the professional level can play the game brilliantly and has established the fact over many years. Coaching at the professional level is more a matter of motivating the players and establishing a chemistry among them that can withstand a long, hard season and many games. Jack Ramsay was a bit of an egomaniac, always emphasizing the "Dr." in front of his name, the only Ph.D. among NBA coaches. He was very methodical but at the same time intent on the creative. He wanted us to have a trapping defense, which is extremely difficult to work in the pros because of the speed and agility of the opposing players. Actually, I think Ramsay tin-

kered too much with every team he coached: Philadelphia, Buf-
falo, Indiana—even Portland after Bill Walton went down with
his foot injuries in 1977–78. Coaches like Ramsay put in too much
stuff and try to control the game from the bench, which they simply can't do in the NBA.

In Philly, he put in too many plays and took the game out of
the players' hands. I became the third or fourth option on plays
for the 76ers in 1968–69. NBA players have to feel free to take a
shot or move instinctively on their own. That's where and how
games are won and lost in the last few minutes. Coaches like
Alex Hannum realized this fact. Alex had played in the league.
Often it's the certified college "geniuses" like Ramsay and Hubie
Brown who frustrate a team's confidence and growth. Despite
the supposed handicap of never having apprenticed as college
coaches, former NBA players who turn coach are closer to the
rhythms of the pro game. Testimony to this is the success of Billy
Cunningham, Phil Jackson, Lenny Wilkens, John Lucas, Don
Chaney, Kevin Loughery, Matt Guokas, Pat Riley, and others.

The best coaches are master psychologists and manipula-
tors. Red Auerbach sold the Celtics on the fact that winning was
the most important, the only thing. One ploy he used to keep
players focused on the play-offs was to keep their salaries low.
Year by year the Celtics were hungry for the play-off money,
which, in some cases, was a healthy percentage of their salary.
Nowadays, when ten thousand dollar fines constitute walking-
around money, I don't know what could keep a team hungry.
The coaches' challenges have to be greater.

The coach is part of the management team, so he has to
manage. He satisfies the owners when he shows he's in control.
To be an NBA coach, you don't need to be a rocket scientist, but
you must "keep the players in line."

To do that, most coaches rely on at least one player to keep
them informed. On every team I played on, black players always
sensed one white player had a direct line to the coach and would
report what we said out of the coach's earshot. In Chicago, I suspected one guy in a good-natured way. So if I wanted to say

something to Motta, I said it to this other player. Once in front of him I did an imitation of Motta as the Japanese general Tojo. Next day, Motta eyed me and muttered, "Tojo, huh?" Former Bulls Jerry Sloan, Bob Weiss, and Matty Guokas have all been head coaches in the league now—so is Rick Adelman, who played fourth guard for us in 1973–74. But where are Bob Love, Chet Walker, Norm Van Lier, Clifford Ray? Certainly not head coaches.

It's hard for black and white players to gain each other's trust. Black players are always looking over their shoulder at someone who wants to keep them under control. It's strange and becomes ingrained, so that you don't even consciously acknowledge you're doing it although it affects your work and daily life. Teams used to try and counteract this division between white and black players by having them room together on the road. But it never quite worked out. I roomed with Cunningham for a while when he first joined the 76ers and with Bob Kaufmann when he played a year with the Bulls, but we just ran out of things to say to one another when we got down to basic interpretations of our lives and views. An exception was Tom Boerwinkle, a Nixon Republican when we were on the Bulls. He and I argued politics in a friendly way. The truth is, black and white players go their separate ways after games. We meet up again at practice the next day.

I knew I wouldn't miss Philadelphia, a city in which I never felt particularly welcome. Philadelphia was a cliquish town, and despite our championship season, I hated it. So on to Chicago, the City of the Big Shoulders with a suspect basketball team. I had conflicting emotions heading west. I'd known and liked Chicago ever since I'd been at Bradley and had come up from Peoria to hear jazz artists with college friends. Chicago was hip. It was on the lake. It was a place where I would find many black communities, but then again, it was one of the most racist cities in the country. The 1968 Democratic Convention and Dr. King's frustrating forays into the city made me wary of Chicago.

Like other players, I found my first trade traumatic; and the Bulls were not a team I admired. First, I had mixed emotions going from a winner to a loser. The Bulls had the growing pains of any expansion team but didn't look as if they were about to shake their losing ways. I had been in the play-offs for all the seven years I had been in the NBA and didn't look forward to finishing out of the money. Second, I always considered the Bulls a team that played hard but just well enough to lose. They didn't have any confidence down the stretch of games. Finally, there was the coach Dick Motta, a fierce guy who wanted his players under his total control.

I toyed with the idea of jumping to the ABA but knew I had to fulfill my one-year obligation to the Bulls. The ABA was a wild, rogue league in its third year of existence and seriously challenging the NBA to sign both hot collegians and established players like me. My attorney, Shelly Starks, was working on a package deal that would bring Cunningham, Luke Jackson, and me to the Carolina Cougars. The Cougars were an ABA franchise reassigned from Houston and eager to make a big splash with its new Carolina fans.

Upon hearing rumors of my defection, both Motta and the Bulls general manager Pat Williams came to see me in Philly to convince me the Bulls were on the move and I would play an important role in their plans. I asked about rumors that the Bulls were moving to Kansas City because Lamar Hunt, who owned a chunk of Bulls' stock, wanted to have a basketball franchise to go along with his football Chiefs. Williams assured me the Bulls would stay put in Chicago. I didn't necessarily believe him. Motta and Williams went with me to a Holiday Inn near Kennedy Airport in New York. There we met with Starks and hammered out a new agreement by which I would consent to join the Bulls and stop playing the ABA card. We wrote in an escape clause that I would be a free agent if the Bulls moved. Needless to say, we outsmarted ourselves because the Bulls stayed put.

With the leverage of the ABA alternative, I did manage to negotiate my best-yet NBA contract for fifty thousand dollars.

And since the Bulls turned things around so quickly once I arrived, I didn't have much to complain about. Winning is contagious.

Chicago would be a decided challenge, a new phase in my career. I didn't know if I was up for it, if I could be a leader there. I'd been part of something so fine in Philadelphia that I wondered what Chicago could offer me. The Bulls' operation didn't impress me much. Their games in the Amphitheatre and the Stadium were poorly attended, forcing management to practically give away tickets. In 1969–70, you could cut out the back of a milk carton, send in a coupon, and receive a free Bulls' ticket! Their mascot, Benny the Bull, had this pitiful moth-eaten costume. The team had a lot of holes, too.

Yet the idea of coming back to the Midwest, to my roots, intrigued me. I also saw my chance to be the bellwether of a team. I'd always been in someone else's shadow in my career: Dave DeBusschere in high school; Bobby Joe Mason and Mike Owens on our most successful Bradley team when I was a sophomore; Dolph Schayes, Johnny Kerr, and the veteran Syracuse group when I was a young pro player. Then I was part of the Philadelphia machine that was driven by Greer, dominated by Wilt, and on which Cunningham was the media interest. Perhaps it was time for me to be the leader. I didn't seek the role, but I had a sense of what would be expected of me.

And I had to take the reins fast, or I would be buried on a losing team that wouldn't turn it around fast enough for me to be of value or to reap the benefits before I retired. I was almost thirty years old when I went to the Bulls. I'd seen many veteran players cast off to expansion teams or to cellar teams because they were making too much money or didn't fit into the new coach's system. In a sense, this had happened to me in Philadelphia.

In the expansion setting, veteran players are often worked to death to provide bridges or continuity while the team builds on youth. Coaches want established players from other teams to come in as a transition toward respectability while the younger players learn the ropes and take their lumps. Expansion coaches also don't want to raise fan expectations by winning too much too early during this development so they can keep their jobs through the inevitable losses.

These veterans then become identified as losers on a losing team, no matter what their careers were before. This prospect galled me. I'd always been a winner. I hadn't been on a losing team since I began playing in Benton Harbor. I knew that if I went to Chicago I would have to be wary and ready to counteract any impression that I was borrowed to provide grey-bearded respectability until my string ran out.

When I came to the Bulls, they saw me as one of those veteran transition players who would take them along until they reached the next plateau. But I wasn't satisfied with that role. If I had been, I would have become a journeyman player working out the string. I knew that if we could keep the game close for forty-five minutes, then I had a chance to take over the last three minutes offensively. I knew I could be the go-to guy. Chicago had no Wilt Chamberlain, no Hal Greer. But there was me. I'd been on a World Championship team. I had confidence in my one-on-one skills. It was my turn to be a leader on the court, and I was ready for the challenge.

Chicago had always been a political city. If you play ball there, you're affected by the politics that are its lifeblood. Mayor Richard J. Daley, although best known as a White Sox fan, was also a basketball fan.

But most high-profile Chicago black athletes were not involved in politics. When I first came to Chicago, Operation PUSH was a very dynamic young organization that the Reverend Jesse Jackson used as a base from which to gain influence first in local, then national politics. If you were a black athlete in 1970 in Chicago, you were not encouraged to hang out with political activists like Jesse. Little hints were dropped that it was unwise, that we were to stay away from politically controversial groups, that it wasn't smart for our careers. However, we were all encouraged to eagerly respond to anything the mayor's office sent the Bulls' way. Through the mayor's right-hand man, Edward Kelley, head of the Chicago Park District, I would visit kids' groups all over the city. I only attended one Operation PUSH meeting in my six years in the city, a Saturday morning affair, although I was asked on numerous occasions.

Players are expected to support what the team feels is in the team's best interest, as in any other business. Management wants to determine a player's participation in community affairs and to channel it through the club's name and reputation. Most players are very comfortable with this symbiosis and see it leading to more endorsements and media opportunities and therefore more dollars. It becomes very difficult for a player to see his potential power apart from that of the team.

I didn't protest very much. Coming from Philadelphia at the end of the 1960s, I had a political hangover from the King and Kennedy murders and the agonies of the decade. So had Chicago after the bitterness of King's Chicago crusade, the brutal theater of the 1968 Democratic Convention, the farce of the Chicago Seven trial, the burning of the west side after King's death, and the assassination of the Black Panther leaders Fred Hampton and Mark Clark. Chicago had a better-run political machine than Philadelphia. Even the black politicians in Chicago were allied to Mayor Daley, including those who broke out of local affairs and were elected to Washington like Ralph Metcalfe, the Olympic teammate of Jesse Owens in 1936.

In speaking to kids I felt that we professional players had a lot to offer, having come out the other end of the process. After I retired, I addressed a McDonald's All-Star camp at UCLA at the request of Sonny Hill. I told the players that their next four years would determine how they would function in society for the rest of their lives. I speculated that only four of the twenty-four would make the NBA and 75 percent of them wouldn't make it through college. They didn't believe that. I was just another older man telling them about the war.

I told the McDonald's players that before they made a decision on college, they should think about the total environment at that school. Could they survive in a place across the country from their homes? What emotional support did they need? I told them to find out about a coach from other players, from that coach's history. If he's a screamer and an autocrat and you feel you can't take that or don't want it, don't go there. I said to remember that every coach is your best friend when recruiting you. But what does his track record show? What does the team's graduation record show?

Richard Lapchick at the Center for the Study of Sport and Society in Boston is trying to make colleges take responsibility for players who drop out of school or who flunk out. He wants the schools to take the players back if they wish to finish their degree even several years later. He hopes to develop the colleges' sense of obligation to these young men. There's a new National Basketball Retired Players Association (NBRPA) that we've established, which we would like to use as a platform to tell the truth about college and life after basketball.

In Chicago, Dick Motta always convinced the writers we were the underdog, so when we did start to win and win big, the writers pointed to his coaching ability. Once the press picks up on that notion of the plucky loser, the underdog, the team is always portrayed that way. This stereotype of the Bulls changed soon after I joined the team. When the Bulls' attitude changed, we became one of the league's top contenders from 1970–75.

I respected Motta because he respected my judgment. We would often talk in airports and walk back to the hotel together discussing the team. We only talked when we had something serious to say. He knew I could help us win right away, but I wasn't his creation and that bothered him. He hadn't found me on some free-agent scrap heap or waiver list, and I wasn't obligated to him. So we were wary allies.

We started off well in the 1969–70 season but then faded a bit in the stretch. We were adjusting to each other and setting higher goals for ourselves and the team. A key change came when Motta put Bob Love at forward in the starting lineup. Love was such a good jump shooter that he forced the defense to play us even and took the pressure off me. A year later we got guard Norm Van Lier, a high-spirited, high-strung kid, a player fueled on emotion and guts but in some ways self-destructive. He was Sloan's tireless accomplice on defense, and both of them took their cue from Motta's "us against the world" philosophy. Officials often started a game with the Bulls just waiting for Van Lier or Sloan or Motta to explode. Yet, on balance, the mad-dog quality of the Bulls worked in our favor by allowing us to compete for years when we were only the fifth or sixth best team and not even that on paper. I couldn't get myself to play at that pitch. It just wasn't my game. So I became what was best for me: the veteran who could take over the offense. I felt that if the game remained close, I could take over offensively.

Motta would never tell me, "Take over, Chet," even when he wanted me to. He simply gave me the freedom to make my own decisions on the court. I never padded my average. I had played on outstanding teams and didn't need to be high scorer. I was prouder of becoming, while I was with the Bulls, the fifth player in NBA history to reach one thousand games played. In Chicago, I had the ball more often than in Philly; it was as simple as that. The clock would wind down in our grind-it-out, half-court offense, and I would go to work. I brought to Chicago all the one-on-one moves that I'd spent fifteen years perfecting in schoolyards, in college, and in Philly.

I could really jump when I was in high school and early on at Bradley. I had a vertical leap that would have made headlines today. But after my kidney problems began at the NIT, I never felt as much strength in my legs. I could only get that spring periodically. In my years at Bradley, I often had to play center against much taller players in the Missouri Valley Conference. Consequently, I developed my whole series of head, arm, and body fakes, which I guess most people think of when they remember my game in Chicago. They were a veteran's bag of tricks. Nobody ever taught me those moves. They came from trial and error and observation. A little Maurice Stokes and Elgin Baylor in them, I guess.

With the Bulls it was my ball in all the pressure moments, and I loved it. I always had a sense of how to get a defensive man down low on my back and hip so I could feel his rhythm, figure out what he wanted or expected me to do. I could adjust, wait, wait, then go up when he was coming down and draw the foul or square my body off a slight push. Shot blockers simply don't have the patience to stay with these moves. Even though they're told to stand their ground, they all want to leave their feet and go after your shot, especially when you stay on the floor as long as I did before putting it up.

In Chicago, I liked to work the baseline, where it was difficult for the defense to find any way to double-team me. I would tranquilize them with a minimum of body movement. Then I would spring up quickly and smoothly like a cobra. It didn't even bother me when at times I felt I was almost falling over the baseline to lean back in and get off a short jump shot. The angle was always congenial to me even when it appeared I was almost behind the basket. Guys wondered how I could be so consistent on that shot.

Every player develops his own stuff. It's an expression of more than style. It has to do with who he is, down deep, more like a blueprint of character coming through. In a way, my one-on-one game *was* me: wary, testing, keeping the defender off balance, sly, determined, patient, then going up at just the right moment and coming through. I never tried to think too far ahead against one team or one opponent. That's a way to exhaust yourself mentally. I adjusted to each situation that presented itself.

At the end of my first year with the Bulls, we squeaked into the play-offs with a 39–43 record. We went against the quick and talented Atlanta Hawks, who had won the Western Division title. These play-offs were extremely important to the Bulls, giving the franchise a legitimacy. Pro basketball failed twice before in Chicago in different eras and could have failed again because Chicago fans loved the Bears and Cubs and saved any leftovers for the White Sox and Black Hawks. Chicago was a conservative, blue-collar grind-it-out town. Basketball as an up-tempo, exciting game was always a tough sell in Chicago.

Near the end of the regular season in 1969–70, the Bulls were still battling for the last play-off spot in the Western Division when I suffered a severe groin injury in which the muscle actually separated from the bone. I couldn't remember the exact play on which it occurred, but that night I woke up in excruciating pain. I remember driving to Northwestern Memorial Hospital in agony, unable to get out of the driver's seat; the nurses and orderlies had to drag me out. The team was desperate for me to play. The whole season came down to our making the play-off slot. Each game night they shot me up with two painful cortisone injections to deaden my whole groin area. Each morning I could hardly get out of bed. I would take five or six Tylenol, anything to stop the pain. At night it was frightening to play with no feeling in part of my body. How could I know what I might be doing to myself? I played ten games on one leg. Finally, we had four or five days of rest, and I got over the worst of the injury.

Except for the Milwaukee Bucks, who became instant championship contenders when they signed Lew Alcindor in 1970, no expansion team ever had as much consistent success as the Bulls did in the six years I played for them. The Bulls won an average of 50 games per year from 1970 to 1975 and went to three bruising seventh-game losses in play-off series. Our main rivals included the Knicks, Lakers, Celtics, and Bucks—all dominant teams in this period, all of whom we fought tooth and nail every season. The Bulls didn't always match up in talent with these opponents. The Knicks played a lot like the Bulls, so our games were often masterpieces of half-court execution. Fans expected real nail-biters with low scores. Walt Frazier and Earl Monroe always pushed Sloan and Van Lier to the limit. Bob Love and I would battle DeBusschere and Bradley. Against the Lakers, we faced a sleek, fast team with Wilt providing the rebounding and defense on his third championship-caliber team. They won 33 straight games in 1971–72 as Jerry West, Gail Goodrich, Happy Hairston, and Jim McMillian feasted off the fast break.

In 1970–71, the Bulls won 51 games, 12 more than in my first season with them. I'll never forget the afternoon of February 6, 1971. I went into another zone and scored 56 points against the Cincinnati Royals. What a Sunday afternoon in Chicago Stadium! Those were the most points I'd ever scored anywhere at any level of basketball. I felt as if the basket was as big as a fireman's net. No way could I miss. The Royals sent about half their roster to guard me at different points, but nobody stopped my onslaught.

Two weeks later we solidified a hold on the play-offs in one of the most exciting games I ever played in. On February 19, 1971, we played the Pistons in Chicago Stadium. A half-game behind the Pistons in the battle for second place in the Midwest Division, we were scheduled to play them again Sunday in Detroit. So the next forty-eight hours would go a long way toward settling things in our play-off future.

Friday night at the Stadium, the crowd kept building and building until they had to sell standing-room only tickets, a first for the Bulls. In 1995, or whenever the Bulls' public address announcer records the "five-hundredth straight sellout for the Bulls," I'll think back to that first sellout. I believe it was the night professional basketball was established in Chicago.

For most of the game, we played catch-up with the Pistons. Their smooth guard, Dave Bing, would use screens from massive Bob Lanier and pop jump shots or cut past him for lay-ups. Bing's backcourt partner, Jimmy Walker, was another sharpshooter. Midway through the fourth quarter, our 18,545 fans were stunned watching the Pistons build a 10-point lead. I was spent and went out for a short rest. Then from somewhere, we revived as my sub, John Baum, scored 6 points and Bob Weiss added 4 more. We had ourselves a game again.

With forty-five seconds to go we trailed 101–97. The Bulls cleared out a side for me, and I went to work. I fouled out Terry

Dischinger with a pump move and made two foul shots to bring us within two points. Then Detroit missed, and Sloan grabbed the rebound. I had the ball at the top of the foul circle and went up with the tying shot. It hit nothing but net to even the score with six seconds left to play. When the Pistons called time-out to set up their last shot, a gargantuan roar came down from the ancient stadium rafters and washed over all of us like a sonic wave. The noise didn't let up until we came back on the floor. Even then, it only subsided, never stopping. And all this was purely excitement-driven emotional release. No stadium had hammering loud music in the early seventies or giant screens inciting the fans to pump up the volume. This great game itself generated the passion.

Six seconds were left on the game clock. I correctly anticipated the inbounds pass to Bill Hewitt, stole it cleanly, and called another time-out. The crowd's thunder reverberated once again. Now I was as pumped as I can ever remember. I wanted it to end right there in regulation time because Detroit had too many offensive players to chance an overtime. I was ready to go out and win it with a shot at the buzzer: that's how confident I felt. But the Pistons knocked away two of our inbounds passes, and big Bob Lanier squeezed the ball. Regulation time expired without my ever touching the ball.

My jump shot in overtime put us ahead 105–103 to stay. Then I drove and faked repeatedly and knocked down 7 free throws to keep us comfortable. Detroit came on at the end of overtime, but we prevailed 115–114. I scored 44 points, and the local papers were proclaiming the game an "emotional orgy." I still hold the Bulls' record from that night with 11 points scored in overtime. Motta told reporters in the locker room that I'd brought the Bulls "back from the dead." Two days later in Detroit, we beat the Pistons easily in Cobo Hall and never looked back.

Games like that you remember all your career. Big crowds in and of themselves don't mean a great game nor do high stakes. Then again, personal accomplishments begin to pale if the team isn't doing well or if you're not appreciated. This game had everything. I took it over to make it a perfect blend of personal and team victory. I had brought my game to Chicago, and we were winners.

After the game outside Chicago Stadium, I used my car roof to sign autographs on programs or pieces of paper fans held out. A really gorgeous woman sidled up to me and purred, "You were so fantastic out there tonight that you gave me an orgasm." I was embarrassed standing there amid all those kids. Just as she walked away, I gulped and turned around, blurting out "Thank you!"

As a player, you never really know what fans are thinking. All of your mail comes in care of the club and is opened before you get it. Most of the obscene or hate mail is kept from the players. The fact that so many off-the-wall threats are sent to players is not publicized for fear that wide-spread knowledge of these letters would only lead to more copy-cat letters and more anxiety for the players.

My personal life in Chicago was put on hold. I had several girlfriends but no intense affairs. I never felt that being an athlete was a proper time to think about getting serious and marriage. An athlete at home (or not, as is so often the case) is a difficult person for any woman to live with considering the adulation pumping him up, his physical life, his many absences, the women constantly available to him.

After games, win or lose, I was not a nice person to be around. I didn't want to talk or be with anyone. I would generally go off and sit in a corner of a restaurant by myself until I cooled down. There was a place at State and Division streets called Mitchell's that would always save a booth in the back for me after a home game. From a big window there I could see the nightlife hustling by in the Rush Street area, people having fun, guys and their dates, and I would wonder what it would be like to feel that elated late at night. My body would be racked and

just coming down after most games. Hell, I know it was, in most
respects, just the workingman's blues, but any job can get to you,
even the athletic career of many men's dreams. I was paid pretty
well for my isolation and sorrowful thoughts.

I never could eat after a game; I would just sit in Mitchell's
and nurse a drink. Before a game, I would try to keep to a schedule. About four and a half hours before a game, I would have a
meal of steak and potatoes at Mitchell's. That was the traditional
athlete's training meal back then. I would walk the six or seven
blocks to the restaurant from my apartment, eat, and then walk
back and take a nap, get up and listen to jazz, Miles Davis or
Sarah Vaughan, to settle me down. Then I would drive down
Ogden Avenue to Chicago Stadium.

Time was running out for me in basketball. That's probably
why I tried to have a separate life from sports in Chicago. Most of
my friends were professional people or schoolteachers at the city
colleges. Part of me wanted to be an executive in a high-rise
building behind a big desk making big deals. That's one reason I
wanted to be a player rep in the NBA: to see the sport from a
business point of view.

Another part of me wanted to get away from cities, jobs,
and responsibilities. I was reading Carlos Castaneda at that time,
a mystical Latin American writer who was into ancient American Indian culture and meditation. His writings fit my fantasies
of chucking my sports career and finding a new place away from
everyone and everything.

Generally, I became even more cautious and private in Chicago. I was always extremely careful about what I said to the
press as I measured my words. As for fans, I always felt that if
they paid their money, they had a right to cheer or boo or sit on
their hands. As long as they weren't personally abusive. I think
many players have too thin a skin when it comes to hearing the
stands. Screaming and yelling is just part of the atmosphere at
games. Fans need to let off steam. If a player is on the road,
chances are it's directed right at him. That's big-time athletics.

It's simply the tone that's set. If, at a concert, a cello player misses a note, no one boos the musician. That's not the culture of concerts. But in sports, you pay the price of letting people have at you, giving you the raspberry on the court or monitoring your actions off. Your privacy disappears at work. Your freedom comes from the way you handle yourself in the new situation. If you go out to a nightspot, you have to be prepared for anything that might happen, for someone to call a contact in the media and say you were acting up.

Halftime of a game is when you regroup mentally. If you're behind, you attempt to recapture any momentum or just gain some. If you're ahead, you need to recharge to maintain an edge. High school and college coaches become different creatures at halftime. If the first half has been rough, they try to psych you up or, depending on their mood and your sins, degrade or bullshit you into some belief or another. Pro coaches don't try to hustle their players or scream at them. Pros *know* when they're bad; and if you're to be successful, you must be able to make your own adjustments. Besides, pro coaches and players have to live together intimately for six to seven months of the year. Self-motivation just has to be assumed. Midcourse corrections, pacing, smoothing a team out, treating each other like grown men—all this makes coaches and players into winners, whether the standings reflect it or not.

The third quarter is when you establish momentum. You must come out and set a pitch of physical aggressiveness and movement, capture it and keep it. I never trusted anyone else at game's end. I only trusted myself to get the job done. This may sound selfish, but it was true. When you know you *have* to shoot the ball, that gives you confidence. It's worse to not have the ball in your hands. That's when fatigue can set in, mental and physical. That's why some teams look so enervated standing around watching superstars go one-on-one with the ball for a great percentage of the time. Only fatigue got to me in a game. After those early games in the Deep South at Bradley, I never let any crowd affect me. Most of the time you're inside a zone called the game, and if you're concentrating on your job, that's where you stay.

What do you do when some nights the game just becomes another job you have to go to? When it's mid-February, say, and you're in the middle of a ten-day road trip and it's fifteen degrees and snowing outside? That's inevitable, of course. I would try and find something or somebody to get angry at, something to focus on to kick into gear. It might be an opposing player or coach or even something one of our guys did. About 10 percent of the time, you have to find ways to keep from mailing in your performance. It's important because the fans are owed that much at least. A father might bring his son once a year to see the fabled NBA stars at work. It's an expensive evening for them. For us to go out and sleepwalk would be an awful thing to do. And once we begin to pretend, our competitive life is gone, we can't just snap it back. No team knows how to lose, but plenty of teams have slowly forgotten how to win.

I never understood why any fan would want an autograph, for I never wanted one from anybody in my life. I received lots of requests for autographs, especially from older people, who seemed to gravitate toward me. Maybe they thought I needed some parents or grandparents. A lot of fans wrote that they just knew I was a spiritual man. They thought I had an inner calm and would write, "God bless you, son!"

Other fans wrote that they felt sorry for me because I didn't look as if I was having any fun on the court. They would ask, "Why are you so sad?" That's not how I *thought* I looked, but these people might have been on to something. I always wanted to get out of the arena. I never wanted to be in that glaring light, except in the last few minutes of games. By the Chicago years I reckoned I'd seen the best at Bradley and Philadelphia and was now a seasoned pro who was just very good at his job. I was looking at the other end of my career.

By my Chicago years I felt that NBA players were like circus performers in short pants, doing the same routines over and over. I gave the Chicago fans all I had, but I was losing my passion for the game and relying on my bag of tricks. It had never been a glamorous life to me. Now I concentrated more and more on how I felt playing hurt, on how I never got enough sleep or the right food. I had so much physical fatigue that some nights on the road it wasn't until the second half that I woke up and got into the game. Do these sound like burnout symptoms? We didn't use the phrase then, but it's a good one. What carried me through my years as a Bull was my rock-bottom pride in being a true professional. I'd been working at this job, in effect, since I was fifteen years old. But no one needs to shed any tears for the poor basketball star. I could just as easily have been weary of being a car salesman or carpet shampooer or hunting guide.

The Bulls became serious challengers in the NBA play-offs beginning in 1971. Until we faced down the Lakers that spring, we'd been "the nice little expansion team that could." We made the NBA take notice that the Bulls had arrived. When we lost the seven-game series to the Lakers, I averaged only 15 points, 7 less than my regular season average. I bore my share of blame for our loss. Chamberlain and Bill Bridges double-teamed me, taking away my best moves down low. I couldn't take advantage of the double-teaming by passing, because Wilt was going up against two hobbled centers in Clifford Ray and Boerwinkle, and Dennis Awtry, our third center, was no scorer. But this seven-game series shocked the basketball world. Our upset of the Lakers would have been historic since they desperately wanted to shake the shadow of the Celtics and win their first World Championship.

I thought my position might be secure as a team leader. But I had no time to rest on my laurels. Instead, it appeared the Bulls wanted to get rid of me. That's the mentality of the NBA. An experienced player is used to make expansion teams better, as was Adrian Dantley for a number of years or Mark Aguirre. Then, when his salary gets too big, management tries to move him. The problem was, I wasn't so easy to get rid of.

Even though 1970–71 had been a great year for the Bulls and for me personally, sure enough, my concerns as a veteran on an expansion team proved valid in the fall of 1971. The Bulls ran in three young forwards to try and take my job: Kennedy McIntosh, Howard Porter, and Charley Paulk. Porter was the star of Villanova's NCAA team, and Pat Williams was close to Porter's lawyer, Richie Phillips. I was disgusted by the ploy. I guess I should have worried about the epithets "old pro" or "statesmanlike veteran." Even some of my teammates quietly suggested I was over the hill. I didn't think so. What I thought was perhaps my teammates didn't relish my role as the go-to guy. They just wanted me to go.

In September preseason practice Motta had me running with the second team. Here I was a nine-year veteran and five-time All-Star playing with the second team. It didn't sit well with me. I couldn't believe I was going through the same shit I had with Ramsay in Philadelphia. Didn't things ever change? Plus, that fall I'd been working out with a Chicago fitness guru, so I was in great shape. I was doing things on the court I hadn't done in years. I kicked Porter and McIntosh all over the gym and dunked on them. I took it as a personal challenge and abused them pretty good. They'd been told that all they had to do was go to training camp and they would have my job. But they said I was as good a player as they'd seen. Motta finally took pity on the kids, suggesting blandly, "Chet, why don't you run with Sloan and Love?"

In the Bulls' six play-off appearances from 1969–75, we'd alternated between being blown out one year and making a great play-off run the next year. Either way, every year ended in enormous frustration. In 1969–70, 1971–72, and 1973–74, we went quietly as a team, winning only a single play-off game in 1970 and being swept in four games in 1972 and 1974. The early play-off loss in 1971–72 hurt the most because the Bulls had a regular season record of 57–25, a club record that was not to be bettered until the Bulls won 60 games in their first championship year in 1990–91. Despite the great season, we wound up first-round fodder for the Lakers, primarily because we had lost Boerwinkle to a torn knee tendon. Clifford Ray had to contend with Wilt almost by himself. Love had a swollen ankle, and I had a pulled hamstring.

Health is often the deciding factor in the NBA play-offs as we proved again in 1974. Crippled teams go home. In the 1974 play-offs we had to face the Bucks in the conference finals without Sloan, who had torn the protective covering off the arch of his left foot. We lost three of the four games by 15 points or more. None of these injury reports is meant to be an excuse. When teams meet in the play-off round, you have to compensate if people are missing. It's tough to do that in basketball though because losing one starter means losing 20 percent of your continuity. Each lineup change, each little injury prevents you from doing what you normally do out on the floor and changes everyone's role. Sooner or later in the NBA, a series of injuries catches up to you. In football, you're one of eleven or twenty-two. In baseball, you're one of nine, and your availability in your position basically affects that position alone.

The pain of losing those close play-off series lingered in the mind as well as the body. Three times the Bulls came very close to making the NBA take notice, but we couldn't win our key seven-game series. In 1971, we caught the Lakers with Jerry West on crutches but couldn't take even one game in Los Angeles though we won all three games in Chicago Stadium.

The 1973 Western Conference semifinals found us back against the Lakers. We thought we would be getting a new play-off partner in the Bucks, but they won 14 straight games to catch the Lakers with a 60–22 record. The NBA had wanted the two teams to square off in a tiebreaker, but the Players' Association balked at the idea. Thus a coin flip set up a Milwaukee–Golden State series whereas we had to go out to the Forum yet again. Motta was beside himself, calling the coin toss a farce and blasting Pat Williams for giving in to the idea. We got even closer to victory this time. On April 15, in game seven, we scored 18 straight points in the second quarter to take over the game from the Lakers on their home court.

With three minutes to play, I put in a jumper to give us a 90–84 lead. But then we brought the ball up court four times without getting off a shot, and the Lakers won 95–92. Wilt blocked a key shot of Van Lier's with thirty seconds to go and

winged a football pass the length of the court to a flying Gail
Goodrich, who laid it in to give the Lakers a 92–91 lead. We lost
even though this had been our game all the way. Van Lier had
fought like a tiger and had 28 points and 14 rebounds. This loss
matched the Havlicek game in 1965 as the toughest of my career.
Some games never go away.

It's odd how in retrospect so much hinges on a single decision. If I hadn't joined the Bulls in 1969–70, the franchise, which
today is one of the most visible and lucrative in all professional
sports, might never have survived in Chicago. I helped save the
Bulls for Chicago. The NBA achieved stability there. Instead of
the Bulls, Kansas City finally got the Cincinnati Royals in 1972–
73, where they became the Kings. The Kings moved to Sacramento in 1985. Can you imagine the Sacramento Bulls with
three NBA titles?

14.
A Free Man

In Chicago, I started to think about my life after basketball but didn't formulate any specific plans. I took acting lessons but was far too shy to project enough emotion to consider a career. Flirting with the idea of becoming a sportscaster, I worked one summer for WCFL radio in Chicago. I also started a scholarship program at Malcolm X College and thought about getting involved with kids in some way. Even in my last years with the Bulls, I still got a big kick out of playing at the Lawson YMCA. I would take three or four of the worst players, spot another team eight to ten baskets, and then help my guys win. Such off-hour games still rekindled all my love for basketball itself.

Chicago Stadium was an old barn from the 1920s. The Stadium had seen circuses, ice shows, political conventions, marathon dances, three-day bicycle races, championship fights—even an indoor Chicago Bears game in 1933. The Stadium sat in a dismal wasteland on Chicago's west side, especially barren since the burning and looting after the death of Dr. King in April 1968. Housing projects circled the Stadium, and the kids outside always surrounded us. Waiting near the players' gate after the game, they would shout, "Give us your shoes, man"; and Bob Love and I would often oblige knowing they would broker those sneakers right away. One kid informed me with a sly grin that my shoes had brought him $15 whereas Love's had been worth $20!

Although I'd become a very well-known sports figure, such attention always took me by surprise. When Wilt Chamberlain and I toured Italy in the summer of 1971, I realized sports was popular worldwide. Wilt, who says he knows everybody and just about does, introduced me to some owners of the Maserati company who took us roaring through the streets in one of their fabulous models. Later that summer in a tiny town south of Naples, I cashed an American Express Travelers Cheque. The guy behind the bank window looked at the check, looked back at me, and then grinned. He pumped my hand and announced, "Chet Walker . . . Chicago Bulls . . . Kareem Jabbar!" I was amazed that my name had reached so far and didn't even mind that he had added Jabbar's name. And all this before ESPN and TNT and world satellite feeds of games.

When we stayed in Paris that summer, we met three little American girls staying at our hotel with their folks. Wilt and I taught these kids how to swim in the hotel pool. Their father was the head of Pepsi-Cola International. Many years later, at the U.S. Open at Forest Hills in New York, a woman came up to me and said, "You know, you taught me how to swim." She was now a writer and asked *me* to write a letter so her friends would believe her. Sport is truly the common language.

Officials and broadcasters, as well as the players, are part of professional basketball. Fans often just take them for granted, but players can't. Officials know they are part of the entertainment so when the game is close, they must let the players play. You can't have too many games ending with players standing on the foul line. You get to know which referees are going to give certain calls.

Today, players such as Alonzo Mourning seem to take an Olympic triple jump to the basket without any referee blowing a whistle. But that's the imperative of entertainment. You can't fly without a takeoff on a launching pad. When the NBA wants to feature slam dunks with players taking off at the foul line, how many steps does that take in an approach to the "runway"? Pragmatism and dollars prevail.

Actually, this is nothing new; only the scope has changed. Bob Pettit established his moves in 1955, and the NBA let him get away with a shuffle step on his way to becoming an all-time great. Michael Jordan was given the same leeway three decades later. Karl Malone backs in like an earth-moving machine as he waits to receive the entry pass in the low post. The Shaq can probably camp out in the lane until the year 2000. Why should kids learn fundamentals any more when they see how loose the game is at its highest skill level? The only imperative is entertainment.

However, the referees always had it in for the Bulls because Motta, Sloan, and Van Lier were so pugnacious. And Bob Love and I had to pay for that tactic. Other teams would really slam us on the offensive end in retaliation for the clawing we did on defense and the way the coach showed them up. Red Auerbach was a coach who could use referees to control the game. He would take a technical foul just to change the pace of the game. Alex Hannum was slicker in the way he worked them. He was a former NBA player, an actor in a way. But Alex was a big guy, over six feet seven inches, and the referees could always *see* him. He couldn't get away with many gestures whereas Red was a little guy with stumpy arms and so could rage a little easier. And the Celtics were gods compared to the rest of us as far as the referees were concerned.

The three I remember best were very distinctive in their styles. Sid Borgia was a little guy with a small, bald head. He loved to jump into a play and take it over with theatrics. He and Wilt hated each other. When Sid called a foul or traveling, he would jump and twist his spindly little body. Mendy Rudolph looked like a Latin leading man or a hit man. He was so smooth and never lost his cool. His arm motions when making calls made him look like a symphony conductor. Earl Strom was an intimidator with an iron jaw but very sensitive to pressure. We hated to have him referee a home game because he would go out of his way to prove he couldn't be influenced by the crowd.

Broadcasters were a different story. They traveled with the team and went out for drinks and dinner with us. Johnny Most was the gravel-throated voice of the Celtics for over thirty years and only added to the list of Boston irritants. We could hear him as we passed midcourt with the ball, rasping out his shamelessly home-team biased commentary. But he was a true pro. His presence was part of the Celtic mystique, and it was a pleasure to be interviewed by him.

The sportswriters also traveled with the team. Like any family member, they would also become part of it and tried to protect its members. Reporters always know more than they print. Back then the rules were unspoken. If the writers came to you for an interview, what you said was okay to print. But if they heard stuff on the plane, in the restaurants, in the hotels, they were expected to keep their silence. Players are always aware of where the writers are in the locker room or on a trip. Sometimes you would say something just so they would hear it and maybe ask you about it later. Other times you might notice them and keep quiet. It was a cat-and-mouse game.

Arenas had their quirks as well. The famous parquet floor at Boston Garden was a visiting team's nightmare. It was full of dead spots, especially in the corners and on the sides, where the ball didn't come up to you on a true bounce. I think Auerbach worked his trapping defenses to pin teams in precisely those places. Convention Hall in Philadelphia was a vintage palace from the 1920s like Chicago Stadium.

I was always careful to get my rest because if I didn't, my body betrayed me in the fourth quarter; but playing on the road was something my body never adjusted to. Some mornings when I woke up in a hotel room, having flown in at 2 A.M. the night before, I had to call the front desk to find out what city I was in.

It was also important to have a routine on the road. I read a lot, mostly history and fiction. I also needed to get *out* of the hotel and mingle with people, breathe fresh air, and sense the pulse of the city. I went to the movies all the time on the road. I would watch anything and everything, but my favorites were comedies; I didn't care for heavy dramas—the games had those. I was beginning to be intrigued by the movies, not by the acting as much as production, the control aspect, the planning. I no longer wanted to get behind that screen as in Benton Harbor when I was young, but I did muse on what went on in the film business behind the scenes.

When Clifford Ray joined the Bulls in 1971, we quickly became best friends. Clifford was and is an incredibly versatile and interesting man. It was always a pleasure to be in his company. He's a gourmet cook and a fine musician. He had studied theater in college and could mimic anyone. One night in Seattle, when we had nothing to do, Clifford went out in the hallway after dinner and began preaching. I came out to testify in his amen corner. Soon we had a crowd out in the hall, and Clifford was so good at it that no one seemed to feel their peace and quiet had been disturbed!

Clifford got a big round of applause when he ran out of steam, but the evening wasn't over yet. Downstairs, we rented a car and drove to Vancouver, where we went to a nightclub, met some ladies, stayed up all night, and had breakfast with them at a coffee shop. We tore back to Seattle to catch the team bus for a 10 A.M. practice and just made it by a hair.

Clifford and Wilt Chamberlain could pick up women faster and more efficiently than any other men I've ever seen. Their techniques were totally different. Clifford was smooth and clever; he would charm ladies in airports or restaurants and have their phone numbers in ten minutes. Wilt was bold, brash, and intimidating. They both put me in the shade.

However, I feel that life on the road is basically a family affair and very personal. I don't want to make it into a public record after all these years. Yes, a lot goes on in terms of sexual and other misadventures. But it's not my nature to kiss and tell, and the bookshelves are full of such accounts already.

***

My seasons with the Bulls began to mount. Living with Dick Motta was an interesting experience over the years. Motta was a good organizer who carefully chose his players to fit into his system. But he was an insecure bench coach once the game began. He wasn't at his best on game strategy but was able to hide the deficiency while coaching the Bulls, because Jerry Sloan and I held the team together at crucial moments on defense and offense, respectively.

Jerry Sloan always got a hell of a lot of press coverage in Chicago. Some writers focused on Jerry because he was the leader on the team. But Jerry deserved everything he received. He was tireless, fearless, an amazing competitor, and also a very fine guy. His background was something like mine. He grew up in a large family on a farm in downstate Illinois. His five older brothers were all married by the time he was in high school. Jerry had to get up at 5 A.M., work in the barn, feed the cows and hogs, and then get to school by hitching a ride into McCleansboro, Illinois, to get to 7 A.M. basketball practice.

Motta was another small-town guy. He was a very sensitive man who had a Mormon upbringing in rural Utah. He was small town, small college, and insecure about suddenly finding himself in the NBA after a few successful years at Weber State in Utah. He just hadn't been around that many black people. When I was traded to the Bulls, another player told me that Mormons think all black people are cursed as the children of Ham in the Old Testament. I said, "So what? That only gives them something in common with millions of other Americans!" But Motta was nothing like that with me.

Motta had good sense about how to use me. He basically let me do what I wanted on offense. He knew and respected me as a veteran who could help him learn how to win in the league. I persuaded Motta to go after Matty Guokas, my 76er former teammate, when we needed a big guard in 1971 to back up Sloan. I begged him not to trade Clifford Ray for Neal Walk. In my later years with the Bulls, he thought of asking me to become a player-coach but was worried that some people would think Sloan had been passed over. Eventually, Motta won a World Championship with the Washington Bullets and built the expansion Dallas Mavericks for one of the more impressive coaching records in the NBA in the past twenty-five years. Later, in his years at Sacramento in the late 1980s, he asked if I would be interested in a front-office job. I told him no. By then I'd completed my break from the game. Too bad he hadn't asked me when I first retired.

Motta was good with a player like Bob Love, whom he utilized to best advantage. Butter had a deadly corner shot. With his long skinny arms, he could release the ball just over the defensive man flying at him. Motta's offense featured forwards who could score, and we maximized it. Boerwinkle was a heady, steady player. Van Lier was unstable to the point where it worried me because he was often emotional and out of control. But he could take over a game at what is now known as the point-guard position. Through it all, Sloan was the rock, the rebounder, the defensive stopper, the emotionally intense extension of Motta on the court.

My last season with the Bulls, 1974–75, looked to be one of our last chances at making a run in the play-offs. Although the Bulls had been a powerful team for four years, the owner Arthur Wirtz and Motta didn't feel we had enough horses to put us over the top. So they made one last gamble to find the missing piece to the championship puzzle. They traded my buddy Clifford Ray to the Warriors for Nate Thurmond. I missed Clifford, but knew that Nate had been a defensive tower for a decade on the West Coast. I had to admit it looked as if the Bulls had finally secured the dominant player for the center position that we had always lacked. But the deal didn't turn out right for us.

Nate was in his twelfth season and simply made an old team that much older. His huge salary made the Bulls' other veterans feel even more unappreciated and underpaid. I'd almost retired but was lured back by a $200,000 contract, the best I'd ever had, plus the chance to play with Nate for a title. Love and

Van Lier demanded a salary adjustment and held out at the beginning of the year. Both insisted that Pat Williams, the departed general manager, had promised them new deals. So they got into a wrangle with Motta, who was now functioning as general manager and coach. Also, a series of front-office moves hadn't worked out. Another of our first-round draft picks, power forward Maurice Lucas, evaded the Bulls and signed with the ABA. The vaunted Howard Porter had contributed little. Veterans were missing as well. Weiss was gone. Dennis Awtry was gone. Boerwinkle and Sloan were injured a lot. I didn't have the stamina at thirty-five that I had had five years before. We had some good young kids—Cliff Pondexter, Leon Benbow, Bobby Wilson, Mickey Johnson—but as usual, Motta didn't feel they were game tested, so he left us old-timers out there too many minutes.

Not only did Nate Thurmond not fit into our offensive scheme but he'd also lost his shooting touch. He became a tentative rather than dominant center, and the Bulls struggled from the start. Except for one good stretch in January–February when we won 22 of 27, we were a below .500 team and finished the season at 47–35, our worst record in five years. Our usual gritty performances alternated with some incredibly flat games. We could never tell what we would be like from one night to the next, usually the sign of a young team, not a veteran one. Some nights we would be lucky to score 80 points. Other nights the veterans would snarl their way through in the patented Bulls' style. We could only hope that our experience would tell come play-off time and that everyone would be on the same page. Motta continued to instill the view in us that no one had any respect for us, not other teams, not the league, not the referees, not the sportswriters. As always, it was the Bulls against the universe year after year.

I played 105 play-off games in my thirteen seasons, or about an extra season and a quarter. I was gearing up for one last run in the spring of 1975. We thought we might have a fairly easy first-round opponent in the Kansas City Kings, but they extended us in an acrimonious six-game series. In the fourth game I was driving to win the game in regulation time and put us up 3–1 when Scott Wedman just plowed into me with no whistle. I'd never been run over like that with no call. I was flattened again by center Sam Lacey as time expired and made two free throws to send the game into overtime. But we lost 104–100 when Love fouled out, joining Van Lier on the bench. Sloan was already in the locker room, ejected by Jake O'Donnell. After that frustrating game, we just got madder. Love, Van Lier, and Thurmond accepted all challenges on defense and shut down the hot-shooting Kings, who scored just 77 and 89 points in games five and six. We won going away.

We flew west to meet the Golden State Warriors in Oakland. The Thurmond-Ray trade, the one I had had grave doubts about, would finally come back to haunt us in a major way in this series. Clifford Ray knew our offense as well as any player in the league, having been our high-post center for several years. Motta's offense was like assigning parts in a play. Clifford knew how much we wanted to run plays through the center position to create shots for the forwards. With his intelligence and strength Clifford was able to consistently deny the ball from reaching Boerwinkle and Thurmond, thus clogging up everything we were trying to do. Clifford was also perfect for the Warriors as he set great picks freeing Rick Barry for jump shots.

Although Love scored 37 points, we were soundly whipped 107–89 in the opener. I had only 10 points, a pulled muscle limiting me to thirty minutes and 7 shots. I certainly didn't make Rick Barry work very hard on defense, and he hit for 38. I gutted my way through game two at the Stadium and drove repeatedly on Barry, scoring a perfect 16–16 at the line on my way to 28 points. We prevailed 90–89 as Van Lier found Boerwinkle for a lay-up with two seconds to play. Even so, we weren't playing well; we simply hung on and got a huge break when Barry turned the ball over to us with about ten seconds to go. The third game went to us in Chicago 108–101 as Van Lier dazzled everyone with 35 points. We raced to a 39–20 lead in game four in Oakland but then lost 111–106. We were getting no help at all from the bench and missed 20 of 44 free throws. No veteran team should be so wildly inconsistent and that worried me.

We clamped down on the Warriors 89–79 in Oakland as Thurmond clogged the middle and came through with 13 rebounds. We were just one game away from the NBA finals. Love hounded Barry all over on defense and I made him work when we were on offense. My leg was feeling better, but Rick had really quick hands and was always checking me with them. Sloan was relentless all over the court. We felt that this veteran Bulls team was about to cap six years of growth and hard work. We were going back to Chicago to finally win a fourth play-off game in front of our fans. Chicago would then be on the basketball map for sure.

Game six at Chicago Stadium on Sunday, May 11, 1975, was one of the strangest games I ever played in. We came out of the first quarter ahead 25–18 before a crowd that passionately yearned for us to break through to an NBA final. But we scored only 47 points in the next three quarters. Rick Barry broke loose on offense, and the Warriors defense led by the old-timer Bill Bridges, Clifford Ray, and George Johnson just throttled us inside. They took us out of all our offensive patterns. Van Lier couldn't penetrate the defense. I scored just 12 points. On one rebound scramble I could swear that Bridges actually kicked me in the head.

We headed back to the West Coast for game seven. Even though we'd collapsed at home, we came out fighting with our backs to the wall. We had a 14-point lead with three minutes to go in the first half and led 47–36 at intermission. But again the Warriors stiffened one final time. We scored 32 second-half points and lost the series 83–79. Using our unit of five or six players against the Warriors' ten-man rotation finally wore us down and out. We were a little too old and much too tired. I tried to suppress the awful feeling that our whole team had suddenly aged too much and that our last best chance together had been taken away.

After the game, Motta really went after Love and Van Lier, suggesting that their early-season holdouts cost the team dearly and they should not get a full share of the play-off money. That was absurd, of course. Motta had worked Butter and Norm like mules all season long. In fact, Love played forty-eight minutes in the seventh Warrior game, shot 6–26, and was so tired he could hardly jump at the end. But Motta was just totally frustrated as we all were.

In a way, the overachieving Bulls finally became victims of our own considerable success. Motta had become restless for that elusive championship and traded away Clifford Ray, not our best player but one who played one of the most important roles in our successful offense. Some other players began to play out of their roles. Some became jealous of my having the ball down the stretch. At the end I just didn't have the motivation to contest them for the ball. I backed off, and we fell into a pattern of no pattern at all. I'm not making excuses or pointing fingers. The Bulls, myself included, just stopped producing.

About a week after this wrenching play-off loss, I checked into Northwestern Memorial Hospital. I was again experiencing the chronic kidney infection that had plagued me since the NIT in 1962. This time I was furious when the Bulls refused to pay my hospital bill, claiming that my ailment was "not game related." I couldn't believe they could be that petty. A real chill was coming between me and the Bulls management.

As the 1975–76 season approached, I was wary about rejoining the Bulls. It would have been my fourteenth season in the NBA. Already the year before I'd been tempted to retire, but the arrival of Nate Thurmond and the promise of a bigger salary kept me motivated. The wear and tear of that confusing season made me even more eager to leave now. I had some personal goals that might have kept me interested, like playing the one or two more years it would take for me to reach an NBA milestone of 20,000 career points. What made me less than eager to continue after thirteen years of aches and pains were the big minutes

I had always played and growing team dissension. I didn't know how I could make the Bulls a better team.

Players don't have much power to influence changes in our own game. We have nothing to say about the game's on-the-court play or its rules changes. We don't participate in conferring honors on our peers, selecting All-Star rosters, or Hall of Fame voting. Our power is largely symbolic and lasts only as long as we are deemed useful to the team. But what made me decide not to play, what made me walk away from the game, was Bulls' owner Arthur Wirtz when I found out just how little my power might be.

Of course, there's also another story within the story of my departure from the NBA. That is the story of two lawsuits. The first was a Players' Association antitrust suit against the NBA aimed at freeing up player movement, particularly by eliminating the draft and breaking the reserve clause that bound a player to a team for life. Some players called it the "slave clause," and we weren't joking. The second suit was mine against the Bulls with the intent of achieving free agency.

The first suit had been hanging fire since 1970. It was commonly called the Oscar Robertson suit because, as president of the Players' Association, Oscar's name was first on the list of eighteen player representatives. Technically, the plaintiffs were the player representatives from each club. And since I had been a player rep for eight years, two years with the 76ers and all six that I'd been with the Bulls, my name also appeared as one of the plaintiffs in this suit.

This antitrust litigation was a class-action suit begun in April 1970 when the players charged the NBA with violation of their freedom of movement by means of the draft and restrictive trade practices—all outlined in the Sherman Anti-Trust Act. The key issues were modification of the reserve clause, elimination or modification of the college draft, and compensation for years of restricted movement. Players entered the 1975–76 season without a contract partly because they wanted to see what the results would be of this suit scheduled to go on trial in June. The owners, too, were eager to see this suit resolved because the NBA was looking to absorb the rival ABA; but until the suit was settled, the NBA was stymied by a 1970 injunction preventing any merger with the ABA on the charge that such a merger would constitute a conspiracy to restrain competition for player services.

Twice in the fall of 1975, I met with Mr. Wirtz in his suite of offices at the Merchandise Mart. In September, I told him that a salary increase could keep me playing, but he shook his head. He countered that I should be content with my current salary because Motta didn't have a place for me in the lineup anyway, that he didn't think the team needed me. Didn't need me? I'd been in thirteen play-offs in my thirteen years as a pro. I was always a big offensive threat, and in the spring of 1975, I became the tenth leading scorer in NBA history. And the Bulls didn't need me? I thought about the series we had played against the Warriors. We took them to the seventh game, giving them their toughest opposition on their way to the championship. I remembered the sixth game of the series in the Stadium when we held the series in our hand, up 3–2 and playing at home. That was one of the toughest losses in my career; and, as it turned out, one of the toughest on my body because I'd forced myself to play with a bleeding kidney. And now they thought they didn't need me?

"Play with us on my terms or retire," Wirtz seemed to be basically telling me. And Mr. Wirtz didn't mince words. He was your classic bully, about six feet five inches and 350 pounds. He really enjoyed his power over athletes. He had a reputation for playing hardball. The Wirtz family had virtually thrown away Bobby Hull, the star of his Black Hawks hockey team, and Hull was a white guy. I tried to remain amicable, letting him calm down. When he did, he told me he wasn't the villain in this situation. He said he wanted me to play for the Bulls, but the coaches needed persuading. He offered to speak to the coaches about working something out. Was it the coaches who didn't want me? Motta who had me busting my tail for thirty-two minutes a game during the last season? I left Mr. Wirtz's office confused, suspecting I'd been had by someone, perhaps everyone.

That night at my apartment, I found messages from every

sportswriter in town plus a few from across the country. I needed to get away from all their questions because I had no answers. I had a lot of sorting out to do in my own mind and not just about the Bulls.

The next day I woke up both restless and weary. I set out for O'Hare. I had no ticket in hand, but I knew I had to get out of Chicago. I had to go. So I got on the first flight I saw scheduled: a plane to Puerto Rico. Once we landed, I knew San Juan wasn't the place for me. I'd been there before and hadn't liked it much. An hour later I hopped aboard a commuter flight to St. Croix, the last flight of the day to the Virgin Islands.

I caught a cab to a St. Croix hotel advertised at the airport, only to be told there was absolutely no room available so late. I sat down in the lobby to regroup while the hotel clerk called other hotels for me. No luck. It was late. I was tired and depressed. I had no place to stay, no place to go, and no place I wanted to be. Brooding over the fix I got myself in, I could hear somebody flirting with the hotel receptionist and looked up to see a white kid trying to make some time. When the kid saw me, his eyes lit up. I knew I'd been recognized but didn't have the energy to elude him. He came over and asked, "Is your name Chet Walker?" I nodded a weary yes, anticipating a pen and paper for the inevitable autograph request. Instead, the guy went on, "Well, I'm Eric, and I can get you a room in this hotel because my uncle owns it. But the deal is that tomorrow you'll have to go with me for lunch at my father's farm." I could live with that. In fact, I'd never been so glad to be a celebrity as I was in that little hotel lobby in the middle of the night.

The next morning I went with Eric in his Land Rover into the St. Croix hills near an old sugar mill. To my amazement, his radio was picking up the signal from WIND, all the way from Chicago, just where I didn't want to be! Eric told me he loved coming up into the hills at night to listen to the Bulls games. It was strange to sit there listening to the squawk of Chicago radio wavering in and out of the frequency as we sat in the warm nighttime air by the sugar mill.

The Bulls were losing badly with all my old teammates still in tow. They would free-fall to a 24–58 record in 1975–76, the worst in the NBA. My emotions were very mixed. I felt sorry for the guys on the one hand but vindicated on the other that clearly I had been the player that had driven the team.

Eric's father's family was Dutch and had been in the islands for generations. The farm we were going to was his father's farm, where beef cattle were raised for the Nelson Rockefeller family. When we arrived, I couldn't believe my eyes. A golf course was carved out right in the middle of this cattle farm. Once a year, every year, he explained, some of the wealthiest men in the world came to play this course and discuss the world economy. Right now these golf links held men with more concentrated power than did any single boardroom. Here they were, these old, white-haired white men dressed in white against a soft, pinkish background. I mused that some of these golfers were powerful enough to buy and sell Arthur Wirtz.

I stayed in St. Croix for two months, resting my body and spirit. The island was lush and green. I loved the outdoor cafés and the gentle breezes. I walked the paved streets until they would veer off into dirt lanes where instead of small, pastel-colored houses I saw shacks and huts. In town I played checkers with old black men relaxing in the cool, green shade. It made me think of an exotic Mississippi—the old white men high on the hillside, the old black men down in the rich valley. I was as close to my fantasy of being a Paul Gauguin as I would ever get.

By the time I returned from St. Croix the 1975–76 basketball season was well under way, and the Bulls had tumbled to a 3–10 start and apparently looked even worse than the record showed. Not surprisingly, I found five or six messages from Arthur Wirtz waiting for me. I guess he was frantic about my whereabouts because no one outside of my family and a few friends knew where I was, certainly not the sportswriters.

We arranged a second meeting. By now I was convinced Wirtz knew as well as I did that I was the backbone of the Bulls. He knew it, Motta knew it, and I knew it. Van Lier's ego probably wouldn't admit it. I thought the Bulls' stumbling start would make Wirtz more eager to hear my point of view. I was wrong. He seemed to blame *me* for the Bulls' bad record.

Our second meeting was hostile from the start. He did offer me a slightly bigger contract, but right off the bat Mr. Wirtz told me, "Chet, the league has sent us a statement from David Stern, the NBA attorney. You are legally the Bulls' property. Play with us or nowhere. This is your last opportunity. I'm not going to change my mind on this." With that, Mr. Wirtz rumbled out of the room, the space emptied of his huge bulk. He probably didn't know, but I could see his reflection in a mirror when he paused in the next room, watching for my reaction to his ultimatum.

I sat there reflecting on the word *property.* I thought about my father, grandfather, and great-grandfather, and how they must have felt living in Mississippi where they were looked upon as property. Their experience had now become mine—the disgust at being in bondage and under the control of an owner. Making $200,000 a year, I knew I was a slave by perhaps no one's definition but my own. I knew that millions of people would love to be in my shoes. Yet with Mr. Wirtz's claim to own me, I felt that two hundred years of my family's history in America had suddenly become real to me. Precisely because I was making that much money, because I had some investments to cushion the shock, I was in a position to choose. I didn't have to listen to Wirtz or accept his claims of ownership. Until this moment, I had always been afraid to challenge the authority of white people in control over me. But now I had a decision to make. The outcome of this decision was critical because it would define Chester A. Walker for the rest of his life.

I decided not to play. I clearly understood the game on the conference table. I had to walk away from the game on the court. Let Arthur Wirtz take *his* ball and go home. I couldn't maintain my self-respect and play for his team. Mr. Wirtz represented the person to whom I had to say no at this time in my life because I had to do it for all the times I'd been called "nigger," real or imagined, all the times I'd been turned away or judged in advance. There, in Mr. Wirtz's office with him peeking at me from a mirrored anteroom, my career came to a climax: all the negatives over the years gave me the push to say *no!* And when I did, I felt a powerful relief. The oppression I'd felt for years just rushed out of me. Every other time I'd figured out too late what to do for my own self-respect. But now I knew what to do, and I was ready.

I left him standing there in his mirrored office. I never said another word to him but turned and walked out the office door. I felt emancipated. I left the Mart and flagged a cab to the lakeshore. The cold Chicago wind cut right through me as I sat gazing across the water toward Benton Harbor where my basketball days had begun. I had always reacted to racism in the acceptable way, staying in the traces for the sake of my family or so I could play on a team. Now I knew clearly that it wasn't worth rationalizing this time. Nobody owned me.

The same day in November 1975 that I left Mr. Wirtz' office to sit on the shores of Lake Michigan and reflect on my decision to leave the Bulls and the NBA, another old pro was in the sports news. The Cubs announced that Ernie Banks would not be named manager because he was "too nice a guy." Some people accuse star players of wanting to become instant executives without working their way up the ladder, paying their dues. But that's not so. We just want the same chance given any other players without such experience. How do you explain it when a former player goes by the book and still doesn't get the breaks? Take the former Bear Gale Sayers, the greatest running back I ever saw. He planned for a career in athletic administration, so upon retirement, he went back to Kansas, earned a master's degree, and eventually became athletic director at Southern Illinois University. But pro football? No, the NFL is closed to Sayers. It has no place for him except in the record books.

There I was, thirty-five years old, a young man in any other professional career. But in my chosen profession, I was expendable. For years I was the player everyone else counted on, and now I wasn't going to be even counted in. I had served my masters well. I made money and a reputation for my high school and my college. Certainly, I had brought in a bundle for the 76ers and the Bulls. But my contributions during more than twenty years of high school, college, and NBA basketball didn't much matter to the number crunchers—the coaches, general managers, and owners who kept tabs on the bottom line and knew that, if I wouldn't accept what they offered, somewhere on a lonely court next to a housing project another boy was busy creating something unique with a basketball, something they must have for their show.

That kid is still there. He's playing to replace me and all the other players who've come after me. He's making moves worthy of an Erving or a Jordan or even a Baryshnikov. Moves you don't learn in summer camp or in suburban driveways. Moves you make to entertain but also to break people down in a physical struggle. He's learning to compete and to survive. He's playing for his dream of becoming a star, of helping his brothers and sisters obtain better food, clothes, and shelter. Like I did, he is also looking for a way to express his rage, to suppress his anger. He hopes his talent will bring him freedom, equality, and respect. But he must realize it will only bring him recognition. He'll have to find freedom, equality, and respect somewhere other than on a basketball court.

The gray lake water churned sluggishly in the November chill. I thought about myself in Benton Harbor. I looked across the water and could almost see the projects in my mind. I could almost see the Bradley coach arrive to snatch me to Peoria via Chicago and start me on the road to this spot. Little Meigs Field was on my right where we'd crammed into that plane for the ride to Peoria. I turned around and faced the big, brawling city that I'd represented so well for six years.

I thought of Jean Baptiste DuSable, half-mythical figure who'd explored these shores hundreds of years ago. Like many black men in history, he is a shadow, more honored in his absence, a convenient reference during black history month. DuSable was a Haitian trader, the first permanent settler in Chicago who was not a Native American. When people speak of Chicago history they talk of Daley, Wrigley, Halas, Frank Lloyd Wright, Carl Sandburg, maybe Ernie Banks, if black athletes sneak in. Would I get even a memory or a mention in a year or two?

When I left the Bulls in 1975, I had finally come into possession of my full manhood. I would not allow myself to be owned or mistreated by anyone. Basketball had served its purpose in my life, and it was time to move on. This didn't become clear to me all at once but bit by bit. I pulled away from the game and from its owners until I found myself standing alone. I liked myself that way.

Epilogue

M ost players have no idea what will happen when they retire. Neither did I, but I was lucky. I stumbled onto St. Croix, left basketball cold turkey, and landed on my feet in Hollywood. A pro-basketball career follows no set path. No player knows where the game will lead him on the court or where it will leave him when his playing days are over. We do know at the outset that we'll be facing two sure things: a short playing career and a long afterlife trying to fit in as a successful someone else.

I didn't know what I would be like without basketball, either physically or emotionally. For twenty years competitive sports had been my outlet. As far back as Benton Harbor, when I wanted to express something and couldn't or when I was frustrated and needed a vent, I could play ball. I would hit the playground and leave everything on the court. I wasn't sure what might replace that outlet in retirement. I had to face myself for the first time without sports, and I didn't always like what I saw. I was fortunate to be single, because many marriages don't survive the difficult times after a player retires. When players become former players, they sometimes become different people. Even their wives don't always recognize them after the cheering stops.

My body didn't want me to let go of my basketball past, either. After years of irregular starting times, haphazard sleeping schedules, bizarre eating arrangements, you would think that you could just say good-bye to it all. My mind did, but my body couldn't. It missed the competition, the adrenaline charge. When I first retired, I needed to run five miles at a stretch just to wake myself up. Sometimes, around three in the afternoon, an urgent need to exercise would propel me outdoors to jog for a few miles so I could get back to work with full concentration. Now I'm a little older, and I've adjusted. But I still carry the scars of battle that remind me of my life on the court—the damaged kidney, the gimpy knees, the swollen arthritic ankles. All I have to do is get up in the morning, and I remember.

After leaving the Bulls, playing again in the NBA seemed remote and then impossible. In February 1976, a settlement was reached between the NBA and all named plaintiffs in the Oscar Robertson suit—except for me. I just couldn't sign off on this settlement because I was convinced the players were being short-changed in a big way. On January 30, 1976, I had already filed my suit against Arthur Wirtz and the Bulls, seeking free agency. This action was enjoined in February by a federal judge who ruled that I couldn't press my suit because I was already a named plaintiff on the same issue in the Robertson suit.

So I was stuck. I was being pressured on all sides to go along with the agreement. My fellow players and the association lawyer, Larry Fleisher, argued they had made an enormous breakthrough. And they had. It would take years before other professional players' groups followed our lead. I just didn't think we'd won it all.

In time I felt coerced into dropping my appeal to the Robertson lawsuit, allowing it to come to a conclusion in July 1976. Why? I had heard some sorry stories about retired players like Gus Johnson in desperate financial straits. They needed the money and weren't prepared to quibble about what they saw as some of the finer points. That tore me up, thinking I was hurting old warriors like Gus.

I never got my day in court. Even so, this whole process was a landmark in my life. I had taken a stand for my rights against both the Players' Association and the Bulls. I really felt like a free agent in the best sense. When all was said and done, the Robertson suit did eventually break the reserve clause and benefit succeeding generations of NBA players—just not soon enough for me and the players who had fought the system for years, in effect since the proposed All-Star game boycott of 1964.

With a return to the NBA definitely out of the picture, I phoned four teams about working in a front-office capacity. I also wrote fifteen letters. I was willing to start out in one of the lower positions and learn the business from the ground up. My calls weren't returned. My letters weren't answered. I even planted an article with Bill Gleason in the *Chicago Sun-Times* about my desire to work in sports management. That didn't stir up any interest in me either. I'm convinced management had branded me as a disruptive influence.

It was clear I had no future in basketball. I had to find a new profession, one that would allow me to maintain the same energy I had on the court and provide me with the same stimulus, the same pressure. I had other things to say and do. I needed a stage. Even though I would be out of sports, I didn't want to be the "poor player who could strut and fret no more upon the stage."

Zev Braun, a neighbor of mine in Chicago, had been a producer with Hollywood connections. Over the course of several years he and I had spent countless hours discussing the film business. Since nothing now held me in Chicago, I took him up on his offer to come out to California.

I wanted to learn not only how to make films but also how to play this new game. I found Hollywood a place with few rules but susceptible to many strategies. The bottom line, as in all business, was to get things done, regardless of how. I was used to rules, so at first I found this wide-open approach disturbing. I coped by becoming more aggressive as well as shrewder in my approach to my work. I was able to do this without sacrificing my principles, those of a nice country boy raised by Regenia Walker, overlaid by twenty years of success in a highly competitive arena.

I took to heart Wyatt's advice of long ago, "If you stop and listen, you can hear everything." I opened my ears and applied what I learned. One thing I learned was Hollywood people didn't expect much from a guy whose main claim to fame was basketball, so I used this piece of information, turned it around to my advantage. Just as I used my background and my basketball skills in this new game, I found ways to use other miscalculated assumptions about me—that I was unsophisticated, that I was another ex-jock without a lot of gray matter between my ears. I lead people into negotiations, and by the time they discover I'm a real professional, it's too late. The deal on the table is made. It used to bother me that I had to set the table for a deal by talking basketball, but now I'm secure about using sports as a tool. Just as I use the fact that I didn't grow up in Bel Air or Beverly Hills to my advantage, I draw on the strengths I gained as a kid from southern poverty and northern projects.

As years passed by, fewer fans wanted to reminisce about my games and seasons. I was no longer introduced simply as a basketball star. I had a new identity. It felt good to stand on my nonathletic, postbasketball accomplishments. It felt comfortable. I was free.

I am free from basketball, but as a man I will always have battles to win. Occasionally, all the demons will return after an experience like the one that brought me up short in June 1991 when the Bulls won their first NBA championship. When the Bulls defeated the Lakers in Los Angeles to take the title, I was elated to be in the Forum cheering them on. I felt as if I had a little piece of them in my heart, and I was glad to have been invited to the Bulls' postgame celebration. The party was at the Ritz-Carlton, but when I arrived, the Bulls' representative who invited me was nowhere in sight. An attractive blonde at the door looked me up and down, and she coolly informed me the Bulls' party was only for players, family, and friends. When I told her, "I'm Chet Walker," she insisted, "I know Chet Walker, and you're not him." Behind her, I could see Jerry Krause, the Bulls' general manager. He corrected her, saying "That's Chet Walker, but this party is closed."

I was devastated. Apparently, I was not a part of the Bulls' "family." Standing at that door was one of the most embarrassing and distressing moments in my life. I was probably there for only a minute and a half, but it seemed like a long time, long enough for painful images from my past to come flooding back: images of all the places where I'd been refused entry. I had seen quite enough of such incidents, both in the North and South. But this was the Bulls, my team. I couldn't help but remember all I had done to put the Bulls on the map, to keep the franchise alive in Chicago and wedge the door open for the current success.

Then, too, I had a long history with Jerry Krause that I had to try and understand. I'd known Jerry for years, as far back as Bradley, where we were both undergraduates. Jerry was a gofer in the athletic department. He was one of those people who wanted to hang with athletes. He'd always make a point of eating with us in the cafeteria. Of course, back then we suspected he was the coach's snitch. I used to feel a little sorry for Jerry and didn't join in when the others taunted him. Now I had some sense of how the memory of that undergraduate ribbing must have burned into him, branding him as an outsider. I see Jerry's decision to exclude me from the Bulls' celebration, not to let me in the door on the night of the team's crowning achievement, was a way to kick the past and finally prove that Jerry Krause was a winner. I was an ex-player with no credibility on *his* stage. He was showing the guys at Bradley who stiffed him in the gym and never let him play that he was a somebody, that he could play his own game at the highest level. But it was the same old story for me. That night I didn't care much about Krause's psyche. His behavior brought back unwanted memories of other doors shut tight.

Krause's decision to keep me out stunned a lot of people

besides me. One amazed Bulls' official overheard Krause at the door and blurted out, "Jerry, . . . that's CHET!" It didn't help. A former NBA star told me later that he saw Krause in the hotel lobby mumbling "Chet, Chet, I'm sorry."

I didn't hear him. I was back home by then. I sat in the dark staring out into the night. The ringing phone jarred its way into my mind. Twice I listened to Krause's voice offering a disjointed apology on my answering machine. The third time, I picked up. I listened to Jerry ramble on, sorting through our past relationship, reminding me how long we'd known each other, emphasizing the strain of the moment, and so on.

When I hung up a half hour later, I was still very hurt and angry. I had no wish to rain on the Bulls' parade, but what happened to me could not go unnoticed. I stayed up all night reviewing what had happened, considering what I should do. In the morning I called Lacy Banks of the *Chicago Sun-Times*, and he got my story out.

When you're black, you fight just to walk through the front door. You keep passing through successive doors until you *think* you've arrived. But there are always more doors. At the Bulls' hotel my mistake was having no Wyatt from Benton Harbor as my lookout, on the watch, the man to let the Bulls know I was there. To let me in. Wyatt wasn't "on the door."

My self-possession told me that now, when I understood my own motives, I had to tell the truth. All my life I have been looking for freedom, respect, and equality. I have finally learned that to find equality I had to prove to *myself* that I was equal. I had to win my own respect.

Taking control on the basketball court was my forte. Doing the same thing off the court is a lot harder. I have always searched for my boundaries—within my family, within the dimensions of the court, the rules of my game. I was graced with the talent to test my limits within those boundaries, and I have used what I learned there in other arenas.

If I had to live my life over again—the struggles in Mississippi, Benton Harbor, Peoria, Philadelphia, and Chicago—I could do it. In fact, I would make very few changes. I would still choose to grow up in the same town, attend the same university, and play for the same professional teams. After all, these places are just spots on a map. I had to find "my place" anywhere I happened to be. Thank God, I know now that "the place" the old folks were talking about when I was a child was not under the farmhouse in Mississippi, not in the South, not in the North. It wasn't in the structure of American race relations or in segregation or integration. It was within myself. The place that I was seeking for such a long time was where I could feel at peace. And I have found it.

DATE DUE